When The HolySpirit Reveals

New Insights Into Old Controversies

[Expanded Edition]

by

Gregg N. Huestis

When The Holy Spirit Reveals—
New Insights Into Old Controversies

Copyright © 2011 by Gregg N. Huestis
Expanded Edition—First Printing January 2011

All rights reserved under International Copyright Law. Contents and/or cover may not be reproduced in whole or in part in any form without the express written consent of the publisher.

ISBN: **978-0615439303**

All Scripture quotations, unless otherwise indicated, are taken from *The Amplified Bible, Old Testament.* © Copyright 1965, 1987 by The Zondervan Corporation. *The Amplified New Testament,* © Copyright 1954, 1958, 1987 by The Lockman Foundation. Used by permission.

Scripture quotations marked KJV are taken from the *King James Version* Bible

Scripture quotations marked NKJV are taken from the *New King James Version,* Copyright © 1979, 1980, 1982 by Thomas Nelson, Inc. Used by permission. All rights reserved.

All Scripture verses, dictionary and concordance; definitions containing *added emphasis* have been added by the author.

Published by: Blessed To Be A Blessing Ministries
E-mail: **info@b2bablessing.org**
Website: **www.b2bablessing.org**

Blessed To Be A Blessing Ministries
Ft. Collins, CO 80524
All Rights Reserved

Printed In the United States of America

Dedication

I dedicate this book to
Emily P. Huestis,
*my beautiful wife and best friend,
who gave of her time and editorial talents.
Without her wonderful devoted support, this
book would still be just a manuscript.*

Acknowledgements

The Holy Spirit for His guidance and counsel, for without His *flowing* revelation I could not write. The late Bill Godwin, a fellow author, who challenged me to finish this book sooner than I'd ever thought possible.

Table of Contents

A Personal Introduction From the Author vii
CHAPTER 1: 1
What's In A Word?
CHAPTER 2: 15
Visualization: Is It Scriptural?
CHAPTER 3: 31
Romans Reconciliation Revelation
CHAPTER 4: 45
Temptation: What's Its Purpose?
CHAPTER 5: 57
Waiting In His Presence
CHAPTER 6: 69
What About Paul's Thorn?
CHAPTER 7 81
Who Said, "Women Can't Preach"?
CHAPTER 8: 95
The Unanswered Prayer of Jesus
CHAPTER 9: 105
Is Bible School "Required" For the Great Commission?
CHAPTER 10: 117
Too Tithe *Or* Not Too Tithe?
CHAPTER 11: 129
Eschatology 101
CHAPTER 12: 151
Spiritual Death & The Cross
END NOTES 191

A Personal Introduction From The Author

For almost ten years I have dreamed about putting this book into the hands of God's people. When the Lord instructed me to write, immediately I *attempted* to start working on my newly given directive. However, all of my efforts were as filthy rags. Every word that **I** wrote was *lifeless*. I even questioned the Lord concerning His instructions about writing a book, because the Anointing was *absent*.

Then, in September 1995, the Lord birthed within my heart a **Rhema** word, *a word of revelation*, which I had never received before during *my* previous attempts at writing. At once, the words I wrote were not coming from my head, nor were they mere ideas. These words were coming from within my spirit. The Holy Spirit came upon me in an awesome, personal manifestation, with the sole purpose of guiding me as I wrote. He gave me insights into controversial issues within the Body of Christ, and guided me to Scriptures that would impart answers to God's people.

When I asked the Lord why I could not seem to write in previous years, He gave me some verses of Scripture:

(John 8:31b&32) "...If you abide in My word [hold fast to My teachings and live in accordance with them], you are truly My disciples. And you will **know** the Truth and the Truth will set you free."

He explained that it was not the "Truth" of His instructions that were going to set me free, but rather my *knowing* (understanding) of the truth; which would set me free to write under His anointed guidance. I can say Jesus loves me, but until I *experience* the love of Christ, I will never truly begin to **know** His love in an intimate, personal way.

There are two conditions stated in this passage of Scripture which will guide us into *experiencing* this kind of freedom and revelation.

1. We must be His disciples: (*be disciplined ones*).
2. We must *know* the Truth [Truth *alone* won't set us free but the Truth that we **know** will.]

What Is Our Input Into Knowing The Truth?

(John 14:16;26) "And I will ask the Father, and He will give you *another* (Comforter, Helper, Intercessor, Advocate, Strengthener, and Standby), that He may remain with you forever...But the Comforter (Counselor, Helper, Intercessor, Advocate, Strengthener, Standby), **the Holy Spirit**, Whom the Father will send...He will teach you *all things*...."

The first condition is that we must make a 100% commitment to being a disciple of Jesus. The next condition is that we rely totally upon the Holy Spirit to guide us and teach us *all things*. *However*, He will not do His part in us if we never invite Him to do so. He is a gentleman, and will not go where He is not welcomed or acknowledged. Surrender to God's Spirit is the key. Dear Saint of God, when you begin to live these two truths; then you too will experience what happens...*When the Holy Spirit Reveals*!

Gregg N. Huestis
Blessed To Be A Blessing Ministries

1

WHAT'S IN A WORD?
(Learning the Power within Our Words)

Ever since I gave my life to Christ on 1 January 1979, I have witnessed a sometimes-hostile debate surrounding the *power* of words. Some believe that words are very powerful and therefore should be chosen carefully. Still others believe that our words have little or no effect upon the outcome of our goals in life. Hence, this subject has always been of great interest to me, but also a source of confusion. Then I received a revelation! "Do some Bible research and learn *what's in a word?*" I desired to know what God's Word says about words. I hoped that this would alleviate my perplexity. I thank the Lord that I was obedient to His Voice.

In chapter one I would like to share with you the results of my research from God's Word in faith that it will help clear up any misunderstandings you may have experienced concerning what's in a word.

Before we go further, I want to define what is meant by the question, "*What's in a word?*" A word is not simply one word that you or I speak in a day. A word, (my word), is the whole course of words that I speak each and every day. In this sense, we can call a word our *daily testimony*. **Who am I praising the most?** Am I praising the devil for his attacks on my life or am I praising God for His strength that has made me more than an conqueror even in the face of defeat? **Whatever** we glorify the most in our daily conversation **will be** the very thing *that controls our thoughts and actions*. On that account, *what* is in a word?

(**Proverbs 18:20,21**) A man's [moral] self shall be filled with the *fruit of his mouth*; and with the **consequence** of his words he *must* be satisfied [whether good or evil]. **Death and life** are in the power of the tongue, and they who indulge in it shall eat the fruit of it [for death or life].

According to Proverbs chapter eighteen in *the Amplified Bible,* "we will be filled by the fruit of our mouths; and by the consequence of our words we **must** be satisfied." This says that if I do not want to be filled and satisfied with evil consequences, then I must pay attention to the words that I speak. Also, this tells me that I am the one who has control over my words, and hence control over the kind of fruit that my words will produce. *We are responsible for the words we speak not God or the devil.* God our Father has given us His Word to help us control our thinking and henceforth our speaking. We are not expected to be the ones to do it all alone. He has given these tools to us in His Word, but *we* must use the tools. God will not force us to change our vocabulary. He has simply given us His Word and left the choice to us. The Holy Spirit is a gentleman—He will not come into our lives without our invitation and cooperation.

The previous passage of Scripture clearly states that *death* and *life* are in the tongue. Moreover, please consider what James said about the power of our word.

(James 3:2-6) For we all often stumble *and* fall *and* offend in many things. And if anyone does not *offend in speech* [never says the wrong things], he is a fully developed character *and* a perfect man, **able to control** his whole body *and* to **curb his entire nature.** If we set bits in the horses' mouths to make them obey us, we can turn their whole bodies about. Likewise, look at the ships: though they are so great and are driven by rough winds, *they are steered by* a very small *rudder* wherever the impulse of **the helmsman determines.** *Even so* the tongue is a little member, and it can boast of great things. See how much wood *or* how great a forest a tiny spark can set ablaze! And the tongue is a fire. [The tongue is a] world of wickedness set among our members, *contaminating and depraving the whole body* and setting on fire the wheel of birth (the cycle of man's nature), being itself ignited by hell (Gehenna).

Here in the book of James we have a much more detailed description of the productive *as well as* destructive power of our word. He clearly tells us that if we do not cause offense with our tongue we are perfect or **mature** in God's eyes, able to control or determine the actions of our bodies. In other words, we will stop being *body dominated*, which is the instrument of sin (Rom. 6:6 TAB). Domination by our bodies keeps us in slavery to sin. The book of James says that the tongue is **the key** to curbing the nature of man. He is not referring to unregenerate man because he goes on to say that *no man* can tame the tongue. Please realize that James didn't say, "the tongue **cannot** be tamed." He said that man *in himself* could not do it. However, a child of God who is living in the Word, with the Word *living* in him, **can** surrender to the direction of God's Word by the Holy Spirit. God's Spirit has the power to keep our tongues operating in line with the will/Word of God.

Now that we have laid a foundation for what's in a word, let us move on to a more in depth study of the power of a word itself.

Can A Word Create Its Own Reality?

Words are very creative tools. They can be used to paint a mental picture of love and peace or one of fear and abuse. Verbal abuse is one of the most common forms of mistreatment in relationships today, and a leading cause of divorce. Countless relationships are damaged beyond *human* repair simply because of the way someone used words to destroy another persons self-esteem. The spirit of man can be wounded and broken because of cruel words.

On the other hand, words can also be used to paint mental pictures of good things. If I were to say, "flower," instantly a picture of a flower would form in your mind. The more that I defined that picture, the more your mind would create the kind of picture that I was imagining. Thus if I said, "long stemmed flower" or "long stemmed red flower;" or even more detailed, "a long stemmed red rose," you would know exactly what kind of flower I was thinking about. Now what do the Scriptures have to say about this?

> **(Genesis 1:1,3;9 NKJV)** "In the beginning God *created* the heavens and the earth…Then God **said**, "Let there be *light*"; and there was light Then God **said**, "Let the water under the heavens be gathered together into one place…and it was so."

God spoke a word, and created every natural thing that could be seen. His words created this natural world *according to their own reality*. God literally painted a picture with His words, and created this whole natural world. God knew exactly what He wanted to create, and He used His words to properly form everything that became visible. Scientists have been quoted as saying, "the most perfect word that one could use to describe this whole universe is **light**." "*Let there be light*" was the first command of creation which God spoke, thus perfectly framing the universe. The New Covenant speaks of this same phenomena in the book of Hebrews chapter eleven; by telling us that God spoke the word of command, and what God said had to appear.

> **(Hebrews 11:1,3)** "NOW FAITH is the assurance (the confirmation, the title deed) of things [we] hope for, being the proof of things [we] do not see *and* the conviction of their reality [faith perceiving as real fact what is not revealed to the senses]...By faith we understand that the worlds [during the successive ages] were framed (fashioned, put in order and equipped for their intended purpose) **by the Word of God**, so that what we see was not made out of things which are visible."

Here again we see how God used His Word (or words) to frame, fashion and set in order this whole universe for His intended purpose. We note, however, how God brought this all about. He spoke out His word in confidence or *in faith*, knowing that what He said—would come to pass.

God had *faith* (confidence, assurance) that everything He spoke into existence would be formed and fashioned just as He originally intended. God used His words, confident that they would produce what He designed them to produce.

Some believers have a problem with the notion that God Himself has and uses faith. But let's take a brief look at what (Hebrews 11:1) is actually saying to us about what faith is. It tells us that faith is confidence, assurance and the title deed of what we hope for. So would it be too much to say that God the Father had full *confidence* and *assurance* that what He said would happen? Faith is our confidence and assurance that those things that we have hoped for will come to pass.

Thus, God released faith (confidence, assurance), in the words that He spoke believing that they would happen. God believes in Himself. He knows that He can do whatever ever He wants.

Moreover, the word that God spoke created the worlds according to the picture *or reality*, which He had within Himself. He released His word with the intended purpose of creating exactly what He pictured this universe to be; therefore, causing it to come into being *by* and *through* faith. We understand creation *by* faith, but the creation was also created *by* and *through* faith **in God's own words** to bring His intended purpose to pass.

What's In A Word?

Can A Word Change Our Destiny?

(Proverbs 13:2,3) A good man eats good *from the fruit of his mouth*, but the desire of the treacherous is for violence. *He who guards his mouth* **keeps his life**, *but he who opens wide his lips comes to ruin.*

Referring to the question above, can a word really change the very destiny of our lives? I believe (Proverbs 13:2,3) clearly addresses this question. Our mouth *(our word)* produces fruit, good or evil. Furthermore, whoever guards his mouth *will keep his life from* **all** *forms of sin and destruction*. I do not see how this could be made any clearer than by this passage of Scripture. Our *word* has created either the good or the bad situations in our lives. God's Word plainly tells us in the book of Proverbs chapter eighteen verse twenty states, "A man's [moral] self shall be filled *with the fruit* **of his mouth** and with *the consequence* of his words he **must** *be satisfied....*"

In The Mouth of *At Least* Two

(Proverbs 12:14) From the fruit **of his words** a man shall be satisfied with good, and the work of a man's hands shall come back to him [**as a harvest**].

(Proverbs 10:31,32) The mouths of the righteous (those harmonious with God) bring forth skillful *and* godly Wisdom, but the perverse tongue shall be cut down [like a barren and rotten tree]. The lips of the [uncompromisingly] righteous **know** [and **therefore utter**] *what is acceptable*, but the wicked knows [and *therefore speaks only*] what is obstinately willful *and* contrary.

(Matthew 12:34-37) You offspring of vipers! How can you *speak* good things when you are evil (wicked)? For out of the fullness (the overflow, the superabundance) **of the heart** *the mouth speaks*. The good man from his inner good treasure *flings forth good things*, and the evil man out of his inner evil storehouse flings forth evil things. But I tell you, on the day of judgment men will have to give account for every idle (inoperative, nonworking) word they speak. For **by your words** you will be justified *and* acquitted, and **by your words** you will be condemned *and* sentenced.

How anyone who calls himself a *believer* could read the previously cited verses, and despite what they say go around and speak words that are contrary to Scriptural instruction is beyond spiritual comprehension. I can only say that the words of the prophet Ezekiel still ring true today. "Son of man, thou dwellest in the midst of a rebellious house, which have eyes to see, **and see not** they have ears to hear, **and hear not**: *for they are a rebellious house*" (Ezekiel 12). Ignorance and rebellion could be the only logical answers to why so many believers ignore God's Word. Like it or not, our words will either bless or curse (defeat) us!

What Can Happen When Ignorance Talks?

I want to continue with a practical example of what can, and often times, does happen when we let our ignorance do the talking. I realize for many this illustration may be painful, still, please don't spiritually disconnect.

I would like to do a Scriptural investigation of the life of Job. We've heard so much opinion and theological debate concerning him, but I believe it's time for us to really see what the Bible has to say about Job's trials. Tradition has made Job appear to be *the model* of Christianity, but was Job really the portrait of how a believer should act during a trial?

(Job 1:8-12 NKJV) "Then the Lord said to Satan, 'Have you *considered* My servant Job, that *there* is none like him on the earth, a blameless and upright man, one who fears God and shuns evil?' So Satan answered the Lord and said, 'Does Job fear God for nothing? Have **You** not made a hedge around him, around his household, and around all that he has on every side…But now, stretch out *Your* hand and touch all that he has, and he will surely curse You to Your face!' And the Lord said to Satan, '**Behold**, all that he has is in your power; only do not lay a hand on his person….'"

Let's examine what we have just read. God makes a statement to Satan about Job, "Have you considered my servant job?" *The Spirit Filled Life Bible* uses a side note that says, "Lit. set your heart on."[1] Thus God literally said, "Have you **set your heart on** My servant Job?" Here God is showing us that Satan had *already* set his heart on destroying Job, thus destruction was *the will of Satan* for Jobs life. Satan; therefore, was *attempting* to deceive God into giving him what he wanted (Jobs life) and God exposed Satan's motive before he was even able to open his mouth. Satan goes as far as trying to get God to stretch out His hand *against* Job to destroy him, fulfilling *Satan's will* and *purpose* for Job's life.

However, what was God's response to Satan's attempt? He replied, "**Behold**, all that he has is in your power…." To some this is proof of God giving His "stamp" of approval upon Satan's deceptive plan to destroy the life of Job. Unfortunately, some sincere believers see this as God partnering up with Satan to make Job (and us) miserable. This couldn't be further from the truth. God and Satan aren't allies. He *doesn't* dance with the devil! He doesn't bring evil, through Satan, into our lives to teach us. God uses His Word and the Holy Spirit to instruct His people—*not evil*!

God told Satan "Behold," but what does *behold* mean, and why would God use this sort of wording? According to the concordance, the word *behold* means, "lo, see."[2] Despite this definition, I was still kind of out in the dark as to how *lo* and *see* were being used in this passage. Researching further, I determined how the words *lo* and *see* were used in other portions of the book of Job.

The word *Lo*, is defined as "lo! behold."[3] Similarly, the word *see* means "advise self, behold, consider, discern; gaze, take heed; lo, look; *perceive*, regard; cause to or let see, look, think, view."[4] God told Satan to *see* (perceive, understand) that something had happened to the hedge that He had built around Job *already*, and Satan didn't perceive it.

I finally realized what God said to Satan that day: "And the Lord said to Satan, "Behold (lo, see, advise yourself, consider, **discern**, gaze; take heed, *perceive*, think) all that he has is within your power...." God did not take heed to Satan's *challenge* of lowering His hedge of protection, *no, no, no*! God was literally saying to Satan, "Behold, see, look; perceive, *understand*, all he has is **already** within your ability to attack, but do not harm his life." God **didn't** lower His hedge around Job so that Satan could torment him. God Himself called Job righteous, (because of His covenant). Then why would our loving Father bring torment on a righteous servant? Such reasoning is foolishness and *religious ignorance* of the true character of God Almighty.

Think about this for a moment from an earthly parent's position. How many *decent, godly* parents would take their child and voluntarily put that baby out in the open where wild animals could come in and destroy that child? I can say this with 100% confidence that there *isn't* a **decent**, godly parent in this world who would commit such a foolish act. Therefore *why* in the Name of Jesus, would the Church try and make our heavenly Father *appear* to be so cruel and insensitive? Why would He do something so appalling that even decent human parents would never do? Truth is He would **never** even think of destroying one of His servants. Especially, one who is totally devoted to Him and His will.

WHEN THE HOLY SPIRIT REVEALS
Pruning Away Traditional "Hedge" Work

(Job 1:10 KJV) Hast not thou made *an hedge about him*, and about his house, and about all that he hath *on every side?* thou hast blessed the work of his hands, and his substance is increased in the land.

(Ecclesiastes 10:8 KJV) He that diggeth a pit shall fall into it; and **whoso** *breaketh an hedge*, a serpent shall bite him.

(Ezekiel 13:4,5 KJV) O Israel, thy prophets are like the foxes in the deserts. Ye have not gone up **into the gaps**, neither *made up the hedge* for the house of Israel...."

(Ezekiel 22:30,31 KJV) "And I sought for a man among them, that should **make up the hedge**, and *stand in the gap* before me for the land, that I should not destroy it: *but I found none.* **Therefore** have I poured out mine indignation upon them; I have consumed them...."

In every verse of Scripture cited here, the hedge that is being referred to was *a spiritual hedge* of protection. In addition, (Eccl. 10:8) refers to our own *willfulness* in breaking the hedge of protection; thus allowing our own destruction. Please notice closely (Ezek. 13:4,5 & Ezek. 22:30,31). Both passages of Scripture overtly state that God **desired** that someone would *stand in the gap*, and *make up the hedge*. What gap was God talking about? I believe He was referring to gaps *that the people had made* in their spiritual hedge of protection, thus causing the hedge to be lowered and to acquire holes of vulnerability to the enemy's attack, where *a serpent* could bite them.

Who Lowered Job's Hedge?

Having just read all of the Scriptural evidence concerning God's will on the subject of *hedgework*, if God didn't do it, then who did? To answer this question we need to look at the words of Job himself.

(Job 3:25 KJV) For the thing which I *greatly* feared is come upon me, and that **which I was afraid of** is come unto me.

(Job 1:20-22 KJV) Then Job arose, and rent his mantle, and shaved his head, and fell down upon the ground, and worshipped, And said, Naked came I out of my mother's womb, and naked shall I return thither: the Lord gave, and *the Lord hath taken* *away*; blessed be the name of the Lord. In all this Job *sinned not*, nor charged God *foolishly*.

Referring to Job chapter three verse 25, Job openly states that the very thing he *feared* the most (losing everything) has come upon him. Job said that he received **what he believed** for. That may sound strange but it is the truth. Fear is faith in reverse. It's perverted (twisted) faith. Job had more "faith" (fear) in the *reality* of losing everything than he did in God's ability to protect him and all that he had. Job had "*faith*" in his ability to lose all. Faith in a thing's ability to harm oneself is called **fear**; hence **twisted faith**. He wasn't trusting God's ability to protect him, but rather in a foreboding feeling that he would lose all, *and he got it too*!

Here is the key to how Job lowered his hedge of protection. He was *living in great fear* of losing everything, and without a doubt he was **verbalizing** his fear where everyone, *including* the devil, could hear him. How can I be so certain that Job was verbalizing his fear of destruction?

First, I've never met anyone who did not talk about what they *feared* as well as *enjoyed* the most. This is just part of unregenerated human nature. We all tend to talk about those things that are strongest on our hearts. Since *unregenerate* man has always been subject to fear and bondage, I believe it is precise to say that Job talked a great deal about his fears **prior to** his loss. Jesus also made this fundamental truth clear in Matthew twelve.

> **(Matthew 12:34,37 KJV)** "O generation of vipers, how can ye, being evil, speak good things? For *out of the abundance* of the heart **the mouth speaketh**…For **by thy words** thou shalt be justified, and **by thy words** thou shalt be condemned."

Job's confession of fear, instead of faith in God's protection, gave Satan an opening to walk in and take everything he had. Job spoke (fearfully) *until holes* in his hedge came into existence, thus leaving *himself* open to Satan's attack.

Did Job Sin With His Mouth?

"In all this Job *sinned not*, nor charged God **foolishly**."

This verse of Scripture says that Job did not charge God *foolishly*. I agree that Job did not *knowingly* shout off his mouth against God and sin by cursing God. *That is what God meant* when He said Job **sinned not**. Hence, I *don't* believe that he did anything like that during his entire grueling ordeal. However, I do believe (as I said earlier) that Job spoke out words of fear **in ignorance**. For example, in (1:21) Job says, "the Lord gave *and the Lord* has taken away...." We who can read the verses prior to and after (v:21) can see that the Lord wasn't the One Who took away. Satan was the one who took away Job's possessions. Job's words were *false*, and were spoken in his *ignorance* of the situation, rather than in foolish disobedience. Job spoke *without* full knowledge of the situation, for he couldn't *see* his enemy really was. He was blind to what was taking place in the realm of the Spirit, and Satan took advantage of that weakness in his character.

In order to answer the question, "Did Job sin with his mouth?" I want to pose another question, *What is Sin?* Is living and walking in fear sin? Is speaking falsely in ignorance sin? Again I ask, "*What is Sin?*" There is a very explicit explanation of Sin given to us in the Word of God.

(Romans 14:23 KJV) And he that doubteth is damned if he eat, **because** *he eateth* not of faith: *for whatsoever is not of faith* **is sin**.

Anything we do that is not done in faith (confidence, trust) in God and His Word *is sin*. Thus, from the words of Job's own mouth we can see that he did indeed sin with his mouth. Recall God spoke of him as being perfect, *but* He **did not** speak of him as being some *sinless* icon of perfection as the traditional Church has portrayed him. Moreover, God also sees the redeemed of the Lamb (us) as perfect, but our perfection is through the blood of Jesus. We must *never* forget that Job *was not* spiritually reborn. God in His mercy saw Job as a man who loved Him, but due to ignorance he experienced a temporary setback. It is sad but true that we all experience spiritual & physical setbacks from time to time. Still, God *is not* the cause of or an **accomplice to**, these setbacks. *We're* the ones assisting the enemy. *It's time we take the responsibility for our own weaknesses and stop blaming God!* Grow up!

What *NOT* To Do In Trials!

(Job 7:11/9:20-22) "Therefore I **will not** restrain my mouth; I **will** speak in the anguish of my spirit, I **will** *complain* in the bitterness of my soul [O Lord]...Though I am innocent *and* **in the right**, my own mouth would condemn me; though I am blameless, **He** would prove me perverse. Though I am blameless, I regard not myself; I despise my life. It is all one; therefore I say, **God** [*does not* discriminate, but] *destroys the blameless* and the wicked."

What's In A Word?

In ignorance Job says some pretty strong things *against* the Lord. He attempts to justify himself and make God *seem* to be the One in error. Job was not only living in fear he was also living under the influence of a *self-righteous spirit*. Job was *unwilling* to believe that **he** could have done anything to bring this trial upon himself. This reminds me of many well meaning "believers" who **insist** on thinking they have done everything "right" and God has not *honored* His Word. Listen carefully! God **does not** fail. We humans are the ones that fall short. We must hear the wake up call: **We** *are most times the makers of our own demise!* Until we humble ourselves and get off our self-righteous high horse, God **cannot** intervene on our behalf. Yes, I meant what I said, God *can not* help us if we live in fear and self-righteousness. **Why?** Because, God will *respect* our right to do our own will! He will not rescue one who doesn't want to saved.

God finally intervened, but Job had to take action *first*.

(Job 38:1-3; 40:1,2,8) THEN THE Lord answered Job out of the whirlwind and said, Who is this that darkens counsel **by words without knowledge?** Gird up now your loins like a man, and I will *demand* of you, and you will declare to Me...MORE OVER, THE Lord said to Job, Shall he who would **find fault with the Almighty** contend with Him? He who disputes with God, let him answer it...Will you also annul (set aside and render void) My judgments? Will you *condemn Me* [your God], that you may [**appear**] **righteous** *and* justified.

Reading the above passage, I find it impossible to believe that anyone would argue for Job's side of this debate. It is obvious that God was *somewhat* putout with Job's conduct. In fact God even referred to Job's words as *words without knowledge* (ignorant words). The Lord continued by addressing the self-righteous spirit that was influencing Job. God told him, "Who are you to make yourself appear to be righteous, and Me your Creator to be unrighteous?" Basically He said "Who do you think you are condemning **Me** with all these ignorant confessions of yours?" Finally, *the light* dawned somewhere within Job's spirit. Miraculously, he was able to see *the evil* behind his own words.

(Job 42:1-3;10) "THEN JOB said to the Lord, I know that You can do all things, and that no thought *or* purpose of Yours can be restrained *or* thwarted. [You said to me] Who is this that darkens *and* obscures counsel [by words] without knowledge? Therefore [**I now see**] I have [**rashly**] uttered **what I did not understand**, things too wonderful for me, which I *did not* know...And the Lord turned the captivity of Job *and* restored his fortunes, when he *prayed for his friends*; also the Lord gave Job twice as much as he had before."

Here we note that Job's restoration did not come *until* he did a few things first. What did Job do? First, he *repented* of self-righteousness and his words without knowledge. Then, he also *prayed* for his friends. Repentance and prayer were **the keys** to Job's breakthrough, just as they are for each of us. Repentance and prayer are two important things that we all should take part in when experiencing tragedy in life.

Job is a perfect example of how one *should not* speak to or about God when in a crisis. Without a doubt this crisis would have turned to Job's restoration much sooner had he looked more closely at his own weaknesses. Nonetheless, praise God for His intervention and mercy upon Job's life. When Job's temptation *by the enemy* was completed, **God** restored *double* of what he had before his crisis began. Repentance & prayer caused Job's restoration of double. Without them he *would not* have seen restoration in his life.

I would like to restate *and* answer the question that I posed at the beginning of this chapter. *What's in a word?* Life & death, spiritually and physically, are in the words that we speak. Therefore what we say is in fact *very* important. Our words can ***literally*** change the very direction of our lives.

For example when I said, "Jesus come into my heart and forgive me all my sins. I want You to be my Lord and Savior," those words totally changed my very destiny in life. Because of those words I can share this message with you today. **Glory to God** for His saving *grace* and *mercy*!

Thus as a result, there are basically three types of words in use in all realms of authority. First, there are the words that are confident, faith-filled, life producing words. These are the words that are in line with God's Word/will, plus those words that come directly out of Scripture. Next, we have the fear-filled, death producing words that come to us from the enemy. Finally, there are the empty, inoperative, non-working words. These are the words we say that are *not necessarily* good or evil, but are in reality foolish, empty (void of healthy productive power) words that come from the unrenewed mind. All of us are speaking one of these types of words, or a combination of any of the three.

Consequently, I could confess something 10,000 times (*in faith*), but if that confession is ***knowingly*** not *in line with God's Word/will*, I

won't receive what I have *believed* because that thing never was the will of God for my life.

Therefore, I *must* make wise Scriptural confessions. Speak things that agree with God's Word/will. God won't support confessions that are *knowingly* against His Word/will. However, the enemy will oblige us by fulfilling our willful desires, so we must be careful to only believe for those things that are in line with His Word.

I could confess, for example, that I am the Apostle Paul 100,000 times, and even convince myself that I'm him; but still I will *never* be able to be the Apostle Paul. Why? This is because that would be an empty, inoperative confession that borders on evil and the occult. Confession is a **powerful**, serious thing, and we should not try to play *foolishly* with it. *Remember*, we are admonished to prayerfully guard *the desires* of our heart or spirit (Proverbs 4:23, 24).

Therefore, we *must* confess the Word of God and words that are **in line** with God's Word/will in order to receive the *definite*, godly things **that He has told us** to believe Him for. Words have a creative ability about them, but if we are running around *attempting to create* those things which God has not already **promised** in Scripture *or* privately spoken into our hearts; then we're practicing **a form of witchcraft**. We must be extremely careful about the kinds of confessions that we make, lest we *invoke* our own will. Furthermore, we do not want to *spiritually* partner up with the enemy in order to bring to pass our own selfish desire. Rhema (revelation knowledge) from God is the key to godly, Scriptural confessions. All of the promises of God are His will for us—yes and amen (2 Cor. 1:20). So it is Scriptural for God's people to believe that they *have received* the promises.

Finally, I'd like to close with a thought provoking verse of Scripture. I pray this verse will remain in our hearts, minds and mouths till Jesus comes…May the Spirit of Almighty God grant us ears to hear (*understand*) and eyes to see (*perceive*), the force of good or evil that is released through our tongue—***Amen!***

A Closing Scripture

(Matthew 12:37) For **by your words** you will be justified *and* acquitted, and **by your words** you will be condemned *and* sentenced.

2

VISUALIZATION: IS IT SCRIPTURAL?
(Take Back What Satan Has Stolen—*Your Vision!*)

During the last fifteen years, there has been a lot of debate over the use of visualization in Christianity, as to whether or not it is a Scriptural practice. The overall controversy seems to focus on the fact that eastern religions and the *New Age Movement* use this sort of mental practice. Since these groups use visualization it seems a prevailing spirit of fear has come upon many believers, inspiring them to establish a "Christian" boycott against its use.

Nevertheless, where did the practice of visualization originate? Is visualization evil as some have claimed? If not, what useful purpose does it have in the lives of Christians today? Does the Word of God re*affirm* or condemn the practice of visualization? Before we continue, let's first define what it means to visualize—hence visualization. The dictionary defines *visualize* as: "to make visible, to form a mental image [picture] of."[1] Have you ever noticed how words form mental pictures? For instance, if I say "dog," a mental picture of a dog flashes in your mind. Using yet another example, when someone says "*mother*," instantly a picture of a mother, possibly your own mother, comes to mind. Moreover, each person's mental picture will be different.

The Origin of Visualization

(Genesis 1:1,27 NKJV) "In the beginning God **created** the heavens and the earth...So God created man in His *own* **image**; in the image of God He created him; male and female He created them."

The word *create* means "to select, feed (as formative processes), choose, dispatch, make."[2] *Create* gives the connotative meaning of the way an artist creates a sculpture. The artist forms a mental picture of what he desires to create. He may even draw out a sketch before beginning to mold his sculpture. With this picture firmly in our minds, let us relate this to the creation of the heavens, earth and the first man. How many of you reading this book believe that God knew *exactly* what He wanted to create **before** He started to make His creation?

Of course, God Almighty knew what He wanted to create, because He had a *distinct picture* of His creation *within* Himself prior to starting His work. He had a visualized picture of His creation long before He began the work. People of God—what we have just addressed is visualization. Therefore, without doubt, God Himself is the Originator of the practice of visualization. God selected, chose, nurtured then dispatched and made His inner visual picture, in the same fashion that an artist creates a sculpture. In an imaginative sense, one could say (Gen. 1:1) was God's *thumbnail sketch* of His creation, or the beginning formation of His inner vision. Let's continue to look at (Genesis 1:27) again:

> So God created man in **His own image**; in the image of God He created him; male and female He created them.

Image as defined by the concordance, is "to shade, a phantom, illusion, *resemblance*, hence **a representative figure**."[3] The dictionary defines *image* as; "a likeness or imitation of a person or thing; *a visual counterpart*. **A mental picture** or conception: Impression, Idea, Concept."[4]

Here I would like to offer a little food for thought. Could man have possibly been created in *the same likeness* as God's inner picture (*image*) within Himself? In addition, have you ever thought that part of the image of God was God's own inner picture of His created man? *In other words*, Adam was created to **the exact specifications** that God had already predetermined based on His visual (inner) image of man. Furthermore, what is the most important thing that any builder requires, whether he's building a tool shed or a new skyscraper? He would need a detailed set of blue prints to keep the project on track. God's *blueprints* (so to speak) for creation were within Himself, in the form of a picture.

Allow me to clarify myself before you label me a heretic. I totally believe that God's image is *spirit, soul, and body* (1Thess. 5:23). However, all I'm simply asking is "Could God have also created man according to the inner image, *blue print*, He visualized within Himself prior to His work?" I believe without a doubt that He did. Furthermore, God also revealed to us His redemptive plan (Jesus' Substitute Sacrifice—in our place) in the book of Genesis.

(Genesis 3:15 NKJV) And I will put enmity between you and the woman, And between your seed and her Seed; He shall bruise your head, And you shall bruise His heel.

This passage of Scripture is the very first prophecy about the coming Messiah, our Deliverer, Jesus Christ the Son of the Living God. Our Father was foretelling of Satan's destruction and our freedom, paid for by the blood Jesus. God was releasing *into* man His vision of the coming Savior and the ultimate defeat of the serpent, who *masterminded* their rebellion. Moreover, in this verse, God is clearly showing us how He calls the things that be not (visible to the natural eyes of man), *as though they were*. In God's eyes Satan's defeat and our redemption were as good as done even though neither was manifested in the physical realm. The Father saw (*visualized*) the future coming of the Lord Jesus and our adoption back to Him. As far as God was concerned, this was an established fact—prepared to be manifested.

Visualization In The Life Of Abraham

Let's continue in our study of visualization, now that we have established the foundational truth that God *is* the Originator of visualization. The next portion of God's Word that I want to direct your attention to is the life of Abram, or Abraham as he was later called.

(Genesis 12:1,2,4 KJV) Now the Lord had said unto Abram, Get thee out of thy country, and from thy kindred, and from thy father's house, unto a land that I will shew thee: And I will make of thee a great nation, and I will bless thee, and make thy name great; and thou shalt be a blessing. So Abram departed, as the Lord had spoken unto him; and Lot went with him: and Abram was seventy-five years old when he departed out of Haran.

Can you imagine God coming to you one day at **seventy-five years** of age, saying; "Come on, move out of this city and go to a city that I will show you, and there I will make of you a great nation." Today most people at seventy- five are in retirement, and the furthest thing from their minds is having children and moving. So the fact that Abram even listened to God's directions was a miracle in itself. I truly believe that had Abram not done as God said, he would never have received the promise spoken of in (v:2). Obedience to the vision of God was **the key** to receiving his promised child.

In the second verse of chapter twelve, God begins to reveal His inner visual picture of Abram's life and the fulfillment of His prophetic utterance in (Gen. 3:15). In order for Abram to be able to receive God's vision for his life, he had to be removed from his comfort zone, his hometown, and be brought into a place where he had no overpowering outside influences of doubt and unbelief.

God further unfolds His vision for Abram:

(Genesis 13:14-16 NKJV) And the Lord said to Abram, after Lot had separated from him: "Lift your eyes now and **look** from the place where you are—northward, southward, eastward, and westward; for all the land which you **see** *I give to you and your descendants* forever. And I will make your descendants **as the dust of the earth**; so that if a man could number the dust of the earth, then your descendants also could be numbered...."

Notice here (v:15), God said "*I give to you and your descendants*," instead of saying; "**I will give to you.**" In God's visual picture Abram and his descendants **already** had possession of the land that He had promised, even though Abram was still *childless* in the natural realm—God saw him with many children.

The word *look* as defined by the concordance means "behold, consider, perceive, think, view, visions."[5] God said to Abram "behold, look, see—all this I give unto you **and** your descendants **now**, only see My vision *as yours* from this day forth." God further developed His inner picture for Abram by giving him a **visual aid,** helping Abram comprehend better what He was doing; "And I will make your descendants as the **dust** of the earth."

This was a vivid portrait which God painted in Abram's spirit, "Behold the dust of the earth, how it cannot be numbered; so will your descendants be." From that day forward, each time Abram saw the dust he'd visualize his children. God put Abram in a position where he would be unable to not see himself as a father with many children every **day** of his life!

Despite his visual aid, Abram started to become rather anxious concerning his promised child. What was God's response to Abram?

(Genesis 15:4b&5 NKJV) "...but one who will come from your own body shall be your heir." Then He brought him outside and said '**Look** now toward heaven, and count the stars *if you are able to number them.*' And He said to him, 'So shall your descendants be.'"

God gave Abram *visual aid* number two "*Look* now toward heaven and count the stars...." The Bible says that this time (v:6), "He believed God." I believe with all my heart that God, through these two revelations, was gradually building Abram's *inner vision* of himself as a man with many children. Abram still did not fully understand all of the details, but he received enough to hold on to God's promise and believed Him despite any doubts. Now, day **or** night, God caused Abram to **visualize** his descendants. This brought about an incredible transformation in Abram.

The Most Powerful Factor of Godly Visualization

(Genesis 17:4b,5;15 NKJV) "...and you shall be a father of many nations. No longer shall your name be called Abram, but your name shall be Abraham; for I have made you a father of many nations...As for Sarai your wife, you shall not call her name Sarai, but Sarah shall be her name."

God is so awesome in the way He works. Not only did He give Abram two revelations, but He also changed Abram and Sarai's names, causing them to **confess** who they were in God. Thus, to show that this *principle* is consistent with the rest of Scripture let's look at it in the New Covenant.

(Romans 4:17 KJV) (As it is written, I have made thee a father of many nations,) before him whom he believed, **even God**, who quickeneth the dead, **and** *calleth those things which be not as though they were.*

God called the things which be not (in the natural) as though they were, because when He changed Abram's name to Abraham, he was in the natural realm still childless. **However**, in the spirit realm, God saw or visualized him as already possessing the promise. He called those things that *were not revealed to the senses*, yet still existed, **into** the realm of the natural, which manifested just as God visualized them to be. God changed how Abram and Sarai saw themselves and the way they spoke about who they were.

God put Abraham in a position where he **had** to confess who he was in God's sight, a father of many nations. Through this name change confession, approximately six months following this event, Sarah became pregnant with their son of promise, Isaac. Abraham and Sarah's new mental picture, coupled together with their new confession of faith, brought the supernatural power of God into them to produce the promised miracle. This miracle *did not* happen simply because Abraham received two revelations and began to confess that he was a father of many nations.

Abraham received **Rhema** a (living, saying)[6] Word from God, which he *acted* upon by believing God with his actions as well as his verbal confession. Whenever God gives you a (Rhema) word, dare to believe Him for it, by **seeing** yourself as He says you are; and by boldly confessing the word that God has birthed within your spirit. If we'll apply these truths, we too will receive from God the exact same way as Abraham did.

Look at what the book of Romans has to say about those who follow *after* Abraham's example of faith.

> **(Romans 4:12 KJV)** And the father of circumcision to them who are not of the circumcision only, **but who also walk in the steps** of that faith of our father Abraham, which *he* had being *yet* uncircumcised.

Abraham copied God's example, by calling the things that be not as though they were. We too should copy Abraham's way of applying faith, thus we would receive the same kind of results. God *always* honors heart felt faith.

> **(Ephesians 5:1)** Therefore be imitators of God [***copy Him*** and follow His example], as well beloved children [**imitate** their father].

Moreover, the book of Hebrews also has a powerful passage that expounds on how Abraham applied the practice of visualization.

> **(Heb.11:17-19 KJV)** By faith Abraham, when he was tried, offered up Isaac: and he that **had *received* the promises** offered up his only begotten *son*, Of whom it was said, That in Isaac shall thy seed be called: **Accounting** that God *was* able to raise *him* up, even from the dead; **from whence also he *received* him** in *figure*.

In the concordance, *accounting* is defined as "[to take an inventory, estimate, conclude, esteem, reason, reckon, suppose, **think on**]."[7] Abraham believed God could, and would, raise Isaac from the dead if need be; because he *knew* Isaac was his son of promise. Abraham was absolutely confident that God would keep His word, no matter how his circumstances seemed to appear. He considered not what his natural thoughts and feelings were telling him. This is the type of assurance and reliance that God desires for all believers to have in Him *and* His Word. Sadly, few dare to do so!

The word *figure* is defined in the concordance as, "[a fictitious narrative (of common life conveying a moral), parable, proverb]."[8] Abraham re*ceived* Isaac (from the dead) with the same *visual* narrative (parable) that God originally disclosed to him when he was 75 years old. God used His words to create a mental picture, which birthed the promise of Isaac inside Abraham's spirit. Consequently, he *saw* himself with Isaac, raised from the dead; **before** he was even sacrificed. Why? Because Abraham was fully persuaded that what God had promised, He was able to accomplish. He had one-hundred percent confidence that God *could not* lie.

One final note should be made regarding the name changes of Abraham and Sarah. The very fact that God changed their names proves that God saw them, as they're new names proclaimed: "You are a father of many nations, and she is a Princess with many children." God would not have called them Abraham and Sarah if they were not exactly as their names intended them to be *in His eyes*. Why? Because, God calls the things that *be not*—as thou they were.

Visualization In The Life of Jacob
(Gen. 30:25-43)

We now focus our attention on what I believe is the clearest, most undeniable example of the power of visualization written in the entire Word of God. We are going to examine the life of Jacob and how God taught him to outsmart his father-in-law Laban.

(Genesis 30:27-32;37-41 NKJV) "And Laban said to him, 'Please *stay*, if I have found favor in your eyes, *for* I have learned by experience that the Lord has blessed me for your sake...Name me your wages, and I will give it.' '...the Lord has blessed you since my coming. **And now, when shall I also provide for my own house?**...You shall not *give me* **anything**. If you will do this thing for me, I will again feed and keep your flocks: Let me pass through all your flock today, removing from there all the speckled and spotted sheep, and all the brown ones among the lambs, and the spotted and speckled among the goats; and **these shall be my wages**....' Now Jacob took for himself rods of green poplar and of the almond and chestnut trees, **peeled white strips in them**, and exposed the white…And the rods which he had peeled, **he set before the flocks** in the gutters, in the watering troughs where the flocks came to drink, **so that they should conceive when they came to drink**. So the flocks conceived **before the rods**, and the flocks brought forth *streaked, speckled, and spotted*. Then Jacob separated the lambs, *and made the flocks face toward the streaked* and all the brown in the flock of Laban; but he put his own flocks by themselves and did not put them with Laban's flock. And it came to pass, whenever the strong live-stock conceived, that Jacob placed the rods **before the eyes of the livestock** in the gutters, that they might **conceive among the rods**."

Here we have a man who is tired of being treated as a slave, and always *tricked* into losing, kind of poetic justice, seeing that he cheated his brother Esau out of his birthright. He decides it's time to move on, but Laban begs him to stay. Unfortunately, Laban makes a mistake, figuring he will continue to *use* the blessing upon Jacob in order to increase himself. One can profit at God's expense only so long, and then comes the retribution of God. Laban thought he had the upper hand when in fact God had a miracle plan of His own, one He would use to bring about the miracle restoration of all that Laban had stolen.

The Bible does not say that God *told* Jacob to do all the things that he did, yet I firmly believe God was the source behind Jacob's wisdom and insight. God wanted to display His miracle power through his life so that Laban and all of the land would know that Jehovah is God.

So, Jacob separated all of the speckled and spotted, (cows, goats, and sheep) from the pure solid colored animals. In genetics, the chance of these pure colored animals producing spotted and speckled offspring was nearly impossible and consequently that which took place was truly a total miracle from God.

Also, God gave Jacob a vision of His restoration plan, and **He** showed him how to bring about his own total restoration. God Almighty Himself inspired Jacob to peel stripes into the rods and place them in the **sight** of those animals where they drank and conceived their young. God's plan of restoration for Jacob was a plan that involved visualization. The animals would *see* the rods, and would produce young just like the rods that were before their eyes.

The Bible goes on to say (v:43), that Jacob increased *exceedingly* and had many cattle, camels, and donkeys, as well as servants. He became an extremely rich man by combining visualization with the natural process of animal breeding. Let's see *what* was the Source of Jacob's success.

(Genesis 31:19 NKJV) So ***God*** has taken away the livestock of your father and given them to me...."

God Almighty was the source of Jacob's miraculous success, *not* Satan. Moreover, Jacob received a dream from the Angel of God (v:10-13), telling him to take all that he had and proceed to Bethel. In other words, Jacob had received the restoration of all that Laban had stolen from him and even more. The Word of God is distinctly clear about our control over the mental pictures that we choose to dwell on. We are the ones who determine what we imagine.

Whatever we perceive in our minds will either be a source of strength or a prison of defeat. The mental picture that we hold within ourselves on a continual basis will either widen our horizon of possibility, or it will set the boundaries of the cage we are doomed to live in.

The amazing thing about all of this is that we are the ones who choose which thoughts we receive. We are *ultimately* the ones responsible for our own success or defeat. Since God cannot *force* us to change our thought life, we must make the choice. Having a godly thought life is the will of God, but He will not enforce it upon us; as we have been given a free will.

Visualization: Goliath's Strength Israel's Defeat!

(1 Samuel 17:8-11 NKJV) "'...Choose a man for yourselves, and let him come down to me. If he is able to fight with me and kill me, then we will be your servants. But if I prevail against him and kill him, then you shall be our servants and serve us...I defy the armies of Israel this day; give me a man, that we may fight together.' When Saul and all of Israel **heard those words** of the Philistine, they were **dismayed** and **greatly** afraid."

Israel lived in a cage of defeat, because *the words* of Goliath created a fear-filled mental picture in all the people's minds. Goliath's size and track record were bad enough, but when they heard his words fear came and their horizon of possibility greatly diminished. They *thought* they were defeated thus, they were. They *thought* he was invincible, therefore he was. The process by which one forms mental pictures through words is the essence of visualization. Goliath used his words to create a psychological picture of defeat in their minds. Unfortunately it worked! Goliath's strength was based on *their* perception of his words.

Miraculously, along came a man who could see no defeat (1 Sam. 17: 17-51). David had been commissioned by his father Jesse (v:17) to take some food to his brothers and their commanding officer, and get word from them. This was God's divine appointment to present to the armies of Israel their next king.

> **(1 Samuel 17:23 KJV)** And as he talked with them behold, there came up the champion, the Philistine of Gath, Goliath by name, out of the armies of the Philistines, *and spake according to the same words*: and **David heard them.**

Notice the last four words of (v:23), "*and David heard them.*" Also, bear in mind that these words which Goliath spoke were **the same words** that the army of Israel had heard many times before. Yet those words created a radically different picture in David's mind. David saw Goliath's boasting as a personal offense; not only to himself, but to the God of Israel as well. He also saw Goliath's defeat as a financial opportunity. This victory would mean total debt cancellation for him and his family.

> **(1 Samuel 17:26,25 KJV)** "And David spake to the men that stood by him, saying, What shall be done to the man that killeth this Philistine, and taketh away the reproach from Israel? for who is this *uncircumcised Philistine*, that he should defy the armies of the living God?...And the men of Israel said, Have ye seen this man that is come up? surely to defy Israel is he come up: and it shall be, *that* the man who killeth him, the king will enrich him with great riches, and give him his daughter, and make his father's house free in Israel."

David's cognitive image of Goliath's defeat became strengthened as he received more details of what his downfall would be worth. Unfortunately, Israel could only see themselves' as weak and defeated, but David saw the whole encounter as a profitable opportunity. Following this, David was brought to Saul to receive permission to fight. He explained his triumphs over the lion and the bear, and showed himself to be qualified as a soldier.

> **(1Samuel 17:36 NKJV)** "Your servant has killed both lion and bear; and this uncircumcised Philistine *will be* like one of them, **seeing** he has defied the armies of the living God."

From this courageous statement we can see that David had a crystal clear *visual picture* of his victory over Goliath. It was this portrait of triumph that motivated him toward the fulfillment of this golden opportunity. It was his destiny, *and he knew it*. Therefore, David **received** exactly what he *believed* would take place. David's confidence stemmed first and foremost from his faith and trust in God as his Provider and Protector. David had a deep, intimate relationship with God Almighty. Second, he had the experience of past victories to draw strength and confidence from. David controlled his thoughts by replaying the mental tapes of his victories over the lion and the bear. The thought of previous victories *drove* him on. David also drew confidence by following in the foot steps of Abraham. He called the things that be not as though they were, *"and this uncircumcised Philistine* **will be** *like one of them."* He saw the battle as already won, he boldly confessed his vision and he went forward with the victory already his. He **knew** God's will for his life and he went out boldly took possession of it.

> **(1Samuel 17:37;46 KJV)** "David said moreover, The Lord that delivered me out of the paw of the lion, and out of the paw of the bear, he will deliver me out of the hand of this Philistine. And Saul said **Go**, *and the Lord be with thee*...This day will the Lord deliver thee into mine hand, and I will smite thee, and take thine head from thee…".

David made sure to give the Lord all the glory for his past and present victories, and he *boldly confessed his faith* in God before Saul. Then just a few verses of Scripture later, he makes his most courageous confession. He fearlessly tells Goliath why, and how he is going to kill him. At the close of this encounter, David *puts his faith into action*, killing Goliath with *Goliath's* own sword, fulfilling his inner vision of victory, and displaying to the whole world that God is *Alive*!

We, as people of God, must understand that David was not an extraordinary man. He simply chose not to see *any* defeat. Hence, he lived his life receiving victory after victory. He lived the life of a winner because he focused his spiritual eyes not on who he was; but on who God was creating him to be. We can all walk in victory the same as David did! But, we will have to think and act like David as well.

Visualization And The Promised Land
(Num. 13:17-33/Num. 14:1-10)

God commanded Moses to send a group of men on a mission to spy out the land of promise. The report was that the land was just as

God said it was; however, there was a massive inferiority problem among the inspection team. Victory was not in sight for this motley-crew. It's sad that negative people seem to out number the positive.

> **(Numbers 13:27,28; 31,33 KJV)** "And they told him, and said, We came unto the land whither thou sentest us, and surely it floweth with milk and honey; and this is the fruit of it. *Nevertheless* the people be *strong* that dwell in the land, and the cities are walled, and *very great*: and moreover we saw the children of Anak there...But the men that went up with him said, We be not able to go up against the people; for they are *stronger than we*...And there we saw *the giants*, the sons of Anak, which come of *the giants*: and we were **in our own sight** as grasshoppers, and so we were in their sight."

The ten spies that brought back an evil report had an inferiority complex simply because they had *no real* relationship with God. They knew His power side, but they had no genuine experience with His Father, Provider and Protector side. Therefore, they were weak and fainted when God's challenge was delivered. They witnessed the signs and wonders, but not His *abiding presence* in their lives (Jn. 15:7), on a personal level. Because of this lack of relationship, ten out of the 12 spies saw *themselves* as grasshoppers before the sons of Anak — "...***in our own sight*** as grasshoppers...."

They could not *see* themselves as victorious regardless of what God had said. In their imagination, there was no possible way to possess the land. Hence, they would not even attempt to do so. But Joshua and Caleb ***saw*** that the victory, because they visualized it through God's Word of instruction!

> **(Numbers 13:30;14:6-9 KJV)** "And Caleb stilled the people before Moses, and said, Let us go up *at once*, and possess it; **for we are well able to overcome it**...And Joshua the son of Nun, and Caleb the son of Jephunneh, which were of them that searched the land, rent their clothes: And they spake unto all the company of the children of Israel, saying, The land, which we passed through to search it, is an exceeding good land. If the LORD delight in us, then he will bring us into this land, and give it us; a land which floweth with milk and honey. Only rebel not ye against the Lord, neither fear ye the people of the land; for they are bread for us: their defense is departed from them, **and the Lord is with us**: fear them not."

Visualization: Is It Scriptural?

Joshua and Caleb were men of faith who had a personal relationship with Jehovah. They *knew* that what God said they could do, they would do. They **knew** God would honor His promises. Unfortunately *many* believers today do not believe that God will honor His Word. They think God *can* and **will** change His mind *whenever* He wants, despite all the promises He has given. But God's Word is His oath (bond of commitment) to us. God & His Word are **one** (the same).

Joshua and Caleb believed God at His Word, and refused to *see* any defeat. They saw the battle already fought and won because their God said they were able to win. They didn't understand all of the details involved, but through *the eyes of faith*, they *saw* themselves victorious. It's time that we open our spiritual eyes and begin to comprehend that God does His business much differently than we could ever dream possible. That which *appears* illogical or *ungodly* to us may very well be perfectly normal to God. The religious mind tends to put God into a theological box, by saying God will *only* move within *our* four walls of understanding. In reality our understanding is **extremely** limited in comparison to His. With this thought in mind, let's see what *Proverbs* says about our thought life:

(Proverbs 23:7 KJV) "For as he **thinketh** in his heart, so is he:"

Thinketh, as defined by the concordance means, "to act as gate keeper, to estimate, or think."[9] This verse is literally saying; "Be diligent in the roll of keeping your thought life." Why? This is because that which *you* allow yourself to think on most will determine you're entire life's destiny. Alcoholics think on alcohol, and a pervert thinks only on sex and other perversions. That man (Prov. 23:7), becomes what he programs into his mental computer bank. This same word of wisdom applies to Christians today. Whatever we visualize (*think on*) will be the determining factor of what we become. The saddest part of all is, **even God** cannot help me if I have chosen to set my thoughts on those things which will destroy me. God has given all of us a free will, which He *will not* violate, so the choice is up to us. He has set before us life and death, blessing and curse (Prov. 18:21); the choice is up to each of us. But, Proverbs chapter four gives us another powerful principle of truth.

(Proverbs 4:23 KJV) Keep thy heart with all diligence; for *out of it* are the **issues of life**.

The word *keep* tells us "to guard or protect [our hearts against anything that brings corruption]."[10] The word *heart* denotes "the will, the intellect, understanding and center of anything."[11] This verse goes on to say; *out of it* (the heart), are the issues of life. What are these issues of life that are coming out of the heart? The word *issue, according to the concordance, means* "geographical boundary, source, and border."¹² In essence, this Scripture says: "Keep (guard, protect) your heart (mind, will; emotions and *spirit*) with all diligence; for *out of it* (the heart) come the issues (geographical boundaries or borders) of life."

This verse tells us to protect the soul and spirit, because what we allow our minds to visualize (think on) will set the boundaries or borders of the prison in which we *must* live the rest of our lives. **We** set up our own limits (*not God*), by the thoughts that we choose to think on.

If we continually see ourselves as failures, that is *exactly* what we will become. However, if we see ourselves through the eyes of God's Word, we will be able to do *all things* through Christ Who Strengthens us (Phil. 4:13). The choice is up to us. In order to live victoriously, we must determine to set our thoughts on **the Word of God**, allowing His Word to be the *determining factor* governing our lives. His Word must be first place and the last word *over* our circumstances in our lives.

Visualization In The New Covenant
(What Did Jesus Say About It?)

(John 1:42) Andrew then led (brought) Simon to Jesus. Jesus looked at him and said, You are Simon son of John. *You shall be called Cephas*—which translated is Peter [Stone].

In order to properly answer regarding Jesus' thoughts about visualization, we should start at the beginning of His earthly ministry. Have you ever wondered why Jesus gave Simon the name "Cephas?" Could it be Jesus *looked inside* Simon, saw all of his inconsistencies, then *in essence* said, "Simon you may be weak and without backbone now, but I see you as a *rock* (Peter); this is what I will cause you to be."

Jesus said to Simon; "I see (visualize) you as Peter (rock), a stable man; a man of strength and power." Jesus saw Simon *as God wanted him to become*; rather than as he was. He called the things *that be not* as though they were. This is the same thing God did in the case of Abram and Sarai. Jesus plainly said in the book of John that Abraham **saw** His day and was delighted.

(John.8:56) Your forefather Abraham was extremely happy at the hope and prospect of *seeing* My day (My incarnation); and he did **see** it and was delighted.

In light of the previous verse of Scripture, how was Abraham seeing His day? Abraham saw (visualized) Jesus' day with his spiritual eyes. God already said in (Gen. 3:15), that the Messiah would come; and He would use Isaac to bring this to pass. Isn't it altogether possible that God showed Abraham a detailed mental picture (Heb. 11:17-19), of His plan to redeem the world and Abraham was excited that he had a part in the restoration of all things. He saw, visualized, this by faith given to him through God's promise. At this point I want to pose a question. Did you know that Jesus Himself *practiced* visualization? *Traditional* believers would probably say, "that's heresy!" Nevertheless, they should consider the words of Jesus Himself in Luke.

(Luke 10:18) And He said to them, "**I saw** Satan falling like a lightning [flash] from heaven."

If you have a King James Version Bible, you will probably have the following cross-reference, as well:

(John 12:31 KJV) *Now* is the judgment of this world: **now shall** the prince of this world be cast out. And I, if I be lifted up from the earth, will draw all men unto me.

Remember that when Jesus testified of what He *saw*, He had not yet gone to the cross (to be lifted up), and the occurrence of Satan's *fall* (from access to God's throne) still had not taken place; "***now*** shall the prince...be cast out." The *fall* that is referred to in (John 12:31) has nothing to do with Satan's "fall" from grace. This was in reference to Satan's defeat at Calvary. Jesus was speaking *in advance* about His victory and the destruction of the works of Satan. Jesus was simply proclaiming that He could already *see* the defeat of Satan and our reconciliation with God, just as His Father did in (Gen. 3:15). God is *the author of visualization*, and Jesus practiced it on earth. If Jesus had an aversion to the practice of visualization then He wouldn't have made those statements that we've addressed. Clearly, Jesus visualized the ultimate down fall of Satan by giving His life: spirit, soul & body.

Visualization And The Apostle Paul

In closing, I would like to include some insightful words from the apostle Paul concerning visualization.

(2 Corinthians 5:17 KJV) Therefore if any man be in Christ, *he is* a new creature: old things are passed away; behold (see, realize), all things are become *new*.

(Romans 6:11 KJV) Likewise *reckon* ye also yourselves to be dead indeed unto sin, but alive unto God through Jesus Christ our Lord.

Was Paul telling us the truth in these verses? If so, and if we are all new creatures, why is it that so many of us live as if we are *not*? I believe the answer is found in the book of Romans, chapter 6 verse 11. The majority of believers *do not* see (visualize) themselves as new creatures, victorious **over** Sin, sickness, fear and death. Hence, most do not walk in victory, because they cannot *see* victory. We can't reach beyond what we view as being possible. Paul tells us to reckon ourselves dead to Sin, but alive to God in Christ Jesus. What does he mean when he says *reckon*? The concordance defines *reckon* as "to esteem, reckon, suppose, think (on)."[13] Paul is saying visualize (think of) yourselves as being dead to Sin, but alive to God in Christ Jesus. Unless we think of ourselves in this way we will *never* be able to walk in the reality of these verses. Thus, in the Church, a majority of believers have no vision, no redemptive revelation; and hence live in defeat (Prov. 29:18).

Visualization Kept Jesus On The Cross!

(Hebrews 12:1,2 KJV) Wherefore seeing we also are compassed about with so great a cloud of witnesses, let us lay aside every weight, and the sin which doth so easily beset us, and let us run with patience the race that is set before us, *Looking* unto Jesus the author and finisher of our faith; who *for the joy that was* **set before him** endured the cross, despising the shame, and is set down at the right hand of the throne of God.

In verse 2 of chapter 12, the words *"set before him"* are defined by the concordance as "to lie before the view, to be *present* (**to the mind**)."[14] Therefore, while Jesus was hanging on the cross, there was a joy *set before His mind*. And that joy which Jesus *saw* was **you**...and **me**. He *visualized* our freedom through His sacrifice, and that visual picture gave Him overwhelming joy! He visualized the dominion of the enemy being broken off the human race. This revelation which was *set before Him*, also strengthened Him to endure **separation** from His Father in hell on the behalf of a race of unworthy sinners (See: Acts 2:22-27 NKJV).

A Closing Scripture

"For as he *thinks* in his heart, **so is he**..."

ROMANS: RECONCILIATION REVELATION
(See Yourself As Free From Sin)

What on earth is reconciliation, and how does it concern me? Reconciliation to God the Father meant He would give His **all**—*for us!*

(Romans 5:10 KJV) For if, when we were enemies, we were *reconciled* to God *by the death* of his Son, much more, being reconciled we shall be saved by his life.

Reconciliation is "a change of relationship between God and man based on *the changed status of man* through the redemptive work of Christ," according to the Bible dictionary.[1] God *gave up* the Lord Jesus so that we could receive a new status or position with Him. Hence we have been reconciled (brought back into fellowship) with God the Father through Christ Jesus. Jesus took upon Himself our guilt and punishment so that we could be free. This is the **vital** revelation that the apostle Paul was desiring to instill into the hearts and minds of the Church at Rome. Many believers today *still* need to receive this essential revelation into their entire beings, so that they can walk in the freedom that Jesus' blood has provided. Paul raises some important questions in Romans 6:

(Romans 6:1-4 KJV) What shall we say then? Shall we continue in sin, that grace may abound? God forbid. How shall we, that are dead to sin, live any longer therein? Know ye not, that so many of us as were baptized into Jesus Christ were baptized into his death? Therefore we are buried with him by baptism into death: that like as Christ was raised up from the dead by the glory of the Father even so we also should walk in newness of life.

Paul asked us in verse (2); "How shall we, that **are dead to** sin, live any longer therein?" Have you ever asked yourself; "*If I'm saved, why is my life so messed up*"? Why are so many "believers" still living in Sin? These are some important but puzzling questions that we will endeavor to look at carefully.

Paul said we are baptized into Christ's death, or buried through our baptism. However, he also says we are raised up from the dead *with* Christ, and that we should walk in *newness* of life.

Paul does not leave any loop hole for living a life of sin. He says we are overcomer's. It's sad to say, but I do not know even 500 people who walk in the newness of life that Paul says we should walk in. Also, I wonder what percentage of the Church really understands the significance of these verses?

> **(Romans 6:5-9 KJV)** For if we have been planted together in the likeness of his death, we shall be also *in the likeness* of *his* resurrection: Knowing this, that our old man **is crucified** with *him, that the body of sin might be destroyed*, that henceforth we **should not serve sin**. For he that is dead is freed from sin. Now if we be dead with Christ, we believe that we shall also live with him: Knowing that Christ being raised from the dead dieth no more; death hath no more dominion over him.

Paul uses baptism as a symbol to explain that when Christ died and went to hell, we also died with Him, in a spiritual sense, through being baptized. He goes on to explain that we rose *spiritually* with Christ as He rose bodily, symbolized by our being raised again out of the water at baptism.

Furthermore, Paul uses many past tense words [were, have been, destroyed], to illustrate our death, burial and resurrection with Christ. By using these words he is showing us that the process has *already* been completed and change has already taken place in us. Now it is up to us to realize it and begin to walk in the freedom that is *already* ours. This does not mean that we will *automatically* walk in total perfection. However, until we begin to see ourselves as free from Satan's dominion, we will **never** walk in freedom. For us to walk in His perfection, we must *see* it as possible.

Moreover, consider verse (6), "Knowing this, that our old man *is* crucified with him...." This is where we English speakers tend to miss something in the translation. The word *know* or knowing does not properly display the exact meaning as it does in other languages. In English we say "I know that" or "I know him," meaning to know a fact or to know someone. However, in the German language; for example, there are several words for the English word *know*. For instance, **wissen** (to know about someone or to know a fact), and **erkennen** (to recognize, perceive, to understand well).

Therefore, when Paul says *"knowing this,"* he means we are to recognize, perceive, and understand well that our old man is dead. This problem in Christian circles is better known as "head knowledge v. heart knowledge."

It is the heart knowledge of God that we are seeking hence one understands the title of this book *When The Holy Spirit Reveals*. Heart knowledge is revelation knowledge, and revelation knowledge of the Word of God will set us free (Jn. 8:31,32). Let's look again at verse six of Romans chapter six.

What Is The "Old Man?"

Knowing (recognizing, understanding) this, that our old man is crucified with him (Christ).

What is *the old man* that Paul is referring to? The Bible dictionary, defines the old man as "the former self of a believer **prior to** conversion."[2] The old man is simply the unrenewed spirit which controlled us *prior* to conversion.

Unfortunately, many still think that they have an "old nature," that they must *wrestle* with until death. Nevertheless, Paul goes directly against this *tradition*, by telling us that our old man **is** crucified, (is dead). Mindful that Paul said our old man (unrenewed spirit) is dead; consequently, we no longer have a *carnal nature* to blame if we do not live as Jesus did. The responsibility then ends up on our shoulders.

"...that the body of sin might be *destroyed*, that **henceforth** we should not serve sin..."

In this part of the verse Paul is referring to our bodies as the instruments used for sinning. He says the body must be destroyed. However, Paul is not saying to **literally** kill your body. The word *destroyed* in the concordance means "to be (render) entirely idle (useless), abolish, cease; become of no effect."[3] So our bodies are to be useless for Sin because our old carnal nature *is dead*. We **have been** set free from Sin to serve righteousness, by Christ Jesus. Therefore, we have a choice given to us. We can choose to serve Sin *again* or we can use our freedom to obey the Word of God. He has made us free now the choice is up to us to live free.

> **(Romans 6:6)** We know that our old (unrenewed) self was nailed to the cross with Him in order that [our] body [which is *the instrument*] of sin might be **made ineffective** *and* inactive for evil, that we might no longer be slaves of sin.

Sin therefore, *should* have no dominion (authority) over the blood bought child of the Living God. Unfortunately, this *does not* seem to be the rule, but rather the exception. Today, we have so many believers living under the bondage of Sin, still desperately trying to kill *an old carnal nature* that has already been crucified. Why do Christians still live in bondage to sinful habits? Is freedom even possible? If we really are free from the bondage of Sin, why does it seem as though we are still held hostage by it?

The Solution To Our Freedom Is To *Reckon*

> **(Romans 6:11 KJV)** Likewise **reckon** ye also yourselves to be dead indeed unto sin, but alive unto God through Jesus Christ our Lord.

The word *reckon* is defined by the concordance as "to take an inventory, estimate; conclude, count, reason, think (on)."[4] The apostle Paul is telling us that we must *think on*, or count ourselves as dead to Sin, but also that we are alive to God. *The Amplified Bible* explains it in simpler language.

> **(Romans 6:11)** Even so **consider** yourselves also dead to sin *and* your relationship to it **broken**, but alive to God [living in *unbroken* fellowship with Him] in Christ Jesus.

The Bible dictionary defines *consider* as "to perceive, behold; **see** with one view, to be aware...."[5] We are told to **see** (visualize ourselves) dead to Sin, but we're also told to *see* ourselves living in **unbroken** fellowship with God in Christ. If we are living in unbroken fellowship with God, then Sin cannot be in control of our lives.

The reason why many of us do not live free from Sin is because we have not followed the instructions of (Rom. 6:11). We have been told to reckon, consider, *see* ourselves 100% totally free from all of Sin's demands upon our lives.

Once we begin to *perceive* the revelation of our freedom through Christ, we will start to tear up the devil's kingdom, taking back all of the ground the devil has stolen. This must begin with the restoration of the mind of Christ **in us,** because as we (think) see ourselves, so will we become. If we have no vision beyond today, we will **never** be able to walk in all of the great things God has for us tomorrow.

(Proverbs 23:7 KJV) "For as he thinketh in his heart, so is he…"

The way I see myself is a *major* determining factor in what I will become. If I do not see (*visualize*) that I have victory over Sin, then I **will not** walk as though I do. With this in mind, many believers are not walking in victory *over Sin* simply because they do not know (believe, understand) that they have been set free to walk after righteousness. This is the reason why Jesus went to the cross.

Many people read the Word, and think, "I wish I could live like that," but they look at their experiences of the past and conclude; "*I cannot live free like that!*" Since when do our experiences have more authority and power over us than the Word of God? We need to stop using our experiences as the measuring stick of what we can or cannot do, and start confessing what the Word says we are and in Christ.

The way we see ourselves really does have incredible power over *our actions*, and therefore over our **destiny** in life. For example, if I see myself as being unlovable what will happen to me? Chances are very good that I will never be able to receive someone else's love, solely because I feel I am unworthy of someone's love. On the other hand, if I see myself as God's Word says I am (*not how I feel*), I will be able to do all things through Christ, which empowers me.

I challenge you today to see yourself the way the Word of God says you are, and do not confess anything else about yourself. God's Word on a (daily basis) is *the key element* in transforming our minds into the mind of Christ. Without this transformation, we will never live free from the bondage of Satan.

If I Am Dead To Sin, Why Am I Still Struggling

(Romans 6: 12-18 KJV) Let not sin therefore reign in your mortal body, that ye should obey it in the lusts thereof. Neither yield ye your members as instruments of unrighteousness unto sin: but yield yourselves unto God, as those that are alive from the dead, and your members as instruments of righteousness unto God. For sin shall not have **dominion over you**: for ye are not under the law, but under grace...shall we sin...God forbid. Know ye not, that to whom ye yield yourselves servants to obey, his servants ye are to whom ye obey; whether of sin unto death, or of obedience unto righteousness? But God be thanked, that ye were the servants of sin, but ye have obeyed *from the heart* that form of doctrine which was delivered you. Being then *made free* from sin, ye became the servants of righteousness.

We are not to allow Sin to dominate our lives, because we *have been* made free from its power. Therefore, we can now yield our members (spirit, soul & body) to God as a new person that has been raised from the dead. Paul wants us to *realize* that Sin has no power over us, and can no longer control us. We are **completely** liberated from our old master. We are free from Sin's power; however, we cannot use this freedom as an excuse to yield ourselves to it again and again. Every time we allow Sin to have power over us, we are **literally** giving back a little piece of our *sovereignty* (from Satan). If *we* allow this to continue, we will soon be back in total bondage to him. The reborn man is sovereign from **all** of Satan's influences *if he chooses to remain so*. However, man can **never** be sovereign from God. God is the *only* totally sovereign being and He has *made us* sovereign from the enemy. In other words, He has set us free from Satan's complete control.

This is the reason so many are in bondage to cigarettes, alcohol, enslaving thought patterns, and the list goes on. We are surrendering a part of the freedom that Christ has given to us every time that we give into sinful actions. Remember, we are servants of God now, not servants of Sin. It is unfortunate that so many believers still live their lives as though they never were set free. The unsaved world stands outside observing us, and says *"They said Jesus is the answer, but they live like He's not!"* Then we ask, "Why aren't our churches filled with unbelievers seeking redemption in Christ?" It is time for a change! We need to live and shine the light of Christ in a lost and dark world.

The lost need to see a *definitive* difference in us so that they will realize *they are lost* and they need Christ to make their lives complete. We cannot win the world while living our lives *just like* those in the world. We are to be in the world, but not live like the world. If we continually yield our members to sinful conduct, we will once again become slaves to Sin, meaning **we** put ourselves back under the enemy's dominion. As a result, we are unproductive in winning the lost to Christ. Hence, millions *remain* lost!

(Romans 6:16) Do you not know that if you **continually** surrender yourselves to anyone to do **his will**, you are the **slaves of him** whom you obey, whether that be to sin, which leads to death, or to obedience which leads to righteousness (right doing and right standing with God)?

The apostle Paul uses the concept of visualization to help us mentally realize our freedom from Sin's power.

(Romans 7:1-4 KJV) Know ye not, brethren, (for I speak to them that know the law), how that the law hath dominion over a man as long as he liveth? For the woman which hath an husband is bound by the law to her husband so long as he liveth; but if the husband be dead, she is loosed from the law of her husband. So then if, while her husband liveth, she be married to another man, she shall be *called* an adulteress, though she be married to another man. Wherefore, my brethren, ye also are become dead to the law by the Body of Christ; that ye should be *married to another, even* to him who is raised from the dead, that we should bring forth fruit unto God.

We are to *see* ourselves as being like a woman, once married, but then free to be joined to another (the Lord Jesus) at the death of the husband. The law of marriage is a perfect visual aid for understanding our freedom in Christ. From the woman's perspective, the husband in verse (2) represents the *old man* (unrenewed spirit). Since he has died, she is now free to be joined to another (the Lord Jesus) in marriage.

Therefore, as in the case of a marriage, we were *legally separated from Satan*, and are now **legally** joined to Jesus. Seeing that the old man is dead, the law (of Sin) has no more *legal* hold on us. Hence, Satan no longer has the right to dominate a born-again child of God.

Jesus has set us free, by fulfilling the *legal requirements of dominion*, which Adam failed to do. That is why He is called our Advocate (lawyer). He met *all* of the legal standards, so that He would be *recognized* as able to represent us before the adversary, and before the Father in heaven.

There was a principle of law at work here *because of* Adam's treason. Jesus *had* to meet the standards of the Law in order to redeem us and return us to God. We are the **legal** sons and daughters of God, and it doesn't matter what Satan *tries* to do to stop us from walking in victory. Because Jesus said, *"It is finished"*...Satan's dominion was over.

WHEN THE HOLY SPIRIT REVEALS
We *Were* "In The Flesh"

(Romans 7:5,6 KJV) For when we **were** *in the flesh*, the motions of sins, which were by the law, did work in our members to bring forth fruit unto death. But now we are delivered from the law, that being dead wherein we were held; that we should serve in newness of spirit, and not *in* the oldness of the letter.

Can anyone explain all this talk about "**being in the flesh?**" Paul says, "...we **were** in the flesh...!" Could it be that the majority of times when the word *flesh* is used, it is merely referring to us living **under** the control of the body, rather than living under the control of some *old Sin nature*?

I believe this means we still have the same earthly bodies that **can** be used as the instruments of Sin, just as they were before we were saved. However, *now* we have a choice. We are no longer *controlled* by an evil nature that **forces us** into sinful conduct.

The blood of the Lamb has redeemed us! The body will obey whatever the soul and spirit tell it to do (good or evil). The soul (by the spirit) must to be brought under the control of the Spirit of God **within us**, so we will make proper decisions and stay out of sin. **The mind**; however, is key to all of this taking place. This is because the mind is the *gateway* to the soul.

(1 Thessalonians 5:23 KJV) And the very God of peace, sanctify you wholly; and *I pray God* your whole spirit and soul and body be preserved blameless unto the coming of our Lord Jesus Christ.

The *soul* (Psuche in Greek) is defined by the Bible dictionary as "the seat of personality, that which he perceives, reflects, feels, desires; the seat of the will; the inward man."[6] The soul is where the decision making processes *are chosen* and put into action. The mind is the gateway or gatekeeper of the soul. This is where all thoughts are processed and sent on to the will. The *will of man* will **only** obey the thoughts that one allows to linger and be repeated in the mind. The longer these evil thoughts are allowed to linger in the mind, **the weaker the will becomes**. This is why (2 Cor. 10:4,5) tells us:

(KJV) (For the weapons of our warfare are not carnal, but mighty through God to the pulling down of strongholds;) **Casting down imaginations,** and *every high thing* that exalteth itself against the knowledge of God, and **bring into captivity every thought** to the obedience of Christ.

A man once said, *"All sin begins with a thought."* According to this passage of Scripture, his statement is 100% true. Sin always starts as a thought in the mind. If the thought is entertained for very long then the will will become weakened and sin eventually will be committed! This why we must guard what comes into the mind.

At this point it is time to kill a *sacred calf*. I have seen it in the Church all my Christian life. It is a tough, stubborn, old *heifer*, so it may die hard in many believer's minds. This is because our traditions often make the Word of God of no effect in our lives (Matt. 15:6).

(Romans 7:8,9;14-17;22-24 KJV) "But sin, taking occasion by the commandment, wrought in me all manner of concupiscence. For without the law sin was dead. For I was alive without the law once: but when the commandment came, sin revived, and I died…For we know that the law is spiritual: but I am carnal **sold under sin**. For that which I do I allow not: for what I would, that do I not; but what I hate, that do I. If then I do that which I would not, I consent unto the law that it is good. Now then it is no more I that do it, but sin **that dwelleth in me**…For I delight in the law of God after the inward man: But I see another law in my members, warring against the law of my mind, and bringing me *into captivity to the law of sin* which is in my members. O wretched man that I am! **who shall deliver me** from the body of this death?

The written commandment or Law was the judicial agent that revealed to us our sinfulness. For before there was a written Law, man did not have anything *absolute* to show him right or wrong, and hence was free from any of the Law's demands. However, when God gave the Law, man suddenly realized that he was under **the power of Sin**. Therefore, he was *spiritually* dead to God and righteousness. Consequently, we have Paul's statement, "but I am carnal *sold under Sin*." Bear in mind that Paul was a man who knew the Law well, and he desired to obey it; but he found *no power* to do so because the spirit within him was spiritually dead (v:14). Paul says he was not the one doing it **but Sin** which was dwelling (living) **in him**.

This depiction could only be of a man *before* conversion, simply because a reborn child of God is no longer **under sin** since the spirit within him is alive in Christ. The unregenerate man is *unable* to obey

God's Law because he has no power, no reborn spirit, to do so. **However**, the reborn man is free from the Law of Sin & death and its' demands.

> **(Romans 7:6)** But now we are **discharged** from the Law and have *terminated all intercourse with it,* having died to what once restrained and held us captive. So now we serve not under [obedience to] the old code of written regulations, but [under obedience to the promptings] of the Spirit in newness [of life].

If (Rom. 7:8,9;14-17;22-24), was a picture perfect display of how a born-again believer was supposed to be living, then Paul wasted his time by writing (Rom. 6:1-23; 7:1-6). In these first verses Paul explains that we are already free from Sin, through Jesus Christ. Now, since I am free from Sin (6:11), how can I still be under Sin (7:14); unless Paul is explaining the condition of man **prior to** regeneration?

Dealing With The Wretched Man

> **(Romans 7:24)** O unhappy and pitiable and wretched man that I am! Who will **release** and *deliver* men from [the shackles of] this body of death?

Paul is expressing his desire to be free from the *Sin principle* that kept him from obeying the Word of God. This is not the picture of a born-again believer who walks in victory, regardless of the circumstances, but rather a display of a man *prior to* conversion. This is not the victorious life Christ said a believer would have. Paul shows us that this (v:24), is not how a reborn believer is to be living, by including (verse 25).

> "O thank God! [**He will**!] through Jesus Christ (the Anointed One) our Lord! So then indeed I, of myself with the mind and heart, serve the Law of God, but with the flesh [or the body in control] the Law of Sin (v:25)."

This is saying to us that we can **now** serve the Law of God, with our spirit and soul (mind, **will** and emotions), as an instrument **in unity** with the Spirit of God within us. However, he also says, that we can (*with our bodies in control*) obey the Law of Sin. But the choice has been given to us. Paul wants us to realize that we now have the ability to choose, whereas before our regeneration we were slaves. Now God has set us free so we can choose to serve Him totally, (with our whole being); or we can let our bodies (through the enemy) regain control and die again to righteousness. We can no longer blame any one for our sin except ourselves. Paul also said condemnation isn't for us.

(Romans 8:1) Therefore, [there is] now **no condemnation** (no adjudging guilty or wrong) for those who are **in Christ Jesus**, *who live [and] walk not after the dictates of the flesh, but after the dictates of the Spirit.*

This is a tremendous verse of Scripture. Notice that the last part of this verse is in *italics* meaning that the italicized words weren't in the original language; but were added in by the translators. According to the Amplified Bible, the italicized words were not in the original language. Therefore it should actually say:

Therefore, [there is] now no condemnation (no adjudging guilty of wrong) for those who are in Christ Jesus. [No condemnation **period!**]

If you are in Christ Jesus, then condemnation has no place in your life! **However,** that doesn't mean you will not receive attacks of condemnation (from the enemy), or feel conviction if you sin. Still, condemnation and conviction are completely opposite manifestations. *Condemnation* is a tool of the devil, used in order to separate us from God through guilt and shame. It is the converse of conviction. *Conviction* is a tool used by God to let us know that we've sinned, and to prompt us to come to the Father, to receive forgiveness.

Jesus Paid The Price, So We *Could Be* Obedient

(Romans 8:4-9;15,16) So that the righteous *and* just requirements of the Law might be **fully** met in us who live *and* move not in the ways of the flesh but in the ways of the Spirit [our lives governed not by the standards *and* according to the dictates of the flesh, but controlled by the Holy Spirit]. For those who are according to the flesh *and* are controlled by its unholy desires **set their minds** on *and* pursue those things which gratify the flesh, but those who are according to the Spirit *and* are controlled by the desires of the Spirit **set their minds** on *and* seek those things which gratify the [Holy] Spirit. Now the mind of the flesh [which is sense and reason without the Holy Spirit] is death [death that comprises all the miseries arising from sin, both here and hereafter] But the mind of the [Holy] Spirit is life and [soul] peace [*both now and forever*]. [That is] because the mind of the flesh [with its carnal thoughts and purposes] is hostile to God, for it does not submit itself to God's Law; **indeed it cannot**. So then those who are living the life of the flesh [catering to the appetites and impulses of their carnal nature] cannot please *or* satisfy God, *or* be acceptable to Him. But you **are not** living the life of the flesh, *you are living the life of the Spirit*, if the [Holy] Spirit of God [really] dwells within you [directs and controls you]. But if anyone does not possess the [Holy] Spirit of Christ, he is none of His [he does not belong to Christ, is not truly a child of God] For [the Spirit which] you have **now received** [is] not a spirit of slavery to put you *once more in bondage to fear*, but you have received the Spirit of adoption [the Spirit producing sonship] in [the bliss of] which we cry Abba (Father!) Father! The Spirit Himself [thus] testifies together with our spirit, [assuring us] that we are children of God.

Because of the redemptive work of Christ, the just requirements of the Law have been ***completely*** met in us. In other words, Jesus paid the debt we could **never** pay, so that the Law of Sin and Death would have no legal claim over us. The ransom is paid and freedom is ours.

Notice in verse (5) the words **set their minds.** This implies we are the ones who do *the setting*. We are the ones who choose what goes into our minds and what thoughts we will **dwell** on. A non-believer is under the control of an unbelieving spirit (Satan). Nevertheless, a believer is controlled by a believing Spirit, the Spirit of God and Jesus living in him. However, we have a choice as to which *spirit*, we want to listen to. We can (if we choose), listen again to the spirit of the old man that is trying daily to find *reentrance* into our lives.

In contrast, we can also choose to listen to and be controlled by the Holy Spirit.

Paul says again in verse (9) that we *are not* living the life of the flesh. Why? This is because we are born-again, and can now obey the Holy Spirit which lives **within** us. We need to get Holy Spirit *inside* minded, so that we will never forget that He lives in our hearts and desires to direct our actions. When we were born-again, the part of us that was reborn was the spirit. Jesus came into us, He drove out the outlaw (unbelieving) spirit of Satan, and now **He** lives in us and will control our thoughts and actions *if we allow Him*. If we are still battling with these temptations and always giving in, *that's not God's fault*, it's ours! Why? Because each time **we** give in to those unholy desires that attack us *from the world*, we give back a piece of our freedom (sovereignty) to our enemy. The more freedom that we give up will mean the greater difficulty we will have in obeying the Word, and thus His Voice. Hence, **we** put ourselves back under Sin's bondage by obeying the thoughts deposited in our minds by Satan.

The Holy Spirit will do His *work*, but we must do what **He** says in order to *stay free*. We can't give up. We **will** succeed, because Jesus is praying (interceding) for us so that we will make it to the end **in victory**!

A Closing Scripture

(Galatians 6:9) And *let us not* lose heart *and* grow weary *and* faint in acting nobly *and* doing right, for **in due time** *and* at the appointed season we shall reap, **if we do not loosen and relax** our courage *and* faint.

TEMPTATION: WHAT'S ITS PURPOSE?
(Recognizing The Enemy And How He Operates)

Unfortunately, many Christians believe that God is the Author of *every* test or trial that comes into their lives. Hence, they meet each experience *without* the slightest resistance; all because they believe it is *the will of God* for them to go through these things. What does the Word of God have to say about the trials and tests that we encounter? Is God *really* the Author of **all** our trials and tests, or is someone else trying to impose his will on our lives? Ignorance of temptations origin invites defeat into our lives.

I believe very strongly that God *is not* the Author of every trial and test that we experience. Satan cannot attack our lives without God knowing of it. However, that doesn't mean that God *wills* all of our trials or has brought them upon us. God still *allows* Satan a certain degree of authority to tempt man, because He has given man a free will. And since we have the right to *choose* between good and evil, we are also *liable* to the trials that the enemy brings. Nevertheless, God has given us the Way in which we can be victorious despite the attacks that the enemy may bring. In Psalm 11, there is a verse that *appears* to support the idea that God is the Author of all trials of the righteous. However, is this Psalm really saying what some have claimed?

(Psalm 11:5 KJV) The LORD trieth the righteous: but the wicked and him that loveth violence his soul hateth.

The Lord tests *and* proves the [unyieldingly] righteous but His soul abhors the wicked and him who loves violence.

God Himself, *does* try or tests His people. Yet, He doesn't send us sickness, disease or any other evil to teach us something. The word *trieth* as defined by the concordance means "to investigate:--examine, prove, tempt, try."[1] God is a **fruit** inspector so to speak. He investigates our lives to see how our fruit is growing. God puts pressure on us so that we will reexamine our lives, and get things in order. God does try us, He **never** brings trials of evil or sickness and disease.

I can hear some of the traditional minded people even now. *What about Job and Israel?* Concerning Job, I have already covered his trials in chapter one; so I will refer you back to it. But concerning Israel, I would ask you to think about the lifestyle of Israel. Israel lived a life that was *totally* against God's Law. They did their own thing, and hence disaster came. Older translations leave the impression that God was the author of Israel's destruction. In contrast, Israel brought this destruction upon themselves. This is because of their rebellion, God *allowed* their enemies to attack them. But God's will concerning them was plainly known. He states this clearly in the book of Ezekiel.

(Ezekiel. 33:11 KJV) "…As I live saith the Lord God, I have **no pleasure** in the death of the wicked; but that the wicked turn *from his way* and live: turn ye, turn ye *from your evil ways*; for why **will** ye die, O house of Israel?" (

Here in Ezekiel 33, God made His intention for Israel's future very clear. He asked them to turn from their evil ways. God continued, saying, "why will *ye* die?" He said, "why have you set your heart to your own destruction?" Israel caused their own dilemma and God would not intervene *unless* they repented. Unfortunately, *much* of the Church is in the same condition as Israel was in their day.

Looking back at God and temptation, I know without a doubt that God our Father does not tempt us with evil (sin, sickness, disease or fear). So, who is behind all of the Sin, sickness and disease in the world today? The number one cause of these evil tidings is Satan himself. However, we can open the door to him by our own *ignorance*. This happens much more than most care to realize.

(James 1:13,14) Let no one say when he is tempted, *I am tempted from God*; for God is **incapable** of being tempted **by** [what is] **evil** and *He tempts no one*. But every person is tempted when he is drawn away, enticed *and* baited *by his own evil desire* (lust, passions).

James tells us God is incapable of being tempted by evil. *Thus* He **can not** possibly tempt us with any form of evil. Some are saying, *"But wait a minute, we are not God!"* Of course we are not "God." Yet, please never forget that Jesus lives in our spirits by the Holy Spirit; and He would never tempt Himself Who lives in us; "That Christ might *dwell* in your heart by faith," (Eph. 3:17). Jesus lives in us by the Holy Spirit, and hence God is incapable of tempting Himself or that which *belongs* to Him. James also continues by telling us "*God tempts no one* (to evil)."

Since we have adequately laid the foundation for understanding how temptations to evil come, now let us examine the purpose of temptation.

The Purpose of Temptation Is Multifaceted

(Genesis 1:1,2;26-28 KJV) In the beginning God created the heaven and the earth. And the earth was without form, and void; and darkness *was* upon the face of the deep. And the Spirit of God moved upon the face of the waters. And God said, Let us make man in our image, after our likeness: and let *them have dominion* over the fish of the sea, and over the fowl of the air, and over the cattle, and over all the earth, and over every creeping thing that creepeth upon the earth. So God created man in his *own* image, in the image of God created he him; male and female created he them. And God blessed them, and God said unto *them*, Be fruitful, and multiply, and replenish the earth, and subdue it: and **have dominion** over the fish of the sea, and over the fowl of the air, and over every living thing that moveth upon the earth.

Before we continue let's first establish a background scene of God's original purpose for creating man and placing him on the earth. The reason is found in verse 26 of Genesis chapter one. God said, "...let *them* have dominion over the fish...and over all the earth." The word *dominion* as defined by the concordance means "(come to, make to) have dominion, prevail against, reign, rule (over)."[2] Adam (including Eve) were to take authority over this whole earth. God gave man the authority to rule this earth—to be Lord over it. They were the *lord* over this earth, subordinate only to the direction and control of the Father Himself. One could say before the fall of that "Adam" was the god (ruler) of this world. *They* had been given the authority to direct all the works of God's hand on earth, but God never told them to make a decision apart from Him. Moreover, they faced beguiling opposition to their God given authority.

Within the definition of dominion we saw the words "prevail against, reign, rule (over)." Who was man supposed to rule over and prevail against? **You got it**! Part of God's purpose for creating man was that they rule over and prevail (win) against Lucifer's opposition. However, to man's discredit, he indeed did not prevail against Lucifer and thus he gave away God's anointing upon him to reign over the earth to Lucifer.

Man had been given authority to rule the earth by God Himself he was given a *power of attorney* to take dominion over the earth. However, he used his "power of attorney" to betray God by **submitting** his authority to Satan. Thus, giving Satan lordship (control) over earth that *really* belonged to God. The devil was; therefore, *allowed* by God to **legally** control planet earth because of man's disobedience. He ruled under Adam's God given authority.

Now why did God allow man to be tempted if He already knew that they would fall? Why didn't God inform man prior to Lucifer's attack? Moreover, why wasn't man able to rule over Lucifer and the earth?

Why God "Allowed" Man To Be Tempted!

(Genesis 3:1-5;14,15 KJV) "Now the serpent was more subtle *than any beast of the field* which the LORD God had made. And he said unto the woman, Yea, hath God said, Ye shall not eat of every tree of the garden? And the woman said unto the serpent, We may eat of the fruit of the trees of the garden: But of the fruit of the tree which is in the midst of the garden, God hath said, Ye shall not eat of it, *neither shall ye touch it*, lest ye die. And the serpent said unto the woman, Ye shall not surely die: For God doth know that in the day ye eat thereof, then your eyes shall be opened, and ye shall be as gods, knowing good and evil…And the LORD God said unto the serpent, Because thou hast done this, thou *art* cursed above all cattle, and above every beast of the field; upon thy belly shalt thou go, and dust shalt thou eat all the days of thy life: And I will put enmity between thee and the woman, and between thy seed and her seed; it shall bruise thy head, and thou shalt bruise his heel."

There are many significant issues that we could deal with from this portion of Scripture, but we'll start out by addressing the reasons why God *allowed* man to be tempted by the serpent? I believe the answer to this question requires a three part answer.

1. Man was created with a free will, and God *had* to allow His man to be tested, so that he would have the right to choose between good and evil. [A foundational principle for *all* who are born of a woman—*Spiritual law*].

2. Man needed to be tested to prove he was *capable of taking dominion* over Lucifer and the entire earth, which God had commanded him (*them*) to do.

3. God *knew* that man would fall. Thus, He turned the fall around, by sending Jesus to redeem man and destroy Satan's work once and for all (Genesis 3:15 & 1John. 3:8,9).

Reason #1 was that man was given a free will and he **must** be tested to see if he would be obedient to the will of God or if he would use his freedom to do his own will. God *had* to allow man the chance to choose good or evil. If God had sheltered him from this test, man would have been obedient *as a robot* and **not** of his own free will. God desires that we love Him willingly.

Some may wonder, "How can you prove your point?" As I said in part one of the reasons why man was tempted, this principle of testing the will of all man is *Spiritual Law*. Jesus Himself, our sinless Lord, **had to be** tested to prove His obedience before God and Satan as well (Lk. 4:1-14). Adam's obedience was tested, and Jesus' obedience was tested as well.

There is something that you must understand about this *process of testing*. These tests are not to prove anything to God, because He already knows the outcome before the test. Rather, these tests are to prove the individual, not only to himself, **but also** to Lucifer. This is because Lucifer, *before* his fall into Sin, was "in charge" of the earth; so to speak. It appears from Isaiah chapter 14 that he had a throne on the earth, prior to man's creation and fall; and this may have been what Lucifer was seeking to have again.

(Isaiah 14:12-14 KJV) How are thou fallen from heaven, O Lucifer, son of the morning! *how* art thou cut down to the ground, which didst weaken the nations! For thou has **said** in thine heart, I will *ascend into heaven*, I will exalt **my throne** above the stars of God: I will sit also upon the mount of the congregation, in the sides of the north: I will *ascend above* the height of the clouds; I will be like the most High.

Verse twelve of Isaiah 14, is describing Lucifer's state *after* his sin, and verses thirteen and fourteen are describing his position **before** his fall from grace. It was what he **said** *in his heart* that brought the fall mentioned in verse (12). Lucifer needed to ascend because God had given him a *throne* on earth, until he sinned. Seeing that he sinned, he tried to regain authority over the earth from Adam. Of course Jesus defeated him, but he is still *allowed* to tempt man; because Adam gave him authority over man-kind.

Reason #2 is why God had to allow man to be tested? Was so he could prove to *all* that he was capable of taking dominion over Lucifer and the entire earth. Adam proved that he was not capable of taking the dominion when they listened to the voice of an outlaw spirit.

As I said before, this also is *Spiritual law*. Jesus Himself also had to prove that He was capable of taking dominion over Lucifer and over the entire earth. Jesus is the *Last Adam*. His mission was to redeem man to his original state of dominion, as well as deal with Lucifer by breaking the power of Sin over man (Lk. 4:4,8,12). He came *in the likeness* of the first Adam. This is why He called Himself (the Son of Man). He regained our lost dominion so that we could walk in authority over Sin, Satan and the entire earth. This is why Jesus came to this earth in the first place!

Reason #3, why God allowed man to be tempted, was because God choose to *use* man's fall to *deal* with Lucifer (**Sin** or evil) once and for all by sending our Redeemer the Christ. There is a passage of Scripture that says, "the gifts of God are given *without* repentance."

Hence we see how Satan was much like King Saul. He had a position given to him by God the Father, but he *lost* the anointing of God for that position. Man too was given a godly anointing and he ignorantly gave it over to Lucifer. However, there is a termination date upon man's lease on earth that I believe will end at the millennial reign of Christ.

This is why God has not *completely* dealt with Satan as of yet. Satan won over man in the garden; thus this is why God has chosen not to imprison him until man's lease (charter) is ended. Satan is ruling in Adam's place so to speak and God honored Adam's decision.

Look at God's immediate response after man's disobedience was made known:

> **(Genesis 3:14,15 KJV)** And the Lord God said to the serpent, Because thou hast done this, thou art cursed above all cattle, and above every beast of the field; upon thy belly shalt thou go, and dust shalt thou eat all the days of thy life: And I will put enmity between thee and the woman, and between thy seed and her seed; it shall bruise thy head, and thou shalt bruise his heel.

God immediately takes action by proclaiming the coming of One Who will crush the head of Satan once and for all. Have you ever wondered why God did not send Jesus to deal with Satan before the fall? This has been on my mind for many years then God opened my eyes to see the answer. He would not send Himself to redeem the earth, or even Satan. *However*, when His family was put in the middle of all this; He could not help Himself. God couldn't bare to see His family **separated** from Him; thus He decided to give **His all** to rescue us from the bondage of evil, ending Satan's authority over man and the earth all in one move!

Why Didn't God Inform Man *Prior* To Satan's Attack?

I asked the Lord this question one day in 1995 while preparing to preach this message for the first time. He spoke to my heart and said, "If I had told man about Satan before he tempted him, I would have **exposed my children to *evil*;** that is against My nature." He continued and said, "If I had told man about Satan's evil ways, I would have influenced his decision, and I would have violated man's freedom of choice (man's free will)." God wants His people to serve Him by their own free choice, not because He "stacked" the deck in their favor, or His. If God had influenced man's freedom of choice, then man would have served God as some sort of robot, rather than from the heart. God gave us a free will which He has refused to violate.

Why Was Man Unable To Take Dominion?

There is a *traditional interpretation* of man's creation that has control over just about every part of Christianity that I know. I mean in no way that others have not discovered this same truth as I. Nonetheless, it is predominant in the Church world wide. The traditional interpretation that I am referring to is the doctrine that man when he was created was *totally perfect*. Perfection is a very subjective topic, since men view "perfection" in many different ways. But we're not interested in how men judge perfection. We are only interested in how God views perfection:

> "Reaching an ideal state of *spiritual wholeness or completeness*. It is not a quality which is achieved by human effort alone, nor is it an end in itself. Christian perfection consists essentially in exercising the divine gift of love for God, and for other people…Christians are, however, to grow from spiritual infancy to maturity so as to share the full stature of Christ, in whose image they may become renewed and perfected."[3]

God's view of perfection has very little to do with always doing everything *correctly*. Rather God says that perfection to Him is found in ones wholeness or completion in Him. Moreover, God's wholeness is something one has to grow into. No one has ever come into this world *knowing* everything there is to know...***including*** Jesus. The Bible says that He increased in wisdom, which means He had to *learn* the same as we have to (Lk. 2:52). Please note that He was *Emmanuel*, God in human flesh, but He was also one hundred present human.

This **is not** to say that Jesus was not *perfect* (whole, complete) and sinless. However Jesus, just like the rest of us, had to learn and increase in wisdom. I know to the natural mind that *seems* impossible, because He was God. This is true, but we must *never* forget that He was God *in flesh*. He **voluntarily** limited Himself, by taking on flesh to live *as* a man. He took upon Himself the natural physical limitation as all men have (Phil. 2:6-8 *The Amplified Bible*).

So where does this leave the first man? Was Adam perfect and sinless, or was Adam merely innocent at *birth*, like the rest of the human race. I can write without a doubt that he *was not* perfect and sinless, as our Lord Jesus was, even though he had no Sin nature *until after* the fall. Adam was **innocent** and *without* Sin; the same way that a new born baby is. There's a ***major*** distinction between these terms.

Think about this for a moment. *What is Sin?* Is lying, or at the least stretching the truth, a sin? Well, what do you think? What is Sin? I believe in order to answer these questions we will need to review the account of Eve's first recorded encounter with Satan.

> **(Genesis 3:1-3 NKJV)** Now the serpent was more cunning than any beast of the field which the Lord God had made. And he said to the woman, "Has God indeed said, 'You shall not eat of every tree of the garden'?" And the woman said to the serpent, "We may eat the fruit of the trees of the garden; but of the fruit of the tree which is in the midst of the garden, God has said, 'You shall not eat it, *nor shall you touch it*, lest you die."

Eve said to the enemy that God said, *"nor shall you touch it, lest you die."* Wait a minute! Did God *really* say if they touched that fruit they would die?

> **(Genesis 2:16,17 NKJV)** And the Lord God commanded the man, saying, "Of every tree of the garden you may freely eat; but

of the tree of the knowledge of good and evil you shall not eat, for in the day *that you eat of it* you shall surely die.

Again I ask you these two questions. What is Sin? Is lying a sin? It is obvious when comparing the preceding passages of Scripture that Eve in fact did lie; or at least *misquoted* God's instructions concerning eating the fruit. This leads me to another important question. Did her misquotation take place *before* the fall or *after*? Without a doubt it took place **before** man's disobedience. Therefore, Eve's response to Satan illustrates my point that man was not *perfect* and *sinless* in the same way as Jesus (the Man) was. Eve actually sinned by misquoting God's instructions, which took place before the fall. Since Eve sinned, why didn't God banish her from the garden then?

First of all, God had **only** given one directive: *do not eat of the tree which is in the midst of the garden*. Next, Eve did not even know what Sin was. Third, she misquoted God **in ignorance**, not in outright rebellion.

Man was ignorant of the devices of Satan. Jesus, on the other hand, was not. Man (Adam) was just like a little born baby that goes too near to a hot oven, and burns itself. Why? This is because the child does not know or understand the danger of a hot oven. In turn, man did not know or understand the danger of having a conversation with the serpent. The word *ignorant* means "lacking knowledge, uneducated; unaware, uninformed."[4] Hence, the dictionary defines man's pre-fallen state accurately.

Seeing that man was ignorant, rather than *perfect*, we can understand why man was not able to take dominion over Satan and the earth. I don't believe man realized that he *could have* taken authority over the serpent and cast him out of the garden. God indeed gave him **everything** that he needed to take dominion, but man didn't understand the authority he had been given.

Thus, he ignorantly submitted his crown of authority (*power of attorney*) to Satan. Man's failure to take dominion over Satan and this earth *was not* God's fault. God gave him the perfect weapon to win over Satan, but he simply surrendered his dominion without a fight. *God's delegated authority was his weapon!*

How To Turn Temptation Around

Now is a good time to discuss how to turn temptation around to work for us. You may be thinking, "How could temptation ever be turned around to work for me?" **This** is probably why it never has worked for you! If we always see things as being negative, then we'll never be able to turn evil attacks around to work for our good. The book of James has some insightful wisdom for those who want to turn all of their temptations around to work for them. Yes, temptation can be used to our advantage if we know how to approach it.

> **(James 1:2-8 KJV)** My brethren, *count it all* **joy** when ye fall into divers temptations; *Knowing this*, that the trying of your faith worketh patience. But *let patience* have her perfect work, that ye may be perfect and entire, wanting nothing. If any of you *lack wisdom*, **let him ask** of God, that giveth to all men liberally, and *upbraideth not*; and *it shall be given* him. But let him **ask in faith**, nothing wavering. For he that wavereth is like a wave of the sea driven with the wind and tossed. For let not that man **think** that he shall receive any thing of the Lord. A double minded man is unstable in all his ways.

James instructs us to first of all, *count it all joy*. "Is he trying to tell me that I should be happy because I am going through temptation?" Yes, that is *exactly* what he is saying. However, I don't believe that James meant this in the same context as most believers have thought. I feel James is telling us to turn this attack of the enemy around, by being joyful in the fact that Jesus Christ is greater **in us** than this attack. We are to realize that the very Creator of the universe is inside our hearts *waiting* to assist us whenever we call. I also believe that part of our being joyful is in the fact that we realize that this is *only* a test *of the evil broadcast system*. But remember—this is *only* a test!

When we understand that this trial which we are experiencing is an attack of the enemy, we are much more prepared to use the Word of God and destroy his works. James says, "be joyful and realize that this is only a test." Someone once said, "It's not the things that happen that are most important, but rather it is *the way one responds* to the things that happen." James said the same thing to us. We must use joy, patience and wisdom as our primary *offensive* weapons in order to turn temptation around.

Furthermore, James tells us that we are to know that the trying of our faith works patience. This is part of why we should be joyful in temptation. We learn how to walk in patience. However, this is not the kind of *patience* that most Christians think of. Most believers think of patience as "putting up with the attacks until Satan finally leaves them alone." This line of reasoning has little or nothing to do with *Biblical* patience.

Biblical *patience* from the concordance means, "*cheerful* endurance, *constancy*: enduring, patience, patient continuance (waiting)."⁵ This is a far cry from the world's idea of patience. *Most think patience is just putting up with something.* But, godly patience is "always staying the same no matter what the circumstance." James is telling us to be and act like God constantly joyful **no matter** what happens. Moreover, James says that joy plus patience will bring us into perfection (maturity, completeness, wholeness). And perfection is really what every believer wants to achieve. However, this perfection won't come without temptation.

James gives us one final key to turning temptation around. He tells us that if we lack wisdom in how to handle a situation, we should ask God and He will give us the wisdom that we need. Then we can be successful in winning the victory over the temptation of the enemy. But there is one catch. We must ask in faith, nothing wavering. In other words, we must believe that when we ask God for Wisdom that He will give it. He has promised to give it. And God's assistance always comes by faith!

In summary, James gives us 4 vital keys for victory:

1. ***Let His joy rule in our hearts.***
2. ***Realize that this is only a test.***
3. ***Be patient*** (stay the same *like* God)
4. ***Seek wisdom*** (ask *expecting* to receive)

Finally, I would like to share some other important keys that will keep us **prepared** for all of Satan's attacks.

(Psalm 119:9-11) How shall a young man cleanse his way? By taking heed *and* keeping watch [on himself] according to Your word [conforming his life to it]. With my whole heart have I sought You, inquiring for *and* of You *and* yearning for You; O let me not wander *or* step aside [either in ignorance or willfully] from Your commandments. Your word have I laid up in my heart, that I might not sin against You.

But when the Comforter (Counselor, Helper, Advocate, Intercessor, Strengthener, Standby) comes, Whom I will send to you from the Father, the Spirit of Truth Who comes (proceeds) from the Father, He [Himself] will testify regarding Me. (John. 15:26)

Within these verses of Scripture that you are important keys that will help you remain ready for whatever temptation that comes along. Psalm 119:9-11 says how to cleanse our way or how to keep ourselves free in the trials that come our way. We are to take heed and keep watch of ourselves by examining our lives with the Word of God. We must obey the Word to live free. David continues, telling us that we must seek God with our *whole* heart. Finally, he says that we must store up God's Word in our hearts…and that Word will help keep our lives in line with God's will for us..

Here is why I included John chapter 15 verse 26. The Holy Spirit is our *Secret Weapon*, when fighting against our own lack of motivation. We must ask the Holy Spirit to give us the desire to do what God's Word says.

A Closing Scripture

(James 1:2-8 KJV) "My brethren, *count it all* **joy** when ye fall into divers temptations; *Knowing this*, that the trying of your faith worketh patience. But *let patience* have her **perfect** work…If any of you *lack wisdom*, **let him ask** of God, **that giveth to all** men liberally, and *upbraideth not*, and **it shall be given** him. But let him **ask in faith**, nothing wavering…For *let not that man* **think** *that he shall receive* any thing of the Lord. A **double minded** man is unstable…"

5

WAITING IN HIS PRESENCE
(The *Missing* Ingredient)

About the third week of February 1995, God started dealing with me about preaching a message on waiting in His Presence. As the Holy Spirit began to direct me to various passages in the Word of God, I suddenly felt Him come upon me and speak to my heart: "*Be still **and know** that I am God.*" What happened during this *first* encounter with His precious Presence is almost indescribable with human language. However, during this chapter I will attempt to share some of the extraordinary things that the Holy Spirit began to teach me, as well as a brief experience or two that I've had while waiting in His *awesome* Presence. *Prepare your heart for an intimate relationship with the Trinity*!

Almost everyone remembers the scandals that took place in 1987 involving Jim Bakker, Jimmy Swaggart and various other men of God. During this period, I was attending a Christian college in Southern California. I can remember watching Jimmy Swaggart's teary eyed confession, thinking to myself; "Why did this great man of God give into an attack like this?" Furthermore, I *saw* the media blitz of anti-Christian, anti-church slogans before they were even aired. My heart was broken. I couldn't understand how these men could fall prey to *such* attacks by the enemy. I asked the Lord for wisdom and understanding as to why these scandals had happened. However, due to my own frustration and confusion, *I* failed to receive the insight that I was seeking. Sometimes one can be overwhelmed by so much confusion, that one is unable to hear the Voice of God. Thus I was the one who was unable to hear His Spirit do to my own hurt.

Then, in February of 1995, the Holy Spirit came upon me and gave me the answer that I was seeking. During my first *real* encounter with His wonderful Presence, I began to understand why so many ministers of the Gospel were falling prey to attacks by the enemy. I then realized that many of them had unknowingly separated themselves by other *things*.

Some of you may be thinking, "Isn't that nice, he got filled with the Holy Spirit for the first time, and had a great time with God." Yes, I had a great time with God that day, but I did not receive my prayer language that day. Actually, I was saved and filled with the Spirit on New Year's morning 1979. The encounter that I am writing about was something *much* deeper than when I received the gift of tongues for the first time. I am referring to how I began learning to walk and live on a daily basis with His Presence by my side. This is the kind of encounter that *all* believers need.

This is the missing ingredient from most Christians' daily lives, and it is the main reason why so many believers are unable to live a life of victory. The Holy Spirit has taught me that waiting in His Presence is the missing ingredient which I, and all believers, vitally need in order to live a victorious Christian life. Without a daily refreshing of His Presence it is impossible to live a successful Christian life.

You may be wondering, "What do you mean by waiting and how do I go about learning how to wait?" That is the purpose of this chapter. God wants me to share with you that which He has taught me. Therefore, I ask you in the Name of Jesus, to open yourself up spirit and soul to receive that which God wants to reveal to you from this chapter. Moreover, I encourage each reader to research all the information in this chapter as well as the entire book for themselves.

We'll start off by defining what is meant by "waiting in His Presence." The dictionary defines *wait* so perfectly, "to remain *inactive* in readiness or **expectation**, to act as attending servant."[1] This is the essence of waiting in His Presence. We are to **inactively** wait before Him in *readiness* and **expectation** of receiving from the Spirit of Jesus. This is because the Holy Spirit speaks most often in restful silence.

Waiting In His Presence Causes Restoration

(Isaiah 40:31) But those who **wait** for the Lord [who *expect, look for*, and hope in Him] shall **change** *and* **renew** their strength *and* power; they shall lift their wings *and* mount up [*close to God*] as eagles [mount up to the sun]; they shall run and *not be weary*, they shall walk and *not faint or* become tired.

Here Isaiah reveals to us the secret of receiving spiritual renewal or restoration. Waiting in His Presence is the *secret* to restoration. We are told that if we will wait in and upon His Presence, with *expectation* that we will begin to **change**. This is what every godly believer desires; real and lasting change. Waiting is the secret to *the beginning* of lasting change. The trouble we face is how to get to that point! Waiting in His Presence is a *life long* process. Just any lasting relationship takes time—so too with the Holy Spirit.

(Job 14:14) If a man dies, shall he live again? All the days of my warfare *and* service *I wait*, **till my change** *and* **release** shall come.

The book of Job confirms what Isaiah chapter 40 has already told us: waiting **is** the secret to real, long lasting change. Something happens to us when we are in a quiet position before the Lord…*we start to listen*!

Let's continue with (Isa. 40:31). After He starts to change us, He will begin to renew our strength and power. God *literally* starts to re-charge our batteries. *Strength* represents our physical bodies being renewed or restored, but *power* represents the restoration of our spirit man. Christians become worn down spiritually as well as physically. This is why many of the great men/women of God have fallen. They were not only worn out physically, but they were even more worn out spiritually, because they were failing to take time to be restored by His Presence.

Isaiah also tells us that if we wait before the Lord we will mount up on wings close to God. We will begin to learn how we are to conduct ourselves in this world, *by* walking close with Him in a daily lifestyle. In order for us to walk and talk like Jesus, we will need to learn how to walk with Jesus on a daily basis and not just on Sundays. Waiting in His Presence lifts us up to the heavenly realms, where we obtain adequate fellowship with our Creator. Fellowship is the glue the holds together our relationship with God.

Moreover, we are told that if we wait before the Lord expectantly; we will run but we will not faint or become tired. I asked the Lord "What do You mean by we 'won't become tired'?" He answered, "When you wait on Me, you will not *burn out* physically or spiritually." Thus, waiting in His Presence is **the cure** for *burn out*! The majority of the ministers, who burn out and fall, are doing so because they have not taken the time to wait before His Presence so that He can refresh them. Instead other things have taken His place! Our preachers *must* have His Presence to minister.

People of God, this is just the beginning of the benefits that waiting will bring into our lives. Remember that waiting is not for God's benefit, He doesn't get tired. We are the ones who need restoration: spirit, soul and body (1 Thess. 5:23). If we want to be strong thus avoiding burn-out and defeat, we should take time **every day** to wait.

Waiting—Isn't An Option; It's A *Command*!

(Isaiah 41:1a) "LISTEN IN silence before Me..."

(Psalm 37:7) Be still *and* rest in the Lord; wait for Him *and* patiently lean yourself upon Him; fret not yourselves because of him who prospers in his way, because of the man who brings wicked devices to pass.

(Psalm 46:10 NKJV) Be still, and *know* that I *am* God; I will be exalted among the nations, I will be exalted in the earth!

(Hosea 12:6) Therefore return to your God! Hold fast to love *and* mercy, to righteousness *and* justice, **and wait** [*expectantly*] for your God **continually**!

Perhaps you're wondering, "Why did you use so many verses of Scripture?" Because it is important that we Scripturally establish waiting in His Presence as a *one hundred percent command* of God.

Waiting—*Captures* God's Attention

(Psalm 40:1-3) I WAITED patiently *and* expectantly for the Lord; and He *inclined* to me and *heard* my cry. He *drew me up out* of a horrible pit [a pit of tumult and of destruction], out of the miry clay (froth and slime), and *set my feet upon a rock*, steadying my steps *and* establishing my goings. And He has put a *new song in my mouth*, a song of praise to our God. Many shall see and fear (revere and worship) and put their trust *and* confident reliance in the Lord.

Waiting before the Lord will capture God's attention, because He will incline to us; and He will also *hear* our prayer. When God sees His children waiting on Him, He gives them His attention. Why? This is because He wants to "know" what they want. One's willingness to wait on God stirs Him up with desire to meet the need of that diligent person. Waiting before the Lord captures God's attention, because He is moved to lift us out of the horrible miry clay. This symbolizes God lifting us out of the mire of Sin that we sometimes get ourselves into. Once we are willing to be still and wait, God is moved with compassion, thus He delivers us from oppression and any destruction in our lives. He not only rescues us from oppression and destruction, but He also gives us firm footing. He sets us upon a rock (**Jesus**). Jesus Christ, through the Holy Spirit's help is our solid rock foundation.

David continues with, "And He puts a new song in my mouth…" When we wait in His Presence, we will receive a fresh new song, which will come forth out of a changed heart. The new song that He gives us will remind us of His goodness, and this will keep us from straying back into the old miry clay. This song is a song of joy and praise to God.

This new song that we receive will encourage others to give their lives over to the Lord. In verse (3) it says **"Many** shall see and fear and *put their trust* and confident reliance **in the Lord.**" Waiting will cause us to be a witness to the world of Jesus' saving, freeing power. People will see the change in us and want to have Jesus too. This is the reason why we have not won the world by now. They look at us and our failures and *think* they are better off than God's children. Daily waiting in His presence will change us and hence change the world in which we live; because, they will see the light of God's Presence in our lives.

There are three additional insights that the Holy Spirit has taught me about getting God's attention through patient, obedient waiting. One insight is in Psalm 104 v:27 and 28.

> These all wait *and* are dependent upon You, *that You may give them* **their food** in due season. When you give it to them, they gather it up; You open Your hand, and they are *filled with good things.*

Because of our obedience in waiting before Him, His attention will be turned toward us, and He will give us our food in the proper season. I believe that as we wait before Him, He will give us food from heaven. In other words, we receive *revelation* from the mind of God concerning His Word, plus any vague situations where we need His divine direction. Revelation from the heart of God **will not** come to those who have no time to wait on His counsel. *Only* those who will wait on Him will receive Super-natural guidance and insight from the throne of God! It takes faith and patience.

Finally, Isaiah tells us more with regards to how God's attention is captured by those who earnestly wait on Him.

WHEN THE HOLY SPIRIT REVEALS

(Isaiah 64:4) For from of old no one has heard nor perceived by the ear, nor has the eye seen a God besides You, Who works *and* **shows Himself active** on behalf of him *who* [earnestly] *waits* for Him.

(Isaiah 49:23) "…and you *shall know* [with an *acquaintance* and *understanding* based on and grounded in **personal experience**] that I am the Lord; for they *shall not* be put to shame who wait for, look for, hope for, *and* expect Me."

These portions of Scripture tell us that God works and shows Himself active on behalf of those who earnestly wait for Him. God **rarely** moves fast, therefore, patience is a needed must when it comes to receiving from Him. I believe *impatience* is probably the main reason why so few people take the time to wait in His Presence on a daily basis. Most people want it fast and their way, like at Burger King. However, the Spirit realm does not operate like Burger King. God *longs* to show Himself active in our lives, but very few will do what He requires of them in order to receive this from Him. It comes only to those who thirst after it.

Finally, Isaiah chapter forty-nine, verse twenty-three tells us that those of wait on God will **know Him** with an acquaintance and understanding *based on personal experience*. Because they know Him from personal experience, He *will not* allow them to be put to shame. His promise is not to those who do their own thing. It is only for those who dedicate themselves to knowing their Lord by **personal experience**; which comes through waiting daily in His Presence and through attentive study of His Word.

I trust that you now can see what waiting before the Lord could have done for Jimmy Swaggart and Jim Bakker? We have looked at many of the changes God will cause in and for those of us who wait. These changes were needed in both men during their own hour of temptation. I believe daily waiting would have protected them during these attacks. This should be a solemn reminder to all believers to take time daily to fellowship with the Father, Son and Holy Spirit. Without His Presence, none of us will live victoriously.

Here's a short review of our last several points: Waiting before God captures His attention and He will cause 7 wonderful things to happen:

(1) He will hear and answer our prayer.
(2) He will deliver us from oppression and destruction.

(3) He will give us a new song of joy in our hearts.
(4) He will cause others to see Jesus in us and they will repent.
(5) He will give us spiritual food (revelation).
(6) He will actively move on our behalf.
(7) He will not allow us to be put to shame.

It is seriously important that we continue in our study on waiting in His Presence, because we have finally come to what I believe is the best *experience* offered by God to those who wait. However, this experience does not come to the impatient. As the cliché goes, "Good things come to those who wait." We must patiently wait to experience it!

Waiting—Causes: The *Secret Place* To Open!

(Psalm 91:1-4) HE WHO dwells in the secret place of the Most High shall remain stable *and* fixed under the shadow of the Almighty [Whose power no foe can with stand]. I will say of the Lord, He is my Refuge and my Fortress, my God; on Him I lean *and* rely, *and* in Him I [confidently] trust! For [then] He will deliver you from the snare of the fowler and from the deadly pestilence. [Then] He will cover you with His pinions, and under His wings shall you trust *and* find refuge; His truth *and* His faithfulness are a shield and a buckler.

David begins Psalm 91 by describing the lifestyle of one who waits daily before the Lord. He uses the word *dwell*, which means to live, abide, surround one's self in. A person who daily waits before the Lord is one who dwells or lives in His Presence. Thus, the doors of the secret place of the Most High open to those who fellowship daily with His Spirit. Therefore, because of our dwelling in the secret place, we will remain stable and be fixed (held) under the shadow of the Almighty. I believe the shadow of the Almighty described here is the Holy Spirit Himself. Then, no foe will be able to stand against us. No temptation, no sickness or disease, no oppression of the enemy will be able to stand against us. His is our shield.

Once we have entered the secret place, we will have a new bold confession of the Lordship of Jesus. But this confession **won't** be like our confession here in this natural realm. Our confession of His Lordship will have so much more power behind it. This new bold confession will literally tear down the strongholds that the enemy has built against us through deceptive attacks. David said this will take place because the Lord is our Refuge and our Fortress. In the secret place we're *infused* with a new confidence of His protection and guidance. In verse (3) it states that He will deliver us from the snare of the fowler and his deadly pestilence. We will be delivered from the temptations (snares) to sin. Sin will not have any attraction for us, because we live daily in His wonderful Presence.

Furthermore, in verse (4) it tells us that God will take us under His wings of protection, in the same way a mother hen protects her chicks. Just as she fends off any predators, God will take authority over any presence of evil that would try to attack and hinder our walk with Him. In the secret place, God's faithfulness becomes our shield and our buckler. Another way to put this is that our faith in God and His Word as our shield and defense becomes renewed. We can then go out into the natural realm and take authority over the attacks that the devil brings into our lives. His Word is our shield and sword for battle. We become offensive soldiers.

Perhaps when you read this a thought comes to your mind "This sounds like some sort of fantasy land story." That's probably because you've *never* entered into the secret place of the Most High. This is **only** fantasy to those who have never **experienced** what it is like to enter His secret place. That is why it is called the secret place of the Most High. It's God's best kept secret, and patient waiting opens it up to those who diligently seek His face.

(Psalm 91:5-10,14) "You *shall not be afraid* of the terror of the night, nor of the arrow (the evil plots and slanders of the wicked) that flies by day. Nor of the pestilence that stalks in darkness, nor of the destruction *and* sudden death that surprise *and* lay waste at noonday. *A thousand* may fall at your side, and *ten thousand* at your right hand, but it *shall not come near* you. **Only a spectator** shall you be [yourself **inaccessible** *in the secret place* of the Most High] as you witness the reward of the wicked. Because you have made the Lord your refuge, and the Most High your dwelling place. There shall *no evil* befall you, nor any plague *or* calamity come near your tent...Because he has set his love upon Me, therefore will I deliver him; I will *set him on* **high**, because he knows *and* understands My [has *a personal knowledge* of My mercy, love and kindness—trusts and relies on Me, knowing I will never forsake him, no never]."

David explains in verse (5) that all fear leaves when we enter the secret place. When we enter His Presence all fear must leave, *because* perfect love casts out **all** fear. This is a place where we are protected during every evil attack. No destruction or darkness has the right to come near us when we are dwelling (*remaining in*)² the secret place of the Most High. Please understand, this is not a place that we go into *and leave*. Rather, this is a place that we go into and **dwell**. We can live there, by daily fellowship with Him, through waiting in the Presence of God. This time of fellowship is where we get to truly know God and His Word. It prepares us to walk and live in the Spirit.

David reveals to us what happens in the Spirit realm when we get renewed in the secret place; a thousand fall at our side and ten thousand at our right hand. All of the demon forces of hell don't stand a chance against a believer who *dwells* in God's secret place. This is the place where we receive God's *daily* anointing for living. Without a daily anointing, we **will not** be able to stand against the works of the enemy. We'll be spiritually vulnerable to attack.

Some of you may be asking yourselves, "Where does reading the Word and *normal* daily prayer fit into all this?" Waiting is an important part, the same as they are. However, waiting is the key that will cause all the things we read and pray to *take effect* in our lives. The anointing needed for them to operate in us is received by our daily waiting. Jesus said, "If you dwell in Me and My Word dwells in you, ask what you will and you will get it." Waiting **is** dwelling in Him!

Please notice that in verse (8) God's Word says that we will only be a spectator, *inaccessible* in the secret place of the Most High. This is a real place! That is why it says we will be inaccessible there. In other words, no one and nothing will be able to harm us there. It is a place to rest and be refreshed by the Holy Spirit. Evil isn't there. Confusion isn't there. Depression isn't there. Evil thoughts are not there either. It is a place of total freedom from the attacks of the devil. When we *live* in the secret place, sickness and disease have to turn back when they come near our door. This is because they no longer have authority to plague the children of God who dwells with Him in His secret place on a daily basis. The secret place is not in an earthly realm were Satan reigns.

I've had many wonderful times with the Trinity, in the secret place. It was there that I first experienced the anointing in the form of an *electrical current* running into my hands, down my arms and through my body. One time while I was worshipping **the Trinity** I, also experienced this electrical current as it turned into a *numbing, burning ache* that was unlike anything I had ever experienced in my entire life. I have no doubt that these manifestations were the Holy Spirits' Presence (the Anointing) moving upon and through me!

When I said *worshipping the Trinity*, that is exactly what I meant. The Holy Spirit is God **isn't He**? And seeing that He is God, He is also worthy of worship in the same way as the Father and Jesus. He won't demand it, but He's worth.

Jesus is saying to us, that He will set those on high who know and *understand* Him by personal knowledge. These are those who have *begun* to learn His ways by having daily fellowship with Him through waiting in His Presence. This is *the key* to "knowing" and "understanding" the Trinity. I didn't say we would know and understand *everything*, but it sure is a great way to start. Therefore, we will never be forsaken. Jesus was forsaken by the Father so that we would never have to be forsaken. He took *our* separation (Spiritual Death) from God upon Himself, and its punishment, so that we would never have to be forsaken.

At this point I would like to briefly share this principle from a New Covenant perspective.

Waiting In His Presence In The New Covenant

(**Acts 1:4**) And while being in their company *and* eating at the table with them, He commanded them not to leave Jerusalem but to **wait** for what the Father had promised, Of which [He said] you have heard Me speak.

(**Acts 2:1,2**) AND WHEN the day of Pentecost had fully come, they were all assembled together in one place, when suddenly there came a sound from heaven like the rushing of a violent tempest blast, and it filled the whole house in which they were sitting.

If you remember the story of Pentecost, Jesus told many to go into the upper room and **wait** for the promise of the Father. Did those people just go up there and *wait*? Of course not, they fasted, they prayed; they worshipped the Lord. However, they also *waited* in His Presence. I totally believe that had those people not gathered together, the Holy Spirit probably would not have come. This cannot be proven either way, but I believe He was sent by the Father because there were 120 obedient believers who waited and expected to receive the Promise of the Father, until He filled their lives.

Since waiting is so important to receiving so much from God, does the Bible say anything about Jesus waiting before the Lord?

(Luke 6:12) Now in those days it occurred that He went up in to a mountain to pray, and *spent the whole night* in prayer to God.

I can hear someone now. "This doesn't say that Jesus waited before the Lord." This is true! It doesn't say it in those exact words. However, Jesus went up on the mountain to be alone where He could pray uninterrupted. No one will ever convince me that Jesus was praying (*talking*) the entire time that He was there. I know beyond any doubt that Jesus spent a lot of this time **listening** to His Father and being ministered to by the Holy Spirit.

These were His times of restoration (refreshment). He *needed* to be spiritually refueled just as we do. Prayer and waiting recharges spiritual batteries, and Jesus needed renewed energy, for His earthly ministry. Please never forget that Jesus was as much human as He was God. He was totally dependent upon the Presence of His Father.

At this point I would like to share the things that I do before and during waiting in His Presence. *First,* I take some time and ask the Father to forgive me of any sins that I have committed. Then **if** I have pressing needs that I want to bring before His face I make them known. When I'm finished, I lay on the floor, lift my hands and worship Him; until I come to a *special* point in my time with Him...then I "be still (shut my mouth/mind) and **know** that He is God." At this time I listen for His Voice to direct me in my day or whatever **He** desires to talk to me about. **He** talks...**I** listen!

In closing, I would like to share some Scripture with those of you who are still somewhat skeptical. I simply ask that you take these verses and study them out for yourself.

6 Keys On How To Wait In His Presence

(1) We must repent of sin (1Jn. 1:9).
(2) Prepare ourselves for His Presence (Job 11:13).
(3) Let our words be few (Eccl. 5:2).
(4) Worship God—*Father, Son, Holy Spirit* (Ps. 99:9).
(5) Confess God's Word back to Him (Joshua 1:8).
(6) Rest in His presence, be still and wait (Isa. 41:1a).

A Closing Scripture

(Isaiah 41:1a) "*LISTEN* **IN** *silence* before Me,..."

6

WHAT ABOUT PAUL'S THORN?
(Fresh Insights Concerning Paul's Thorn & Healing)

"What about Paul's thorn? Haven't you ever read where God **refused** to deliver Paul of his thorn in the flesh?" Have you ever had someone make this statement to you? I have heard this statement numerous times.

All right, what about Paul's thorn? The passages of Scripture concerning Paul's thorn appear to be a *sacred calf* to those who, for some unforeseen reason, have failed to receive their healing. Why is it when our *experiences* do not line up with the Word we blame the Word, as if it is God's fault that *we've* failed to receive His promise. Concerning healing and deliverance (2 Cor. 12:7-9), emerges as probably the most controversial passage of Scripture in the entire Word of God; *(with the trials of Job running a close second)*.

People of God—the paramount controversy surrounding Paul's thorn, is not over the question of whether or not Paul ever became sick. But rather it is focused on the notion that God **refused** to deliver Paul from this thorn; which to many traditional minded people was physical sickness. However, chronic sickness was never addressed by Paul. In no way would I debate the possibility of Paul being *attacked* by physical injury or sickness, seeing the injuries he received in his life. Humans can be attacked with sickness by Satan because we are human. However, we do not have to live in those attacks. We can live **above** them in the Name of Jesus. If it were *impossible* to live above the power of attacks by Satan, the apostle Paul **wouldn't** have written for us such a glorious testimony.

(2 Corinthians 4:8-10 KJV) *We are* troubled on every side, **yet not** distressed; *we are* perplexed, **but not** in despair. Persecuted, **but not** forsaken; cast down, **but not** destroyed; Always bearing about *in the body* the dying of the Lord Jesus, that the life also of Jesus might be made manifest in our body.

Does this victorious confession sound like it came from an impotent, frail, disease ridden servant of God; as many traditional people claim? **No!** This is the confession of a man who walked in victory, not in disease and failure. The vast majority of sick people, "believers" *included*, talk more about their illnesses, than they do about their victory in Jesus! This may be hard for some to hear, but the truth that we **know** will set us free (Jn. 8:32). Physical attacks of sickness are *a fact* of life, but we live by the Truth, **not** facts. The Word of God is **Truth**, circumstances are *mere* facts, and subject to change at any moment. Satan can not put sickness or disease upon us *without* out willingness (open door) to receive it!

Let's continue our study by examining 2 Corinthians 12:7-10:

(2 Corinthians 12:7-10 KJV) And lest I should be *exalted above measure* through the abundance of the revelations, there was *given* to me a thorn in the flesh, the **messenger of Satan** to **buffet me**, *lest I should be exalted* above measure. For this thing I besought the Lord thrice, that it might depart from me. And he said unto me, My *grace* is sufficient for thee: for my strength is made perfect in weakness. Most gladly therefore will I rather glory in my *infirmities*, that the power of Christ may rest upon me. Therefore I take pleasure in infirmities, in reproaches, in necessities, in persecutions, in distresses for Christ's sake: for when I am weak, then am I strong.

Mark the word **given** in verse seven in your Bible. This word is defined in the concordance as, "to hinder, smite (with the hand); strike (with the palm of the hand)..."[1] Therefore, one *could* say that this verse of Scripture could be read more accurately as: "...was given [to hinder, **smite** with the hand; **strike** with the palm of the hand], **me**. This was a messenger of confrontation and destruction.

What Was Paul's Thorn?

Look again at verse seven, where Paul defines the thorn as; "...the messenger **of Satan**..." The word *messenger* from the concordance is translated "angel or spirit."[2]

Consequently, we understand that Paul's thorn was a messenger (evil angel or spirit), of some sort, which was from the enemy; **instead of** God. Since this messenger was Satan's undertaking, why does God always appear to be the One blamed for its presence in Paul's life? Moreover, what was the purpose of this messenger?

"...the messenger of Satan **to buffet** me..."

In the concordance the word *buffet*, is defined as "to rap with the fist: buffet."[3] Interestingly enough, the Bible dictionary also defines buffet basically the same way. The purpose of this evil messenger (spirit), was to inflict physical punishment by beating upon Paul with its *fists*. Recognizing that evil spirits *often times* identify themselves by their evil characteristics, one could say that this messenger was a *spirit of persecution*, sent to hinder Paul from preaching the Gospel.

(**A word study of** 2 **Corinthians 12:7)** "...was given [to hinder, smite with the hand; strike with the palm of the hand], me a thorn in the flesh, the messenger [evil angel or spirit], to buffet [to rap with the fist], me..."

Paul continues in verse eight, informing us that he prayed three times that it (the messenger of Satan), would depart. Paul wanted God to stop this messenger from attacking him. Nevertheless, God responded with, "...*My grace is sufficient for you....*"

What did God really mean with this statement? In the concordance the word *grace* is also defined as "**gift**."[4] For this reason, I believe God actually answered Paul by saying; "My *gift* [Jesus in you] is sufficient for your victory." Likewise, the word *sufficient* is defined as to be sufficient, but it's also defined as, "through the idea of **raising a barrier**, *to ward off*, be enough, be satisfactory."[5] I believe with all that is within me that God was literally saying; "My **gift** [grace—Jesus in you] is all you need (sufficient) *to raise up a barrier, and ward off the enemy*." God's desire was for Paul to depend upon the gift of Christ within him for victory. God continued to instruct Paul by saying, "...for *my* strength is made perfect in *your* weakness...." God wanted him to see that His strength was what was making him victorious.

The word *strength* is defined in the concordance as [*dunamis*-Greek], which is "the miraculous power, ability of God."[6] The word *perfect* means "fulfillment, complete,"[7] according to the Bible dictionary. Briefly, this is saying to us, "God's strength [gift] in us is made complete when we realize that we're not our own source of strength.

Subsequently, we shall deal with presumably the most controversial word in this verse. That word *weakness* by the concordance is defined as: "feebleness, malady; frailty: disease, infirmity, sickness, weakness."[8] With this sort of definition, the traditional church seems correct. However, when we examine the Bible dictionary definition, a much different picture is painted. *Weakness* (*astheneia* in Greek) means; "weakness of the body **in respect of** the physical sufferings…of Christ"[9] Therefore, we see that the weakness in Paul's life was the result of physical suffering (beating, stoning, and wiping), rather than the result of a lifelong battle with a chronic disease.

Not only that, think about this for a moment. If *weakness* truly meant sickness and disease, then this type of reasoning would be in line. In order for the (*dunamis*) power of God to manifest through our lives, we would **all** have to have life long sickness and disease. What's more, what about the other apostles? They were used by God; yet there is no record of them having lifelong diseases. Consequently, the healthy people couldn't experience the privilege of being used by God. One can ascertain that this line of reasoning is very **illogical**. In this same manner, the reasoning of the many traditional people is equally as illogical. There is no Scriptural basis for such assumptions.

Yet, Paul said, "I have joy or boast in my infirmities." What is meant by *infirmities* in verse nine? *Infirmities,* according to the Bible dictionary, means "a want for strength, weakness, *indicating inability to produce results.*"[10] Paul took joy or boasted in the fact that through his loss of strength (his own inability to produce results), he was able to draw upon the strength (dunamis—Gift) of God.

(2 Corinthians 4:7 KJV) But we have this treasure in earthen vessels, that the excellency of the power *may be of God*, **and not of us.**

This is the kind of glorying that Paul was referring to when he wrote, (2 Cor. 12:9,10). He was boasting before all that his source of strength and power was none other than the dunamis of Almighty God in his earthen vessel. He **was not** thanking God *for* the trials and persecutions, but rather for His *strength* and *power* being his source.

There's an additional sacred calf that must be put to death. It has been contrived by *traditional theologians,* as proof of Paul's failing health. This bogus doctrine teaches that Paul had a *chronic eye disease.* These traditional theologians believe Paul had an eye disease that God *refused* to heal. However, this line of reasoning couldn't possibly be true; because Paul identified his thorn as the messenger of Satan to **buffet** (beat, slap) him around, to hinder him from preaching. He didn't say it was a messenger from God—did he?

(Galatians 4:13-16 KJV) Ye know how through *infirmity* of the flesh I preached the gospel unto you at the first. And my *temptation* which was in my flesh ye despised not, nor rejected; but received me as an angel of God, *even* as Christ Jesus. Where is then the blessedness ye spake of? for I bear you record, that, if *it had been* possible, ye would have **plucked out your own eyes**, and have given them to me. Am I therefore become your *enemy*, because I tell you the truth?

Paul said he preached the Gospel despite his own want for strength (weakness) within himself. He was acknowledging that in himself he was weak, but through Christ he had *all the strength* he needed to go on in total victory.

The word *temptation* as defined by the concordance, means "a putting to proof by experience of *evil*, solicitation, adversity."[11] Paul is saying, "you Galatian's received me like an angel of God, despite my adversities; **knowing** that you too could have experienced the same adversities for befriending me." In other words, "you risked your lives before, so that my needs could be met by you." During this time, *almost* everyone had heard of Paul's seemingly endless battle with the religious leaders. I believe there were many who wouldn't even talk to him because they were fearful that they too would receive the same type of treatment Paul received. Many were afraid of being persecuted on account of helping Paul.

Paul continued, making one of the most controversial statements that ever came out his mouth, yet one of the simplest to understand.

(Galatians 4:15 KJV) "...if *it had been* possible, ye would have **plucked out your eyes**, and given them to me."

The traditionally minded read this and say, "See, Paul had an eye disease. That's why they were willing to give their eyes." Paul's statement has **nothing** to do with having some chronic eye disease, but *simply* expresses the Church at Galatia's love and devotion to Paul and to God. In order to clarify this point, look at what the Bible dictionary has to say about the word *pluck* (out).

EXOPUSSO: "to dig out or up, is rendered "ye would have plucked out (your eyes)" in Gal. 4:15, an indication of their **feel-**

ings of gratitude to, and love for the Apostle. The metaphor affords **no real ground** for supposition of a reference *to some weakness of his sight*, and certainly not to the result of his temporary blindness at his conversion...their devotion prompted a readiness to part with their *most treasured possession* on his behalf."[12]

In light of the undeniable evidence presented, I believe this part of our case concerning Paul's thorn is closed. Next, let's examine why many try to **over inflate** Paul's thorn.

The Evil Underlying Current Surrounding Paul's Thorn In The Flesh

Waters of a river can be very deceptive. Why? Because of the underlying current which can be very dangerous if one is caught within its grasp. Once caught in the current, one is most surely guaranteed to be swept away in the undertow. How does this relate to our topic at hand? Religious minded people have **created** this entire river of theological *problems* (the evil underlying current), which has swept away millions of unsuspecting *believers*. This river of controversy has stirred up an evil undertow, pulling many believers away from believing that God still wills to heal. Since these questions have been stirred up, many are now questioning the workings of the *Super-natural*.

Thus they see acts of the Spirit as if they were the acts of the enemy, *implying* that the Anointing of God no longer operates in the affairs of men. If God never changes, then why would He do miracles in Israel, but not in the Church age?

The principal evil undercurrent that has been stirred up by Paul's thorn in is in the area of healing and deliverance. Some say God heals, some say He doesn't. And many say He does, *but no one knows when He will want to*. No wonder there are so many believers saddled with sickness and disease, simply because they have *no idea* what God's Word/will tells us about healing and deliverance.

What Does Salvation Really Mean?

In order for us to clearly understand the appropriate Biblical view of Paul's thorn, we must understand what salvation **really** means. Once we are able to grasp this concept, no *religious minded* person will **ever** be able to fill our heads full of theological, philosophical *debris* again!

What About Paul's Thorn?

In the Old Covenant, salvation is defined by (5) Hebrew words. My objective is to share only two of them from the concordance.

[Yesh'-oo-aw] "something saved, deliverance; hence aid, victory, **prosperity**:--deliverance, **health**, help; salvation, save, saving."[13] [used **65 *out of* 114 times** in the Old Testament]

[Yeh'-shah or Yay'-shah] "liberty, *deliverance, prosperity*, safety, salvation."[14] [used **28 *out of* 114 times** in the Old Testament]

These two words together are used **93 out of 114 times** in the Old Covenant, thus an accurate definition. Unfortunately, in the mind of the majority of believers, salvation is only being forgiven of all sin, and an escape hatch from hell. If you were to ask the average *believer* on the street "what does salvation mean?" I believe that most couldn't tell you much more than that. Unfortunately, this is about all most Christians are taught in our churches today!

We should continue our examination of salvation by seeing how the New Covenant defines it.

[soteria] "*rescue*, safety, deliver, **health**, salvation, save saving."[15] [used **40 *out of* 45 times** in the New Covenant]

Salvation means a *whole lot more* than just forgiveness of Sin and escaping hell (although that's a great deal). Salvation really means forgiveness, deliverance from all oppression; healing and prosperity in all areas of life.

(John. 10:10 KJV) "...I am come that they might have life, and that they might have it **more** abundantly."

Think about this a moment. Since salvation also means healing, deliverance and prosperity, *why* are so many believers full of diseases; in bondage and living in abject poverty? It is my belief that Satan has done a very good job spreading his lies via the *theologians* of the past one hundred years or more. This spiritual ignorance has unknowingly spread the enemy's doctrine of fear, depression and disease, thereby holding a great many in bondage.

I am not angry with these theologians, because they are **spiritually blind** to Satan's using them. However, I'm mad at the devil because he has robbed and deceived so many of God's people, by convincing them that God doesn't care about their physical health.

Nevertheless, what did Jesus really accomplish on the cross? Was healing a part of God's plan of redemption? Does God care about healing us physically?

(Isaiah 53:3-5 KJV) He is despised and rejected of men; a man of sorrows, and acquainted with grief: and we hid as it were our faces from him; he was despised, and we esteemed him not. Surely he hath **borne** our ***griefs***, and carried our ***sorrows***: yet we did esteem him stricken, smitten of God, and afflicted. But he *was* wounded for our transgressions, *he was* bruised for our iniquities the chastisement of our peace *was* upon him; and with his stripes we are **healed**.

The Lord Jesus paid an awesome price so that we could be completely free from *all* the power of the devil. Let's investigate exactly what Jesus bought and paid for (in our salvation), from the concordance:

Borne [nasa or nacah] "to lift, carry (away), cast, contain, ease, fetch, forgive, hold up, receive, **take** (**away**, *take up*) pardon."[16]

Griefs [choliy] "malady, anxiety, calamity: ***disease***, grief and (**sickness**)."[17]

Sorrows [makobah] "anguish, affliction, grief, **pain**, sorrow [See Isa. 53:3 AMP]."[18]

Healed "to mend, **to cure**, heal, repair, **make whole**."[19]

Our Lord Jesus bore (carried away), *all* of our griefs (diseases); and *all* our sorrows (pains, afflictions), on the cross. So that we could walk in victory above *all* of these hindrances of life. However, that doesn't mean that we are automatically *immune from attack*; it simply means we posses the victory even before the attack comes.

This is the kind of salvation that the whole world needs to know about. Most non-believers do not become believers simply because they look at our lives and see all of the bondage and think; *"I have it better than they do and I don't even have Jesus."*

This is a total misconception on their part, but nonetheless they do have a understandable line of reasoning. I believe it's time for the people of God to *rise up and display* to the world what salvation **truly** means. But this won't happen until we *live* true salvation before the world.

What About Paul's Thorn?

Refer back at (Isa. 53:5) where it reads: "...the chastisement of our peace was upon him..."

Jesus took the *chastisement,* defined by the concordance as "the discipline or correction;"[20] so that we could live in peace with God. However, the Hebrew word for peace means more than just peace. *Peace* in the Hebrew concordance is defined as "**well**, happy, **health**, prosperity; (*good*) health, perfect peace, prosperity and prosperous."[21]

When the Lord Jesus hung on that cross and proclaimed "**It Is Finished**" that is exactly what He meant, *the end of the rule of Satan and the fulfillment of the Old Covenant.* Unfortunately, despite all that we've just gone over there are *still* those who struggle over whether or not it is God's will to heal today. I believe all of us can agree that Jesus was and is God, but He lived *as a man.* Have you ever investigated what He said on the subject? Let's take a look a Jesus' teaching about healing and God's will.

(Luke 4:18,19 KJV) The Spirit of the Lord is upon me, *because* he hath anointed me to preach the gospel to the poor; he hath **sent me to heal** the brokenhearted, to preach **deliverance** to the captives, and **recovering of sight** to the blind, to set at liberty them that are bruised, To preach the acceptable year of the Lord.

Why did Jesus say He was anointed? Jesus said He was anointed to preach the *Gospel* to the poor, to *heal* the brokenhearted; to preach *deliverance* to those that were captive, and to reclaim *sight* for those who were blind (physically as well as spiritually). Finally, He was anointed to set at liberty them that are bruised, and to preach the year of God's favor toward all men.

What is good news to a poor man? Good news to a poor man is that he doesn't have to live in his poverty anymore, there's hope! What's good news (the Gospel) to a sick man? Good news to a sickly, dying man is that there is a cure for his illness. Jesus Christ is the cure for **every** disease known and *unknown* to man.

There is a lost and hopeless world that needs to hear the good news, that there is *hope* for their marriage, that there is a cure for their alcohol addiction, and that **Hope** is freedom through Jesus. So say this is idealistic, but Jesus is the answer to any problem in life.

Jesus also had something interesting to say about healing in His *instructional prayer:*

(Matthew 6:9,10 KJV) "...Our Father which art in heaven, Hallowed be thy name. Thy kingdom come. Thy will be done *in earth, as it is* in heaven."

Jesus said, "God's will is to be accomplished on earth just **as it is** in heaven." How about this, *"Is there any sickness or poverty in heaven?"* **No!** So why should a believer in Christ be under sickness, disease, or poverty here on earth?

(Galatians 3:13,14 KJV) Christ hath redeemed us *from* the curse of the law, being made a curse *for us*: for it is written, Cursed is every one that hangeth on a tree: *That the blessing of Abraham might come on the Gentiles through Jesus Christ*; that we might receive the promise of the Spirit through faith.

Notice in verse (13), it says that Christ was **made a curse** for us. Why was He made a curse for us? This is because *Adamic Sin* was a cursed thing in the eyes of God. In order for Jesus to pay the *complete price* of our redemption, He had to be made in the likeness of Sin, even though He had lived a sinless life. This caused Him to be made a curse for us. Please remember the price that Jesus paid in our place—He went to **hell** so we could legally come boldly into His throne! He endured the punishment that we deserved.

Before The Fall

Before Adam and Eve sinned in the garden, life was incredible. They had anything and everything they could ever need or want. There were three things in particular that God **never** intended for man to experience:

1. *Sin*
2. *Sickness* (of any kind)
3. *Death* (spiritual & physical)

However, because man used his will to disobey God, Sin was born into humanity. As a result of the fall of man Sin, sickness, and death came into the human race. Please realize that this came *as a result of Adamic Sin*. Therefore, God the Father sent the Lord Jesus *in the likeness* of sinful man to redeem us *out of and from* Adamic Sin. Hence Jesus delivered us from the power of Sin, sickness, and death. All three equal the curse of the Law, (Deut. 28:1-14/Gal. 3:29). But, we are redeemed from the curse of the Law.

This is why Jesus displayed the authority given to Him by His Father, healing a man who had leprosy and showing us that it is His will to heal.

> **(Matthew 8:2&3 KJV)** And, behold, there came a leper and worshipped him, saying, Lord, *if thou wilt*, thou canst make me clean. And Jesus put forth his hand, and **touched him**, saying **I will**; be thou clean. And immediately his leprosy was cleansed.

This is an awesome passage of Scripture. The man said "Jesus *if thou wilt*, you can make me clean." How did Jesus response to that man? Jesus put forth His hand, and *touched him*, saying **I will**. Do you *understand* what this verse is saying? When Jesus put forth His hand and touched the man, He was saying "I have authority over disease, and *I will* that you be cleansed." Leprosy is an extremely *contagious* disease. Yet the Lord Jesus was not *apprehensive* in touching this man. Why? Because He **knew** that the dominion of Satan over man was finished and that Sin, sickness and death were under His (hence our feet). [See: 1 Jn. 3:8]

One final thing in (Matt. 8:2,3), please note that Jesus did not say to the man, "This is the will of God for you, just learn how to live with it. God is using this leprosy *to teach you something* or *to make you strong.*" Jesus never said anything so ridiculous. He touched him, as He spoke. The result of Jesus' actions brought cleansing (healing) to this man's body. What about His disciples. Were they authorized to do the same works that He did?

> **(Matthew 10:1,5-8 KJV)** And when he had called unto him his twelve disciples, he gave them power *against* unclean spirits, to cast them out, and to heal **all** manner of sickness and **all** manner of disease. These twelve Jesus sent forth, and commanded them, saying, Go not into the way of the Gentiles, and into any city of the Samaritans enter ye not: But go rather to the lost sheep of the house of Israel. And as ye go, preach, saying, The kingdom of heaven is at hand. Heal the sick, *cleanse* the lepers, *raise* the dead, *cast out* devils: freely ye have received, *freely give*.

In verse (1) do we see Jesus giving His twelve power over **some** manner of sickness and *some* manner of disease? Many *theologians* wish that was what He said. However, Jesus said **all** (disease), and **all** means **all**. Furthermore, in verse (2) the Word says that Jesus *commanded* them. His command was more than "do not go to the Gentiles..." It included, heal the sick, cleanse the lepers, *raise the dead*. Therefore, we're *commanded* by our Lord to be about His Father's business.

I believe from the context of the Scriptures presented here, that *it is* the will of the Father that we (the believers) walk everyday of our lives in a flow of the dunamis of God. The Lord Jesus Himself wills that we minister the healing miracle power of God to this world, in the same manner as He did while on this earth. When people look into our eyes they should see the love and power of God ready to minister to their needs. If we don't do it...then who will?

To all believers who are searching *desperately* for some answers to their failing health, I say, "Please remember God's Word ***is*** His will, and His Word is **always** true, regardless of what our circumstances tell us. *Don't give up!* He loves you and desires that your body be whole. You **will** receive (reap) **if** you do not give up and faint (Gal. 6:9)."

Finally, to all the critics—*the religious people*: I pray that some of you have seen your old doctrines in a new light. I also pray that you have been able to catch sight of the awesome job that is set before us today. *However*, I am also a realist, and I recognize just as the religious people in Jesus' day **refused** to listen, still many of you have *refused* to hear. I **pray** that you receive ears to hear, and eye to see *once again!*

A Closing Scripture

(Isaiah 53:4,5) Surely He has borne our **griefs** (**sicknesses**, *weaknesses*, and *distresses*) and **carried** our sorrows *and* pains [of punishment], yet we [ignorantly] considered Him stricken, smitten, and afflicted by God [as if with leprosy]. But He was *wounded* for our transgressions, He was *bruised* for our guilt *and* iniquities; the chastisement [needful to obtain] peace *and* well-being for us was upon Him, and with the stripes [that wounded] Him we are healed *and* made whole.

7

WHOEVER SAID, "WOMEN CAN'T PREACH?"
(Restoration Time For The Daughters of God)

Who said, "Women can't preach?" That is an **extremely** important question. Have you ever asked yourself, "Who started the whole controversy, and why was it started in the first place?" I have asked the Lord this question many times, and He has shared with me some insights concerning this problem, which I would like to pass on to you. I've written these insights not in a *spirit of division*, but rather one of **restoration** for the Body of Christ. The devil has robbed us of much through division and strife, and I believe it's time for us to receive the restoration of the *full potential* of the Body of Christ. Men of God, it's time for us to reorganize our lives, and make room for the anointed women of God in "our" ministries. I praise God for many ministers of our day who are not too insecure or full of pride to allow a woman minister to preach beside them. Yet, there are still many ministers who are *resting* their feet on the daughters of God. The Spirit of the Living God says to you, ***"Let my daughters go!"***

I understand that many may not agree with *my* position. However, I ask you to read what follows with an open mind, and most of all with a repentant heart. It's *impossible* for one to receive revelation from heaven without a broken and contrite spirit (heart).

Adam & Eve
(Dominion; The Fall And *Man's* Redemption)

In order for us to establish a Biblical perspective concerning women in the ministry, I believe it is appropriate that we investigate this subject from its origin context. The book of Genesis reveals God's *original* plan for women.

(Genesis 1:26 & Genesis 3:20 KJV) "And God said, Let us make *man* in our image, after our likeness: and let **them** have dominion over the fish of the sea, and over the fowl of the air, and over the cattle, and *over all the earth*, and over every creeping thing that creeps upon the earth…And *Adam* called his wife's name Eve; because she was the mother of all living."

Please mark that in Genesis chapter 1 verse 26, God said "Let us make *man* in our image." Also note that He gave dominion to **them**. Adam and Eve had equal authority (dominion), before the fall of man; but Sin entered in, messing up that delicate balance of power.

Consider (Gen. 3:20), and note further that God never called the woman Eve. Adam was the first to call her Eve, **after** the fall. God called them **Adam** (man) because He saw them as **one**. This is why He said; "Let us make *man*," because in God's eyes they were one and the same (the two were one). Sin interfered with the anointed balance created by our Lord, *thus* the controversy between the sexes ensued.

Moreover, dominion was never meant for just the **men**. Dominion was given to a husband and wife **team**. The husband as leader (*one held responsible*) of the team. Before God created woman, Adam was **only** the caretaker of the garden. But when the two became one, **then** the powerful principle of dominion was put into force. Dominion of this earth was *originally* set in motion by God, in the form of a husband/wife (male & female) unification.

Who was responsible for the fall of man? Some say Eve was, since she was the first to eat of the fruit. But was Eve *really* responsible?

(Genesis 3:11-13 KJV) And He said, Who told thee that thou wast naked? Hast thou eaten of the tree, whereof I commanded thee that thou shouldest not eat? And the man said, The woman whom **thou** gavest *to be* with me, she gave me of the tree and I did eat. And the Lord said unto the woman, What is this *that* thou hast done? And the woman said The serpent beguiled me; and I did eat.

I would like to point out that Adam tried to initially put the blame on God for *his* disobedience; "…The woman whom **thou** gavest to be with me…" Basically, he was saying, "It's your fault, God, because You are the One Who gave me this woman." However, he knew his excuse would not work, so he tried another *brave* endeavor.

He decided to put the blame on Eve. Adam seems to be a true symbol of today's typical *spineless* male, since he was unwilling to accept the responsibility for the problems that his family created. Instead of admitting that he was **ultimately** responsible for his wife's illegal action, he attempted to pass the buck two times.

Perhaps you are asking, "How is it his responsibility? She was accountable for her own actions." This may be true in today's court of law; however, God's legal system is not the same as man's. Look at verse (6) of chapter 3: "...she took of the fruit thereof, and did eat, and gave also unto her husband **with her**, and he did eat." I have heard many preachers say "Eve was the cause of the fall of man." That was just not the case! Adam was made *head* of that team; he was right there **with her** while she was being tempted, and he *allowed* her to be deceived without saying **a word**. At least she was deceived. Adam, on the other hand; had no excuse. He saw the choice Eve made, and committed the same act!

Redeemed Or Re-damned?

An invasive study of Romans chapters 6,7&8 (see chapter 3) would reveal that we have been redeemed from the curse of the Law, which was originally put into effect *as of the result of* man's fall from grace. Since we already have been redeemed (set free) from the curse of the Law, through Christ, we have also received restoration concerning the place of authority which Adam and Eve had *before* the fall.

Through the sacrifice of our Lord Jesus, we have received back **equal** dominion (authority) over all the earth. Since we have been given back our dominion, does that release men from their responsibility as heads of the marital union? **No way**! Paul deals with the subject of **marital** submission in first Timothy chapter 2.

> **(1Timothy 2:11-14 KJV)** Let **the woman** learn in silence with all subjection. But I suffer not **a woman** to teach, nor to *usurp* authority over **the man**, but to be in silence. For Adam was first formed, then Eve. And Adam was not deceived but **the woman** being deceived was in the transgression.

At face value these verses *appear* to make a blanket statement addressing the entire female race. Upon further investigation, however, we find this certainly was not the case. These verses do not speak about just *any* woman. They are **specifically** addressing a married woman or wife. *Woman* as defined by the concordance says, "a woman; specifically **a wife**."[1] Furthermore, "the man" addressed in these verses is none other than the man or **husband**. The concordance defines the *man* as, "a man, husband, fellow."²

At this point one might be wondering, "How can you be sure that this is addressing a husband and wife, not men and women in general?" In the next verse, Paul illustrates this principal by using the first man and wife as a visual example of this important *fundamental* teaching. He says that a woman (wife) is never to usurp her husband nor to teach (instruct) him in an overbearing or domineering manner. *Usurp* as defined by the concordance means "to act of oneself, dominate."³ Paul instructs married women to *honor* their husband's position of authority, but he doesn't expect them to be a *doormat*. This is not because the husband is smarter or better, but simply out of respect for God's authority structure in the realm of **marriage**. It is amazing why some *traditional* people would work so hard to put women back under bondage of the Law of Sin and death, seeing that Christ Jesus has set us free from its control.

Does Speaking Always Constitute Preaching?

(1Corinthians. 14:34-36 KJV) Let *your women* keep silence in the Churches: for it is not permitted unto them **to speak**; *they are commanded* to be *under obedience*, as also saith the law. And if they will learn anything, let them *ask their* **husbands** at home: for it is a shame for women to speak in the church. **What**? *came the word of God out from you? or came it unto you only?*

Just because a verse *appears* to be saying a certain thing does not necessarily mean that that is what is being said! Doing a word study of these verses makes this crystal-clear.

Speak is defined as "to utter words, say, speak, talk, tell, *or preach*."⁴ The word *preach* is included here, but preaching **is not** the context of this passage. The context **is** about wives talking out loud in the middle of a service, questioning their husbands; who were on the other side of the Church. Paul tells us that it is not permitted for a woman to speak (talk, question out loud) in the middle of a service, but to ask their *husbands* at home. He also tells *the women* to remain under obedience, under obedience to *whom*? I've never read a verse in the Bible which tells a woman to remain under obedience to a man, **except** within confines of the verses concerning *the law of marriage*. How would the unmarried women ask questions—they had no husbands?

My wife is *subject* to me, however she **is not** subject to *all* men. No other man can legally or morally tell my wife that she has to sleep with him, or do anything such as that. A **married** woman is to remain *under* obedience to her husband and none other, *besides* God Almighty.

Again Paul is addressing the **married women**, telling them to ask their *husbands* at home rather than interrupting the service and shaming the husband. The word *shame* as defined by the concordance means "to disgrace, feel shame, be ashamed."[5]

What happens when a child acts up in the middle of a Sunday morning service? The answer is simple the parents become ashamed because their child is disrupting the service. This was the same type of situation Paul was attempting to correct. It wasn't an *abomination* for a woman to speak (talk, chatter), but it was disrupting to the flow of the Holy Spirit. Why? This is because it was the wrong place and the wrong time to be asking a bunch of questions. Paul (clearly) was not advocating some legalistic doctrine against women preaching in the Church. He was addressing **married** women!

Furthermore, in Paul's day, there was a separation between men and women, *even in the Christian churches*. Men were on one side and women were on the other during worship, with a curtain separating them. Perhaps this was a reason Paul said that **the middle partition** has been destroyed.

Also remember that women were not formally educated in those days. This is not the case today with most women educated just as well as men, and oftentimes better. God's desire is for the restoration of all godly women to their original positions of authority (dominion). Without these godly women our task of taking dominion would be **totally** impossible since God gave dominion to Adam and Eve. Men our dominion is not complete without our female counterparts.

Moreover, are women only allowed to teach younger women to be good housewives and mothers, or is this just *one* aspect of their ministry?

> **(Titus 2:2-6 KJV)** That the aged men be sober, grave, temperate, sound in faith, in charity, in patience. The aged women likewise that *they be* in behavior as becometh holiness, not false accusers, not given to much wine, teachers of good things; That they may teach the young women to be sober, to love their husbands, to love their children, *To be* discreet, chaste, keepers at home, good, obedient to their own husbands, that the word of God be not blasphemed. Young men likewise exhort to be sober minded.

This passage of Scripture is commonly used to "strengthen" the fight against women in the ministry; simply because of a statement concerning women teaching younger women. It has been assumed that women are *only* allowed to teach other women, and no one else. Upon further examination one can see that the *context* of these verses have no such prohibition over women teaching in the Church, *or anywhere else*, they are not addressing corporate worship!

Paul was instructing Titus to tell the Christian families about how they were to live their lives as examples before the ungodly world. These were Titus' instructions on how to exhort *both* adult men **and** women on how they were to act.

He was exhorting Christian *parents* to be proper godly examples for their children, so that their values would be handed down to future generations. These verses dealt with the proper way families were supposed to live in order to be examples of Christ before the world. Paul in **no way** lays down a pattern for ministry *within* the Church, but rather within **the family unit.**

Are Women Called To Be Ministers of The Gospel?

(Matthew 28:5-7 NKJV) But the angel said to the **women**, "Do not be afraid, for I know that you seek Jesus who was crucified. He is not here; for He has risen, as He said. Come, see the place where the Lord lay. And go quickly and **tell** *His disciples* that He is risen from the dead, and indeed He is going before you into Galilee; there you will see Him. Behold, I have told you."

Wait a minute! I believe someone needs to explain to this angel that these are women that he is speaking with, and that they are not *allowed* by some to **tell** (proclaim, preach) the Gospel, especially *not* to a group of men.

What was the message of the twelve apostles? They told the world that Jesus Christ had risen from the dead. Therefore, these *women* were the very **first evangelists** of the resurrection of Christ. By the way, where were the disciples during Mary Magdalene and Mary's encounter with the angel? They were *hiding* in a little room, *afraid* that the Jews would find and kill them because they had been with Jesus. Jesus used two brave women as His *first evangelists*. This was one of God's acts of **restoration** to the Church. Jesus believes in women ministers, or He wouldn't have sent (*apostled*) these women. Jesus said all of us who want to be great in Him must learn to be a *minister*. We need to realize that God has called every believer to be a minister to those who are need.

(Matthew 20:26,27 KJV) But it shall not be so among you: but **whosoever** will be great among you, let him be your **minister**; And *whosoever* will be chief among you, let him be your servant.

"Whosoever" is the same as whoever (NKJV), which means *anyone* who wants to. In other words, anyone who desires to be great in God's kingdom must be a minister (servant). The concordance defines *minister* as "deacons & *deaconesses*: An attendant, to run errands; to waiter (at table or in other menial duties). **Specific**: a Christian *teacher* and **pastor** (a deacon or **deaconess**)."[6]

Please notice that this definition included women as *teachers* and also as *pastors*. A deaconess is the female counterpart of the male deacon. They were allowed to preach the Gospel, contrary to what *some* may believe. We are all called to preach the good news to every creature. We're not all called to be pastors, evangelists, etc., **but** we are all called to spread the Gospel to every person we meet. **All** believers are kings and priests unto God, not just the males!

The apostle Paul also tells Timothy that he is to commit this Gospel to faithful *men*. What did Paul mean by faithful *men*?

(2 Timothy 2:2 KJV) And these things that thou hast heard of me among many witnesses, the same commit thou to faithful **men**, who shall be *able to teach others also*.

When reading this passage of Scripture *without* further investigation, it could lead one to believe that Paul told Timothy to only allow men to preach the Word. This is not the case! The word *men* is defined as "Man-faced; *a human being*, man."[7] This passage doesn't in any way define gender rather Paul is telling Timothy to commit this Gospel to faithful people of the human race who are able to teach the whole world. I believe Paul was talking to every believer whether they were male *or* female.

There is another way of looking at this controversy. *If* we cut women out of preaching the Gospel, *then* we would cut our army of soldiers by *over* half. Well over half of all people who attend our churches today are women. Women make up over half of the world population. I believe with all my heart that the enemy would love to see the Church's evangelistic force cut by more than half. Then he would really be able to destroy multiplied billions of souls.

WHEN THE HOLY SPIRIT REVEALS
The Prophet And Prophetess

For some mysterious reason, it has been implied that the office of a prophet is functionally different than that of a prophetess. How has this unfounded assumption gained such a foothold in the minds of many traditional churches?

The prophetess is simply a female counterpart of the male prophet. Many of the well known prophets of the New Covenant were also well known preachers. These men preached under the *inspiration* of God, and prophesied. Since a prophet was an inspired preacher of God's Word, why should we assume that the prophetess would be anything different? Let's look at a particular example from the Word of God.

> **(Luke 2:36-38 KJV)** And there was one Anna, ***a prophetess***, the daughter of Phanu-el, of the tribe of Ash'-ser: she was of a great age, and had lived with an husband seven years from her virginity; And she *was* a widow of about fourscore and four years, which *departed not* from the temple, but *served God* with fasting and prayer night and day. And she **coming in** [the temple] that instant gave thanks likewise unto the Lord, and **spake of him to all** them that looked for redemption in Jerusalem.

Anna was an 84 year old woman, who went **into the temple** in Jerusalem, praising God and speaking (preaching) about the arrival of the Christ to all who wanted redemption. She was a godly woman, and I don't believe if it were *unlawful* for a woman to speak in the temple that she would have been there proclaiming the Gospel. Notice also that Anna was a prophetess, fulfilling the same role as the prophet. She was prophesying **and** preaching that the Messiah had arrived, *without* being stoned by the Church elders. Today she would be demeaned in some slanderous book on supposed heresy charges, or asked to leave many of our churches, and labeled a feminist rebel. I find it extremely sad that women ministers are not welcome in *many* of our churches in America, traditional or other wise. Sexism **lives** in our pulpits!

The word *prophetess* is defined as "female foreteller **or** an inspired woman,"[8] and comes from the Greek word for *prophet* "a foreteller **or** an inspired speaker (poet)."[9] The concordance states that the word prophetess comes from the Greek root word for prophet. The prophet and prophetess do in fact have the same job description the only difference being one is male and the other female. Both are foretellers, but they are also inspired, anointed speakers of God's Word. Prophets and prophetesses both spoke the Word of God with God's authority. Still, we have more valuable evidence to examine.

(Ephesians 4:11) And His gifts were [varied; He Himself appointed and gave *men* to us] some, to be apostles (special messengers), some prophets (*inspired preachers and expounders*), some evangelists (preachers of the Gospel, traveling missionaries), some pastors (shepherds of His flock) and teachers.

If you are a traditionally minded person you may be thinking, "See, right there it says **men**." This is true, but *men* is defined by the concordance as "man-faced, *a human being*, man."[10] Moreover, *the King James Version Bible* uses the word *some*. The word *some* according to the concordance is defined as "[including fem.]," *or including the feminine gender*, "the, this, one, he, **she**, it, etc."[11] Females are; therefore, included in the message of this verse of Scripture!

I would like to point out that *prophet*, as defined by *The Amplified Bible*, means much more than the traditional teaching of what a prophet is. It states that a prophet (prophetess) is an inspired preacher and expounder of the Word of God.

Furthermore, in this passage neither gender is assigned to these offices. In Eph. 4:11, Paul does not *in any way* establish either male or female gender specifications concerning these offices. "Men" or "man" is an **all inclusive** word for the human race or the race of man.

What Is Prophecy?

The Bible dictionary defines *prophecy* as "signifies the speaking forth of the mind and counsel of God. In (Jn. 11:51) prophecy is **not** necessarily, *nor even primarily*, foretelling. It is the declaration of that which cannot be known by natural means...(1 Cor. 13:8,9) in this manner the teacher has taken the place of the prophet."[12]

This Bible dictionary defines *prophecy* as a great deal more than what the traditional church leaders have dared to teach us. Thus, here lies the problem which has always separated traditional from non-traditional churches concerning this subject. When using this definition of prophecy, we begin to see a whole new world of opportunity opening up for the prophetic ministry, one which **does not, in any way,** exclude those of the female gender. It amazes me that women *are* allowed to tell the Church what is on the mind and heart of God (prophetically), but they are *forbidden* by some to preach the Gospel in our churches.

Women are physically different than men and somewhat emotionally different too. However; women are still *just* as intelligent and capable of being used by God in prophesy (preaching by revelation) as men. God used many women in the Old Covenant, such as Deborah, Esther, Ruth, and Miriam. In the New Covenant, God used Mary and Mary Magdalene (the first evangelists of the resurrection), Anna (the prophetess), Chloe, and Phoebe; just to name a few.

Phoebe was a very interesting woman of God, and her story has been a source of much *theological* debate. I believe it is important that we look at this controversial passage:

> **(Romans 16:1,2 NKJV)** I commend to you Phoebe our sister, who is a **servant** of the Church in Cenchrea, that you may receive her in the Lord in a manner worthy of the saints, and **assist her** in *whatever business* **she has need of you**; for indeed she has been a *helper* of many and of myself also.

Phoebe was a *servant*, defined by the concordance as "an attendant, (official service), *teacher* or tech. of the dianconate; *minister.*"[13] [*Note*: minister denotes deacon or deaconess, Christian teacher and pastor.] Thus, Paul told them that Phoebe was a minister (servant—possibly a pastor or assistant pastor, teacher), in the Church of Cenchrea. Paul was insistent that the Church at Rome receive her *"in a manner worthy of the saints."* Such a statement *could* indicate that there may have been a problem with receiving women in authority in the past. Therefore, Paul wanted to deal with this problem before it came up. He does this by instructing the Roman church, "...receive her in a manner worthy of the saints, and **assist her** in whatever business **she** has for you..." He said "and assist **her**..."

Paul's statement shows us that Phoebe was a woman in some sort of authority. Perhaps she was Paul's crusade director for his ministry; nonetheless, she was placed in a position of authority by God through the apostle Paul himself. Phoebe was the woman who carried the book of Romans *to the Roman church*; and Paul specifically directed them to **assist her** in whatever business that **she** had for them to do.

Paul also referred to Phoebe as, "...a helper of many and of myself also." *Helper* here is *succourer* which means "a patroness, assistant."[14] The dictionary defines a *patron* as "a person chosen or named as special protector, a wealthy or influential supporter, a regular client or customer, sponsor."[15] Phoebe was an *assistant* to Paul, and possibly a financial supporter of his ministry as well as the Church at Cenchrea. No matter how we look at her Phoebe was a woman of great respect and authority in the eyes of Paul. Paul clearly did not have any problems with women in ministry, or he would not have spoken authoritatively in her favor. If women were not anointed to minister then Paul would not have sent Phoebe.

The apostle John in his second epistle addresses a very special woman. He called her *the elect lady*.

(2 John. 1 NKJV) "The Elder, To the elect lady and her children, whom I love in the truth, and not only I, but also those who have known the truth..."

In the epistle of 2 John, John commends this elect (chosen) lady for the fact that some of her children are abiding in the truth. However, he does not state if these are her physical or spiritual children. He warns her concerning false teachers, and says if they come to her that **she** is not to receive them. This may also indicate that there was a church functioning in her home.

Hence, John told her to not allow them to *speak* or even stay in her home. Nonetheless, she was much respected in her church, as well as by the apostle John.

Submit Yourselves *One* To *Another*

(Ephesians 5:20,21 KJV) Giving thanks always for all things unto God and the Father in the name of our Lord Jesus Christ; *Submitting* yourselves **one to another** in the fear of God.

Paul tells every one of us to be in submission to each other. *Submitting* means "to subordinate, to obey, to be under obedience, subject, submit self unto."[16] We are *all* to be in submission to each other, and not just the women. Men are still the heads of our families; however, they are to put pride and *importance* aside and walk in love, one toward another (*See* 1 Cor. 13). Men must realize that their wives are also their *sisters* in Christ. They are daughters of God **not** the exclusive possessions of their husbands. God has called our wives to stand besides us in ministry—not behind us!

(Galatians 3:26-28 KJV) For ye are **all** the children of God by faith in Christ Jesus. For as many of you as have been baptized into Christ have put on Christ. There is neither Jew nor Greek, there is neither bond nor free, there is *neither male* **nor** *female*: for ye are **all one** in Christ Jesus.

(Romans 10:12 KJV) For there is *no difference* between the Jew and the Greek: for the same Lord over all is rich unto all that call upon him.

In God's eyes we, men and women of all nations, are equal (one). So why are there so many legalistic, *traditional* minded people in the Church trying to put women under the bondage of male dominance? Women are to submit to their *husband's* authority as leaders of the home. This doesn't mean that they are like the family dog and can be ordered around at the whim of the man. It is time for us (men) to clean out the closet of secret sins against our wives, and to begin to **really** love our wives (and all women), as Christ loves us. If we do this then our marriages would be heaven on earth!

The only way for this *sin of dominance* to be cured in our churches, **is for us to first cure it in our homes**. In most cases, men carry the same attitudes toward women *from their marriages into their churches*, thus making a great mistake. In God's house there is **no male or female**, because we are all equal in His eyes! I also believe there must be an authority structure in the Church. However, this does not give men license to *exclusively* dominate church leadership.

Women Ministers Have Come A Long Way

It would be *very foolish* to look at our recent history of anointed women in the ministry, only to say "***That's*** not of God!" Women ministers have come a long way, and accomplished a great deal, despite the *traditional* mind set here are just a few examples of anointed women of God.

Marilyn Hickey is an anointed evangelist who has a popular television show. She also travels and preaches, with Super-natural miracles taking place in her ministry. Her husband Wally is in *full* support of her endeavors.

Gloria Copeland is on the teaching staff of Kenneth Copeland Ministries, and teaches a *Healing School*. Many are healed in her school, and learn how to minister to the sick. Gloria also has the full support of her husband in all ministerial duties. She is also the author of several books.

Patricia Avanzini is the pastor of a successful church in Texas, and an anointed teacher and preacher. Patricia's husband, financial teacher John Avanzini, is in full support of her work as a senior pastor.

Corrie Ten Boom was a survivor of the Nazi death camps. She touched millions of people through her personal appearances and the books she authored, including *The Hiding Place,* telling of her imprisonment in Nazi Germany.

Finally, it could be said that *Kathryn Kuhlman* was the most anointed woman minister *(in the area of healing)* that the Church has seen in the last 100 years of Christian history. The Lord used her greatly in the ministry of healing and miracles. In my opinion, for ***anyone*** to dismiss the miracles flowing through her ministry would be the same as denying the power of God which flowed through Jesus' ministry. We must remember that He is the same Spirit, and that He is always ready to use *anyone* who is willing—***Even A Woman!*** Men—do you have the ears to hear?

A Closing Scripture

(Galatians 3:28 KJV) "…there is ***neither male nor female***: for we are all one…"

THE UNANSWERED PRAYER OF JESUS
(All of Creation Awaits the Answer)

For some believers, the very thought of Jesus having an unanswered prayer *seems* heretical. Considering Jesus' position prior to His incarnation, I understand why many would oppose such a notion. Nevertheless, Jesus ascended to glory with a prayer that is still unanswered. What was His unanswered prayer? In this chapter it is my desire to answer this question, and to illustrate Scripturally **why** Jesus' prayer remains unanswered.

Furthermore, I wish to share some important keys from God's Word, which I believe will *finally* usher in the fulfillment of Jesus' unanswered prayer on the planet earth.

What was Jesus' unanswered prayer? The answer is found in the book of John chapter 17:

(John 17:11; 21-22) "And [now] I am no more in the world, but these are [still] in the world, and I am coming to You. Holy Father keep in Your Name [in the knowledge of Yourself] those whom You have given Me, *that they may be one* as We [are one]…That they all may **be one**, [just] as You, Father, are in Me and I in You, that they also may be one in Us, so that the world may believe *and* be convinced that You have sent Me. I have given to them the glory *and* honor which You have given Me, **that they may be one** [even] **as We are one**…"

Jesus' unanswered prayer was His prayer for **unity** within the Body of Christ. Jesus desired to see His Body living in peace and unity. Having just read this enlightening passage of Scripture, I dare say no one would argue that this is indeed an unanswered prayer. This brings us to a critical question. Why is the prayer of Jesus still unanswered? God (the Father) is not the cause, and neither is Jesus at fault. So who is to be blamed for all the disunity within the Body of Christ?

Why Jesus' Prayer Is Still Unanswered!

(**John 17:17**) Sanctify them [purify, consecrate, separate them for Yourself, make them holy] by Truth; **Your Word is Truth**.

The Bible teaches very clearly that **we**, the Body of Christ, are *solely* to blame for its lack of unity. I say this because we have not and **are not** allowing Truth to sanctify us. The Truth I refer to is the Word of God. God's Word is simply more than the Bible, because God's Word is actually twofold. The Word of God is written (*the Bible*), but the Word of God is also living (***Jesus Himself***). Many believers study and read the Word, but fail to have a daily fellowship with Him. Most believers only pray for *their four and no more*. It is in our times of daily fellowship that God takes the Word we have learned, and by the Holy Spirit uses it to sanctify and purify us.

Unfortunately, the Body of Christ is majoring in minor areas of the Word and minoring in the major areas. Hence, **man made doctrines** are the tools that have spawned this *spirit of division* within the Body of Christ. Man's ideas have become more important than the Word of God for daily living. Denominationalism now attempts to override the simple Truth that the Word of God *clearly* states. Jesus' prayer for unity has not been answered because unity within the Body of Christ *depends* on our surrender to the sanctifying power of the Word of God, written as well as living. Without true, honest surrender, we will never have true, lasting unity.

It is time for us to wake up and shake ourselves free from the spirit of division. I am not insinuating that we must all become Baptists or Word of Faith followers, or even Pentecostals. That is the world's concept of "unity". No way! I'm talking about **all** believers in Christ daring to unify under the Name of Jesus; *rather than* under the different denominations. There is a saying I've heard many times: "*Let us agree to disagree*," meaning we must learn to accept **each and every** believer for who they are, and stop focusing on the *petty* doctrinal differences we have experienced. If we continually over emphasize our differences then we will never see and *experience* the fullness of the Anointing.

Almost every believer loves and admires the writings of the apostle Paul, so let's see what Paul wrote about unity in the Spirit!

The Unanswered Prayer of Jesus

How Paul Said Believers *Should* Live

(Ephesians 4:3-7) Be eager *and* strive earnestly to guard *and* keep the harmony *and* oneness of...the Spirit in the binding power of peace. [There is] body and one Spirit—just as there is also *one* hope [that belongs] to the calling you received [There is] *one* Lord, *one* faith, *one* baptism, *One* God and Father of [us] all, Who is above all [Sovereign over all], pervading all and [living] in [us] all. Yet grace...was given to each of us individually [not indiscriminately, *but in different ways*] **in proportion to the measure** of Christ's [rich and bounteous] gift.

What is Paul attempting to say? Paul is endeavoring to teach the Body of Christ that there is only one (God, faith, and baptism); thus we are to do **our** best to keep the oneness of the Spirit. Realizing we are all *different* and that we see and do things differently. We must comprehend that this doesn't make anyone "wrong," just different. In God's eyes it is not either/or, but rather "all of the above." In this portion of Scripture, Paul is clearly telling us that it is time for us to *take advantage* of our differences by using them to learn from one another, instead of criticizing each other intercede for all.

The next point Paul makes in Ephesians 4 may step on some of our denominational toes. Remember, however, that God's Word **must always** take preeminence, even above what *we* think or teach as doctrine.

No Apostles and Prophets—No Growth and Unity!

(Ephesians 4:11-14a) "And His gifts were [varied; He Himself appointed and gave men to us] some to be apostles...some prophets...some evangelists (preacher of the Gospel, traveling missionaries), some pastors...and teachers. **His intention was** the perfecting and the full equipping of the...[that they should do] the work of ministering toward building up Christ's body...[That it might develop] until we all **attain oneness in the faith** and in the comprehension of the [full and accurate] knowledge of the Son of God, that [we might arrive] at really mature manhood...the completeness found in Him. So then, we may no longer be children, tossed...to and fro between chance gusts of teaching and wavering with every changing wind of doctrine..."

In this long excerpt of Scripture, Paul isn't telling us that Jesus gave us the apostle, prophet, evangelist, pastor and teacher just to set up the Church, then He wanted them to fade out of existence. Further, it *seems* strange that the evangelist, pastor, and teacher managed to survive in most churches, but for some reason the apostle and prophet did not. On the contrary, Paul specifically says that Jesus' intention was for the *full* equipping of the saints, so that we could do the work of the ministry; which is *building up the Body of Christ*. He continues by saying "**until** we all obtain *oneness* in the faith and in the comprehension of the Son of God that we might arrive at *real* manhood." Think about oneness of the Church for a moment. Have we all come into the *oneness of the faith*, and have we all come to **full** comprehension and maturity? Any unbeliever on the street will tell us we are not unified. I'm not saying that we all must think, speak and act like some cult. For that reason, the fivefold ministry needs to be complete and effective **in every part** of the Body of Christ.

I understand some will not want to hear such a message, so let me clarify myself. I am not in any way saying, "If the fivefold ministry gifts are not functioning in your church, then it's dead." I am simply saying *this was the original plan of Jesus Christ our Lord, when He established the Body of Christ*. I am not giving you my opinion I am restating the Word of Almighty God. Unity **depends** on the ministry gifts functioning properly in the Church.

Verse fourteen of Ephesians chapter 4 says; "So then, we may no longer be children, tossed to and fro between chance gusts of teaching and wavering with every changing wind of doctrine." Here Paul exhorts us not to allow our doctrinal differences to *blow* us apart. We are should not allow our doctrines to cause division. We are to be established **by** the fivefold ministry gifts, so we will grow into the unity of the faith. Sadly, many churches view this as past history, and marvel at the nearly nonexistent oneness within most of the Body of Christ.

I believe the reason there is so little unity in the Church today is because so many of us have rejected the very foundation on which Christ built His body. The Word of God says in (Eph. 2:20 TAB), "You are *built upon the foundation* **of the apostles** and **prophets** with Christ Jesus Himself the Chief Cornerstone." How can anything function accurately and effectively using a different set of standards than the inventor intended?

The Body of Christ is no different. If we do not play by **His** rules, we will hinder the outcome of "the game." This makes as much sense as trying to repair your Mercedes Benz using a BMW owner's manual. This is precisely what has taken place in the Church. Most of the believers are operating on *their own* set of standards therefore many are virtually unproductive for Christ. Thus, the world stays away from the Church and God by the billions.

We are The Joints And Ligaments

(Ephesians 4:16) For because of Him the whole body (the Church, *in all its various parts*), closely joined and firmly knit together **by the joints *and* ligaments** with which it is supplied, when each part [with power adapted to its need] ***is working properly*** [in all its functions], grows to full maturity, building ***itself up*** in love.

Here, Paul compares the type of unity that the Body of Christ should function in with the way the human body is held together (unified) by its joints and ligaments. The sad commentary is that **we** are the very joints and ligaments holding the Body of Christ together, and hence we know why the Church is in such disunity. Most believers think Jesus *alone* holds the Church together, but that is not what Scripture teaches. Of course, Jesus *holds* the body together, **but** He is doing this through its members. Recall the verse that speaks of the Lord working with them. That verse doesn't say *for them*, but **with them**. We are the ones to blame for our disunity. People fail, but **He** doesn't! As we live the Word, He works with and in us by confirming the Word with signs and wonders of Christian love and unity.

Verse sixteen says; "When each part is working properly…grows to full maturity, **building itself up** in love." If every part is working properly, then we will have an efficiently running machine. But what if all the parts aren't working properly; what do we have then? Then we have the condition that the Church of Jesus Christ is in today. Paul tells us the Church is to build *itself* up in love. Notice this doesn't say, "Jesus will build it up in love." Like it or not, we are responsible for holding together the Body of Christ.

Jesus is capable and will do most of the work. Nonetheless, we are the ones who must be obedient to do what He says, so we will be able to love and live in the unity of the Spirit in the bond of peace.

We Must Stop Thinking Like The World

(Ephesians 4:17-19) "…you must no longer live as the heathen (the Gentiles) do in their perverseness [in the folly, vanity and emptiness of their souls and the futility] of their minds. Their moral understanding is darkened *and* their reasoning is beclouded. [They are] **alienated** (estranged, self-banished) ***from the life of God***…because of **ignorance**…In their spiritual apathy they have become callous *and* past feeling *and* reckless and have abandoned *themselves* [a prey] to unbridled sensuality, eager *and* greedy to indulge in every form of impurity...."

I believe Ephesians chapter four verses seventeen to nineteen is an accurate portrait of the modern day church. We have proceeded in our own ignorance, not understanding that our foundation is based on the fivefold ministry gifts. In our disobedience we fail to walk in love and unity, and the world fails to see Jesus in us.

They end up in hell as a result of our apathy and ignorance. It is time for us to repent and clean up our lives, so the world will see Jesus in us. We need to allow the Word of God to renew (transform) our minds. Then we will think in line with God's will/Word, instead of the enemy's. Repentance is the main key to healing the wounds caused by the spirit of division. Paul said in (Eph. 4:22 TAB), that we are to strip ourselves of our former nature.

Before continuing, let me state that I am not against believers who do not understand unity as God has taught it to me. I am simply asking all believers, whether you agree with me or not, to please start *respecting* one another's gifts, talents, and styles of worship and prayer. Begin to learn from your brothers and sisters of other denominations. No one of us has **all** wisdom and revelation, thus we can learn from each other. It is time to stop criticizing and begin to love one another. When I say these things I am directing them at Pentecostals, the Word of Faith as well as Evangelicals.

What About Spiritual Gifts?

(1 Corinthians 12:1) NOW ABOUT the spiritual gifts (the special endowments of supernatural energy), brethren, I do not want you to be misinformed [*ignorant*].

This is the prime reason the majority of churches are in confusion and disunity. Paul writes that he **doesn't** want us to be misinformed or ignorant about the spiritual gifts. Nevertheless, we have still failed to listen, and therefore have run headlong into ignorance. Some are into **extreme** emotionalism, while others have scrambled completely away from all manifestations of emotional worship.

There must be a point of middle ground where we can accept each other, not in spite of our differences, but rather because of our differences. Ignorance concerning the **variety of ways** God's Spirit is manifested has always been a source of contention.

Different Ways of Operating...But The Same Spirit

(1 Corinthians 12:4-7; 11) "Now there are **distinctive varieties** *and* distributions of endowments (gifts, extraordinary power distinguishing certain Christians, due to the power of divine grace operating in their souls by the Holy Spirit) and they vary, but the [Holy] Spirit **remains the same**. And there are *distinctive varieties* of service *and* ministration, **but it is the same Lord**. And there are distinctive varieties of operation...but it is the same God Who inspires *and* energizes them all in all. But to each one is given the manifestation of the [Holy] Spirit...for good *and* profit...All these [gifts, achievements, abilities] are inspired *and* brought to pass by one and the same [Holy] Spirit, Who apportions to each person individually [exactly] as He chooses."

First, direct your attention to the beginning of verse four: "Now there are *distinctive varieties and distributions*." Again, Paul stresses there are many different manifestations of the Holy Spirit **within** the Body of Christ. I believe Paul says this so we will *not* be ignorant when we see new and different manifestations of God's Spirit. His Spirit is so much greater than our ability to comprehend Him. I believe as the time of the rapture comes even closer, we will see many *new* and wonderful manifestations of the Holy Spirit. I am not talking about **extremism**. I am referring to new varieties of manifestations which the Spirit desires to make known within the midst of His church. The revival of holy laughter is only one part of these new varieties. We have hardly begun to see all of the new manifestations that the Holy Spirit will reveal.

Next, I want to stress that there are *many* different varieties and distributions, **but** they are all under the direction of the same Holy Spirit Who lives in each one of our hearts, by faith. This is a vital point which the Church needs to begin to grasp. He is the same Holy Spirit Who anoints one to sing as well as another to heal the sick. No one can sing a song that impacts the spirit of man without His anointing, any more than an evangelist can heal someone without the anointing. The Anointing is still performing the healing, not the person.

In both instances it is the Holy Spirit using a vessel to sing or minister healing to a disabled person. Without the anointing no miracles will ever take place; no salvation, no healing, **nothing**!. Until we wake up and realize this, we'll continue to live in disunity, and the lost will remain lost. Unity in the Spirit is up to us, but if we do not start living it, many more will spend eternity in hell's fire, and God will require their blood at our hands. I don't know about you, but to me this is a seriously sobering thought.

Different Anointings—Different Ministries

I would like to point out a few examples of modern day ministries that have different manifestations of the Anointing, but the same Holy Spirit doing the work.

Billy Graham has preached the miracle of salvation to probably more souls than any minister alive today. Salvation has been his major area of emphasis for while *over* 50 years.

Kenneth Hagin [who went to be with the Lord in 2004] and **Kenneth Copeland** are evangelists of the Word of Faith. God has called them to minister to the Church *predominately* in the areas of faith and prosperity (spirit, soul and body).

Rod Parsley is a man who some call *the Preaching Machine*. He is famous for his no compromise, hell fire and brimstone sermons, with which he challenges the Body of Christ to live according to the Word of God.

Benny Hinn is an anointed pastor/evangelist who travels the world introducing believers to daily communion with the Holy Spirit. He also ministers healing and deliverance to the sick and oppressed. He helps to create an atmosphere of worship, and the Holy Spirit does the healing.

James Robison is an anointed Southern Baptist preacher who feeds children all over the world, bringing them medical aid and sharing the Gospel. He also travels the world preaching an anointed message of restoration.

Some may wonder why I listed these ministers and their individual preaching areas of emphasis. I am using this to illustrate the point Paul made in (1 Cor. 12), using modern day examples. Each of these ministers is anointed by the Holy Spirit to preach the message they have received from the Lord. However, notice that each has a different area of the Gospel in which they major. All of them minister the Gospel, but each one is focused on a different *aspect* of the Gospel. Each of these ministers preach and give altar calls, but they do not all *major* on preaching salvation. I believe each of these areas are very important, and none of us has the right to judge or condemn another for **not** preaching the same message that another minister preaches. We need to realize that not everyone is called to major in salvation or hell fire. Thus, we shouldn't *mock* others who do not emphasize *our* particular message (aspect) of the Gospel.

It is extremely unfortunate, but the world can turn on their televisions and hear preachers bad mouthing other preachers and other styles of worship. Equally sad is when an author continually writes slanderous books about other born-again, Spirit filled ministries. Is this sort of conduct an exhibit of love and unity to the unsaved? On the contrary, many use these examples as excuses for *not* giving their lives to Christ. Unfortunately, the Church has provided them these excuses by our late of sincere love and unity.

Preachers and authors everywhere: It is time for *us* to repent of our criticizing tongues. We are the ones who are *supposed* to lead the people, but we cannot lead them to a place *we haven't found ourselves*. Unity begins in the pulpits, then flows into the pews, and finally the river over flows into the streets. We must be the example for others to follow.

Paul tells us in (1 Cor. 12:12), "For just as the body *is a unity* and yet **has many parts**, and all the parts though many, form [only] one body, so it is with Christ." We need to realize that it is our responsibility to live a life of **godly** love and unity. By ourselves we are merely parts of the whole, *but* together we form God's unified, victorious body. Unity in the Spirit has always been a *primary emphasis* which God desired to communicate to His people. Jesus' mission was to teach peace, from God **toward** man. Today we need to ask ourselves, *"Am I heeding the call for unity in the Spirit?"*

In closing I would like to share six keys to Biblical unity that the Holy Spirit taught me. If all members of the Body of Christ would faithfully apply these six keys, I believe victory over disunity would be accomplished in our lifetime. These are very *simple* keys, but for some reason **most** do not apply them to their lives.

6 Keys To Biblical Unity

1. **Repentance**: If I regard iniquity in my heart, the Lord **will not** hear me. (Psalm 66:18)

2. **Allow the Word to Sanctify us**: Sanctify them [purify, consecrate, separate them for Yourself, make them holy] by Truth; Your Word **is Truth**. (Jn. 17:17)

3. **Serve one another:** For you, brethren, were [indeed] called to freedom; only [do not let your] freedom be an incentive to your flesh *and* an opportunity *or* excuse [for selfishness], but through love **you should serve one another.** For the whole Law...is complied with in the one precept, You shall *love your neighbor as* [you do] *yourself.* (Gal. 3:13,14)

4. **Forgive:** And whenever you stand praying, if you have anything against anyone, forgive him *and* let it drop (*leave it, let it go*), in order that your Father Who is in heaven may also forgive you your [own] failings *and* shortcomings *and* let them drop. (Mk. 11:25)

5. **Don't criticize:** "Do not judge *and* criticize and condemn others, so that you may not be judged...Who are you to pass judgment on *and* censure another's household servant? **It is before *his* own master *that he stands or falls*.** And he shall stand *and* be upheld..." (Matt. 7:1/Rom. 14:4)

6. **See our differences as our strengths:** And there are ***distinctive varieties of service*** and ministration, but it is the same Lord [Who is served]. (1 Cor. 12:5)

A Closing Scripture

(John 17:22b,23 KJV) "...that **they may be one**, even as we are one: that **the world may know** that thou hast sent me.."

IS BIBLE SCHOOL "REQUIRED" FOR THE GREAT COMMISSION?

I was fourteen years of age when the Lord called me into the ministry. I vividly remember my pastor at that time. He was an anointed, young, good looking man of God. He was also a graduate of a very popular Spirit-filled university. Since I greatly admired my pastor, I wanted to be just like him. I thought if I went to the same university he did, I would also be an anointed man of God. I later found that the university was not what made him the man of God he is today. It assisted in training him; but he entered that school with a revelation from God already deep within his heart. He had begun a daily fellowship with the Spirit of God long before he walked through the doors of that university.

Years later, I worked with men who were trained at a Bible university. They told me it does not matter if one goes to school or not; what really matters is the *fellowship* one has with the God-Head. They also recounted stories about people they had gone to school with who were only at this same university because their parents had sent them. These students were partying like those at secular universities. I thought to myself, "How could this happen in a Christian university?" Eventually I realized one must be committed to Christ completely or Bible school will not do him or her any good. What grieved me severely is that my coworkers all went to the same university my former pastor had attended.

Finally, the time came for me to attend college. I went to a small Christian college in Southern California, because I knew a few former students. With idealistic stars in my eyes, I started college with the notion that everyone in attendance was *a servant of God*. Was I in for a rude awakening! I saw a lot of the same things my coworkers had warned me about. There were parties, drugs, sex…you name it. Reality hit home, and very hard I might add. Yet the most severe shock of all was yet to come.

WHEN THE HOLY SPIRIT REVEALS

I was attending a New Testament survey class, and my professor proceeded to tell us the book of Mark was most likely **copied** from either the Gospel of Matthew or Luke. He continued, saying it was **impossible** for all three of *the Synoptic Gospels* to be written without one of them copying the other! He also attempted to point out several discrepancies between the writings of Matthew, Mark and Luke. There are many other examples, but I do not want to bore you with the details. Needless to say, I debated with my professor often. He seemed to enjoy having a new fired up freshman, who dared to challenge his doctrine. I realized that if I wanted to learn anything from God's Word, it would have to come by personal revelation from His written Word! Bible school could not be my main *source*.

You may wonder why I've written such a long, some may say depressing, introduction. Am I against good Bible schooling? Absolutely not! I haven't written this to downgrade my former pastor's university, nor the Christian college which I briefly attended. I have written my introduction this way to shock the reader into reality concerning today's Bible schools and universities. I longed to attend a Bible school because that was the thing to do in those days. All I heard was, "If you want to be a minister of the Gospel, you have to go to college." I struggled with this for a long, time. Finally, I was led by the Spirit to research what God's Word has to say about education and preaching the Gospel.

What you are about to read is not, *in any way*, an indictment against anointed Bible schools, universities, and training centers. Rather it is a tool to teach one the proper emphasis from the Bible concerning education and preaching the Gospel. There are many traditional people today who desire to tie us down with four or more years of Bible school before we can be used by God as a pastor or evangelist. I am not saying that going to Bible school is a sin. Rather I am *proclaiming* that all can be used by God with or without **formal** Bible school training. Not all are called to Bible school since God uses the unlearned (*foolish*) to confound the so called learned (*wise*).

I praise God for the wonderful Bible schooling available today like Oral Robert's University, Rhema Bible Training Center and Spirit Life Bible College. *However*, not all "Bible Schools" are training *servants of God*. Many schools today are utilizing a bunch of **man made doctrines** and fables, teaching our future preachers that the Bible **is not** a reliable, error-free book and saying that it's outdated for today's changing times. These schools are breaking down the very faith of those who are teaching the Church.

Furthermore, there are so called theologians attempting to tell us that every preacher must attend Bible school, or they are unprepared and unscriptural.

This is the kind of *bogus doctrine* I desire to dispel, by displaying what God and His Word have to say about education and the Great commission. Having said all this, it is time for us to look into God's Word for answers.

(Proverbs 30:1-3) THE WORDS of Agur son of Jakeh of Massa: The man says to Ithiel, to Ithiel and to Ucal: Surely I am too brutish *and* stupid to be called a man, and I have not the understanding of a man [for **all my secular learning is as nothing**]. I have not learned skillful *and* godly Wisdom, that I should have the knowledge *or* burden of the Holy One.

In Proverbs (the book of Wisdom) chapter 30 we see a man who is in distress. He has finally realized that despite his education, he actually knows *nothing* of real value. He says, "all of my secular learning is as nothing." Is He saying that *all* secular learning is worthless?

Not at all! He is in despair because he has a lot of secular *head knowledge*, but he has somehow failed to receive skillful, *godly* Wisdom. He has failed to receive the understanding of how to use the secular wisdom he has received. Let us continue with Proverbs 3:

(Proverbs 3:13,14) Happy (blessed, fortunate, enviable) is the man who **finds** skillful *and* godly Wisdom, and the man who gets *understanding* [**drawing it forth from God's Word and life's experiences**], For the gaining of it is better than the gaining of silver, and the profit of it better than fine gold.

Here is where the problem lies for many of today's Seminaries and Bible colleges They provide their students with a lot of facts and figures and some wisdom. Yet, only a few teach their students how to get skillful, godly Wisdom *and* the understanding. Wisdom is a wonderful tool; however, wisdom without godly understanding is unproductive.

Understanding is discernment, which can only be produced by abundant time with God. It is totally worthless for a preacher to study the Word of God without respect for fellowship with the Author of the book. Wisdom is knowledge about (facts and figures), but **understanding** is a revelation of how to use the (facts and figures) that we acquire, and revelation is obtained both by studying and by personal experiences.

WHEN THE HOLY SPIRIT REVEALS
The Insightful Words of Solomon

Solomon wrote most of the book of Proverbs, but he also wrote the book of Ecclesiastes. Solomon was a preacher as well as a king, since Ecclesiastes means "the preacher."[1] Let's examine something Solomon said in the book called *The Preacher*, Ecclesiastes chapter one:

(Ecclesiastes 1:16-18) I entered into counsel with my own mind, saying, "Behold, I have acquired great [**human**] wisdom, yes, more than all who have been over Jerusalem before me; and my mind has had great experience of [moral] wisdom and [*scientific*] knowledge. And *I gave my mind to know* [**practical**] *wisdom* and to discern [the character of] madness and folly [in *which men seem to find satisfaction*]; I perceived that this also is a searching after wind *and* a feeding on it. For in much [*human*] wisdom **is much vexation**, and he who increases knowledge increases sorrow."

Solomon seems to agree with the words of Agur in Proverbs chapter thirty. Solomon too had ample secular, scientific, human wisdom, and he closed his statement with "[human] wisdom is much vexation." In other words, human wisdom is nothing but irritation and trouble. The Bible says no one was as wise as Solomon. Until Jesus came into this earth, Solomon was the wisest man to ever live.

However, the Bible also states that Solomon's wives turned his heart away from God. How could a man who was *so* wise allow his wives to turn his heart toward other gods? He did not *take time to receive* the understanding of his learning. He had *much* study, with *little* fellowship.

This is a problem that affects millions of believers. It is sad that many Christians in the Body of Christ are like Solomon and Agur—possessing little *true* understanding. The Bible tells us to learn wisdom, but it also tells us to **get** understanding in order to use the wisdom.

These two Old Covenant case studies are *definitive* proof that knowledge without **fellowship** with the Creator will leave one cold, empty and lost as any unbeliever. As a result, we have many theologians in our schools today who are lost in a fog of theological facts and figures, just as Solomon and Agur were.

We must be extremely careful concerning which school or university we send our children to. Not all educational institutions are worthless. On the other hand, not all *Christian* schools are Bible believing! There is a **vast** difference between the two!

Is Bible School "Required" For the Great Commission?

The Educational Level of The Disciples

(Matthew 4:18,19; 21,22 KJV) And Jesus, walking by the sea of Galilee, saw two brethren, Simon called Peter, and Andrew his brother, casting a net into the sea: *for they were fishers*. And he said unto them, Follow me, and I will make you **fishers of men**. And going on from thence, he saw other two brethren, James *the son* of Zebedee, and John his brother, in a ship with Zebedee their father, mending their nets; and he alled them. And they immediately left the ship and their father, and followed him.

Our Lord and Savior Jesus Christ chose four unschooled fishermen to be on His staff. All the men mentioned here in Matthew's book were not school educated men. That does not mean they were stupid, but they were also not educated in the things of God. Nevertheless, the Father told Jesus to choose four fishermen to be part of turning the world upside down. I believe Jesus did this on purpose. Why? This is because the Bible says that "God uses the foolish things of this world to confound those that would think they are *wise*." These men were surely looked upon by the religious leaders of Jesus' day as foolish, in much the same way today's theologians look down upon those who are not Bible school trained ministers! Of all the disciples, the most educated was Luke, however; he too was not educated in the things of God. Luke's education was in the secular realm, in the area of medicine.

I believe the reason why Jesus chose a group of unschooled men to take the Gospel of the Kingdom to the whole earth, was because He would not have to **retrain** them. They did not have any religious *crust* to break off. They were like a brand new chalk board that had never been written on. Jesus could write whatever He pleased on their lives and, they would not oppose Him based on their past religious experiences. I am convinced the Anointing moved so strongly in their lives and ministries by reason of their childlike innocence and willingness to learn.

Saul Got Knocked Off His *Religious* Horse

(Acts 9:3,4 NKJV) As he journeyed he came near Damascus, and suddenly a **light shone** around him from heaven. Then he fell to the ground, and heard a voice saying to him, "Saul, Saul, why are you persecuting me?"

The light of Jesus' *revealed presence* knocked Saul off his natural and religious horse. It was the blinding light of the revelation of Christ that took Saul and turned him into Paul. The same light that shone upon

WHEN THE HOLY SPIRIT REVEALS

Saul, changing his direction, is the same light of revelation that needs to shine in each and every one of our Bible schools, seminaries and universities. The revelation power of God's Word is the only force that has the power to open *our* eyes, change *our* lives and redirect our course in this life.

Saul was a very devoted religious man. He followed the Jewish Law down to the letter. He even called himself a "Pharisee of Pharisees." Saul was a sincerely religious man. Nonetheless, Paul was *sincerely* **wrong**. Paul gives us some insight into his religious education in the book of Acts which was very extensive.

(Acts 22:1-3 NKJV) "Brethren and fathers, hear my defense before you now,"...Then he said: "I am indeed a Jew, born in Tarsus of Cilicia, but brought up in this city at the feet of Gamaliel, taught according to the strictness of our fathers' law, and was zealous toward God as you all are today.

Paul tells us he was highly educated in the traditional Jewish religion. He was a student under Gamaliel, a highly honored teacher of the Law. Paul was the only apostle mentioned in God's Word who was *well educated* in the traditional Jewish religion. However, there was a problem with Saul's education; hence, a transformation had to take place to fix his educational defects.

Paul Attends Holy Spirit University

(Galatians 1:15-18) "But when He, Who had chosen *and* set me apart [even] before I was born and had called me by His grace...saw fit *and* was pleased. To reveal (unveil, disclose) His Son within me so that I might proclaim Him among the Gentiles...as the glad tidings (Gospel), immediately I did not confer with flesh and blood [*did not consult or counsel with any frail human being* or communicate with anyone]. Nor did I [even] go up to Jerusalem to those who were apostles (special messengers of Christ) before I was, but I went away *and* retired into Arabia, and afterward I came back again to Damascus. Then **three years later**, I did go up to Jerusalem..."

I have heard of theologians who spend much of their time debating what Paul did during his "silent years." I can tell them exactly what Paul was doing during that time period. He was attending **the University of the Holy Spirit**. He was receiving a **re-education** from all of the traditional religious training he had received under Gamaliel.

The Spirit of God had to take Paul into a wilderness experience to teach him the many mysteries of the anointing. The Holy Spirit taught Paul Himself by revelation knowledge from God's Word. Thus I find it strange if one complains against learning by revelation.

> **(Galatians 1:12)** For indeed I did not receive it from man, nor was I taught it, but [it came to me] through a [**direct**] *revelation* [given] by Jesus Christ (the Messiah).

While Paul was in Arabia, he was going through *intensive* reeducation by the Spirit of revelation. The Spirit of God literally sat down and personally revealed the mysteries of the Anointing that Paul describes in his many books. He was taught these things by revelation, Paul says.

The point Paul wanted to stress is that he was not taught the things he learned *by any man, woman or child*. He received Wisdom and understanding from the throne of Almighty God, through **the Spirit of revelation**. If the apostle Paul received his insight by revelation of the Holy Spirit, why in the Name of Jesus shouldn't we? Jesus Christ is the same yesterday today and forever. I believe we too can experience the same revelation power in our lives that Paul did. **Nevertheless**, I am not inferring that we should write some sort of "new" Bible, but rather that we too can understand the Word of God by this same Spirit of revelation. John the beloved disciple illustrates my point perfectly:

> **(1 John. 2:27)** But as for you, the anointing (the sacred appointment the unction) which you received from Him abides [**permanently**] *in you;* [so] then *you have no need that anyone should instruct you*. But just as His anointing teaches you concerning everything and is true and is no falsehood, so you must abide in (live in, never depart from) Him...as [His anointing] has taught you [to do].

By using this portion of Scripture I'm not attempting to say that we don't need the fivefold ministry gifts for instruction. That would be foolishness on my part. I desire to illustrate *the other side* of how the Body of Christ is to receive Wisdom and instruction. We need anointed men and women of God to teach the Word in our churches and conferences. However, these same anointed people are also limited.

Why are they limited? This is because **they** cannot put *their* revelation into our spirits apart from our openness to the Anointing. This is where we need to depend upon the Holy Spirit's revealing power to teach us what others cannot. This truly is the purpose of this chapter. I truly desire to see the Body of Christ walking in the fullness of this revelation. *The Anointing* is our teacher, no matter who or what He uses to teach us. **He** is the One giving us the Wisdom and revelation.

Not In The Wisdom of Men

(1Corinthians 2:2-5 KJV) For I determined *not to know* any thing among you, save Jesus Christ, and him crucified. And I was with you in weakness, and in fear, and in much trembling. And my speech and my preaching *was* **not with enticing words of man's wisdom**, *but in* **the demonstration** *of the Spirit and of power*, That your faith **should not stand** in the wisdom of men, **but** *in the power of God*.

The beloved apostle Paul himself says our faith *is not* to be based on the wisdom of mere man's ideas. He desires that we research *everything* we hear, especially those things that are unfamiliar to us. We won't be able to do this if we do not know what the Word of God says for ourselves. Paul said his preaching wasn't with enticing words, because he had the Anointing upon his life which confirmed the Word; with signs and wonders.

Preaching the Gospel **literally** means, signs and wonders (of some form) confirming the preaching of God's Word in our ministries. I'm not saying all ministers must be like Benny Hinn or Morris Cerullo, but we all need to have some form of signs and wonders *in proportion* to the type of ministry in which we are called. If you teach on financial abundance, there should be people who are becoming debt free under your ministry.

I Count All Things But Loss

(Philippians 3:8 KJV) Yea doubtless, and I count all things *but* loss for **the excellency of the knowledge of Christ** Jesus my Lord: for whom I have suffered the loss of all things, and do count them *but* **dung** that I may win Christ.

Paul said he considered all things loss *in comparison* with the excellency of the knowledge of Christ. In other words, he said there is nothing more glorious than *revelation from heaven*, made possible by the Holy Spirit. In his eyes the only thing even worth discussing is the revelation knowledge that he received from God's Spirit on a daily basis. The only knowledge that will last is **revealed knowledge**, by the Spirit.

Is Bible School "Required" For the Great Commision?
Was Jesus A Bible Schooled Preacher?

(Matthew 13:54-57a KJV) "And when he was come into *his own country*, he taught them...they were astonished, and said, **Whence hath this man this wisdom**, and *these* mighty works? *Is not this the carpenter's son?* is not his mother called Mary? and his brethren, James...And they were offended in him...."

Jesus was in his hometown, where everyone knew Him and His family. These people became offended at what He taught because they knew He was not a *traditionally trained* preacher. They were unable to receive from Him because of their offense at the doctrine and miracles of His ministry. Offense, hinder the power of God from working in their lives. Jesus didn't fit their traditional idea of a preacher. He *was not* in the line of the Levitical priesthood. The Bible tells us in the book of Hebrews that Jesus was a Priest, but He was of another type of priesthood.

(Hebrews 7:11,13,14 KJV) If therefore perfection were by the Levitical priesthood, (for under it the people received the law,) what further need was *there* that *another priest* should rise after **the order of Melchisedec**, and not be called after the order of Aaron? For he of whom these things are spoken pertaineth to another tribe, of which no man gave attendance at the altar. For *it is* evident that our Lord sprang out **of Judah**; of which tribe Moses spake nothing concerning priesthood.

The Lord Jesus truly did not fit the traditional Jewish cast type of a priest. This was one of the main reasons they **would not** receive His ministry. First, He was not of the tribe of Levi, and second, He was not "Bible school" trained by one of their top theologians. He was also ordained a Priest after the order of Melchisedec—*the first* priestly order.

By What Authority?

(Matthew 21:23 KJV) And when he was come into the temple, the chief priests and the elders of the people came unto him *as he was teaching* and said, "**By what authority doest thou these things**? And *who gave thee this authority?*"

(Mark 11:28 KJV) And say unto him, "*By what authority doest thou these things* and *who gave thee this authority* to do these things?

It is extremely obvious that the priests and elders *did not* recognize Jesus' authority to preach and heal the sick. In their minds, He was a rebellious outlaw, attempting to corrupt their sacred system of religious formalism. Our Lord and Savior was neither honored nor respected as an anointed man of God. He was seen as a threat to their entire religious *system*, and was rejected by His church. Therefore, it does not surprise me to see that there are still traditional theologians today who are threatened by those who have not spent their entire lives in Bible school and Seminary. Those educated primarily in *theory* usually become defensive around those who are anointed through personal experience with Jesus.

It is saddening to realize many are still unable to recognize each other's individual calls. Not everyone is called to attend Bible school. On the other hand, not everyone is meant to not attend some sort of Biblical training. The bottom line, however, is that we must all learn to respect each other's individual anointing and calling. Simply because I'm not Bible school educated does not mean I am an unfounded, unscriptural fruit cake. Nor does an educated servant of God have to be a spiritual dud. The time has come for us to see *the balance* between being a Bible school trained person, and one who is trained by revelation that flows from their **daily** fellowship with the Holy Spirit.

The Credentials of Jesus

(John. 10:24,25) So the Jews surrounded Him and began asking Him, How long are You going to keep us in doubt *and* suspense? If You are really the Christ (the Messiah), tell us so plainly *and* openly. Jesus answered them, I have told you so, yet you do not believe Me [you do not trust Me *and* rely on Me]. **The very works** that I do by the power of My Father *and* in My Father's name bear witness concerning Me [**they are My credentials** and **evidence in support** of Me].

The very works that Jesus did by the power of His Father in Him were His **credentials of ministry**. These signs and wonders were the *confirmation* of His call into the priesthood. Yet the Jews could not see this. Isn't it difficult to comprehend how they could not perceive this, with the glory of God shining in Him and everything He did?

If you are reading this today and wondering what is God's will for you, the answer is very simple; *do the works of God* as long as there is still time. Being an educated preacher is fine and noble. However, if you do not have the time and/or the money to spend four or plus years in school, then you can seek other opportunities open to you for ministry. There are many wonderful home study courses you can attend. There is also a mentor program, where one is trained by their pastor or another anointed servant of God. There are other ways to learn God's Word without having to spend several years in school.

To answer the question asked by this chapter: Bible school is not *a requirement* of Jesus for the Great commission. The only element we must have in order to be effective witnesses **is the Anointing** upon our lives and words. As far as Jesus and the apostle Paul were concerned, **the anointing of the Spirit of God** was the most important element to qualify one for success in the Great commission.

If you are considering going into the ministry, but are struggling concerning Bible school or not, I suggest you pray and find out what vision God has given you. Next, follow the example of our Lord Jesus. Pore over the Word of God like a starving man searches for food. Study God's Word and read all the books you can get your hands on, written by other anointed men and women of God. Realize this that no one but God Himself can give you the answer to this question. You must take time daily to **fellowship** with Jesus and the Father by the Holy Spirit. It is in those times of stillness and fellowship that His answers come. Consider once again what Isaiah had to say about this in chapter forty verse thirty-one:

(Isaiah 40:31) But those who wait for the Lord [who expect, look for, and hope in Him] **shall change** *and* **renew** their **strength** *and* **power**, they shall lift their wings *and* mount up [close to God] as eagles [mount up to the sun]; they shall run and *not be weary*, they shall walk and *not faint* or become tired.

A Closing Scripture

(John. 10:25b) "...*The very works that I do* by the power of My Father *and* in My Father's name bear witness concerning Me [**they are My credentials** and evidence in support of Me]."

10

TOO TITHE *OR* NOT TOO TITHE?
(The End Time Harvest Awaits *Our* Response)

Too tithe or not too tithe? Now that is an *extremely* important question, especially when considering that these are the last days. You might be thinking, "How could my financial actions be so important to the last days?" Our financial decisions are **immensely** important, when one considers the impact our giving has upon *reaching* the end time harvest of souls. Our faithful stewardship can *make the difference* between millions walking through the gates of glory and **millions** spending eternity in hell's fire. I trust you're able **to see** the seriousness of our private financial decisions. We all have a tremendous responsibility to God to help finance the end time harvest of souls. The book of Luke reveals the importance of being a faithful steward.

> **(Luke 16:10-12)** He who is faithful in a very little [thing] *is* faithful also in much, and he who is dishonest *and* unjust in a very little [thing] *is* dishonest *and* unjust also in much. Therefore, if you have not been faithful in the [case of] unrighteous mammon (deceitful riches, money, possessions), who will entrust to you **the true riches**? And if you have not proved faithful in that which **belongs to another** (*tithes*) [whether God or man], who will give you that which is your own [that is, *the true riches*]?

The book of Luke is brutally honest concerning what will happen to those who are not faithful stewards. ***It could cost them heaven's riches.***

With this introduction a vivid picture has been painted concerning the importance of our remaining good stewards. Let us now move on and lay the Biblical foundation with which we will answer the question; *Too Tithe Or Not Too Tithe?*

As you know from previous chapters, I love to go back to the beginning of creation for answers to difficult questions. Therefore, we'll start this quest for answers by again returning to the book of Genesis.

(Genesis 2:16,17) And the Lord God commanded the man, saying, You may freely eat of every tree of the garden; But of the tree of the knowledge of good and evil *and* blessing and calamity you *shall not eat*, for in the day that you eat of it you shall *surely die*.

Many Christians try to tell us tithing *isn't* for today. They say tithing is strictly under the Law and that we are under *grace*. However, these same *well meaning* believers have failed to understand that tithing **did not** start with the Law of Moses. Tithing actually began in the garden of Eden. God's commandment to not eat of the tree was for *man*, the same as tithing is for us today. God established these principles in Eden, suggesting that whenever *man* worked, he must also give a tenth back to God. And seeing that, man labored on the Garden; the Bible says that man took care of the garden (Gen. 2:15). Hence, this was the first form of tithing known to man. In addition, if one were to read further into chapter 3 of Genesis, one would find that when they partook of the tree (His tithe); they experienced immediate separation (Spiritual Death), from the presence of God. There is a high price to pay for consuming what belongs to God.

Poor Stewardship Caused The First Murder

(Genesis 4:2b-5a NKJV) "...Now Abel was a keeper of sheep, but Cain was a tiller of the ground. And in the process of time it came to pass that Cain brought an offering of the fruit of the ground to the Lord. Abel also brought of the **firstborn** of his flocks and of their fat. And the Lord respected Abel and his offering, but He did not respect Cain and his offering...."

Some may wonder why I've mention offerings in a chapter about tithing. It is also equally important to firmly establish the fact that offerings as well as tithes were taking place **long before** the Law of Moses was ever written. Furthermore, offerings and tithes go hand in hand in God's eyes. (We'll deal more with offerings later in this chapter).

The point I want to establish with this passage of Scripture is why God accepted Abel's offering, but not Cain's. Some theologians feel this was because Abel gave a blood sacrifice and Cain didn't. This answer may *seem* logical; however, at the time of this incident there was *no law* specifying sacrifices, much less one of blood. God accepted Abel's offering because it was from the firstborn (*first fruits*) of his increase and it was by faith. Cain's offering, on the other hand, was not. It is extremely important that we give first fruits to God, and out of a proper attitude; whether that be our tithes or offerings. Attitude is always extremely important in everything that we do.

The Father of Faith Tithed!

(Genesis 14:18-20 NKJV) Then Melchizedek, king of Salem brought out bread and wine; he *was* the **priest** of God Most High. And blessed him and said: "Blessed be Abram by God Most High, Possessor of heaven and earth; And blessed be God Most High, Who has delivered your enemies into your hand." And Abram **gave** him *a tithe of all*.

Abram had returned from rescuing his nephew Lot from the people of Sodom and Gomorrah. He took possession of all their goods and then *gave* to the priest a tithe of all that he had taken. Some might say, "That's what he should have done, he was under the Old Covenant."

However, this took place approximately 400 years **before** the Law—before any command to give a tenth of one's income to God was written. Abram did this because his heart was close to God, and it compelled him to act by God's nature, *which is giving*.

Abraham's grandson is also recorded in Scripture as making a vow to give God a tenth of everything that He would bless him with.

(Genesis 28:20-22 NKJV) Then Jacob made a vow, saying, "If God will be with me, and keep me in this way that I am going, and give me bread to eat and clothing to put on, so that I come back to my father's house in peace, then the Lord shall be my God. And this stone which I have set as a pillar shall be God's house, and of all that You give me I will surely give *a tenth to You.*"

Again, let me remind you that Jacob made this vow approximately 200 years **before** the Law of Moses. Thus, the history of the tithe is well documented in Scripture as beginning many years *before* it was established as a rule of Law. Therefore, **God** established the principle of tithing (out of love and obedience) *before* Moses wrote concerning tithing in the book of the Law. God had this written into the Law because He wanted us to be blessed in every area of life.

In reality, there is no need to continue writing this chapter, since we have already answered the question at hand. However, for the sake of skepticism we will continue to reinforce the Bible's support of tithing since the beginning.

God included tithing in the Law of Moses, which is found in chapter 27 of Leviticus:

> **(Leviticus 27:30 NKJV)** And all of the tithe of the land, *whether of the seed of the land or of the fruit of the tree,* ***is the Lord's.*** **It is holy** to the Lord.

Please understand this is not some new regulation God put into the Law to torment the Israelites. God had been trying to instill in His people for many years, (this act of love and worship), still many would not listen. **Therefore**, He wrote it down as a requirement of the Law, *so no one could say they didn't know* (Gal. 3:19, TAB). The tithe was to be an *act of love* toward God and our fellow man. Still, many were not motivated by the heart of God to give out of love. Had their giving been out of love, God *may never have* established this principle by Law.

We have now reached a proper turning point, where we can begin to focus on tithes and offerings from a New Covenant perspective. Again, many believers say, "tithing is not a part of the New Covenant; therefore, we are not expected by God to participate." Is this really what the New Covenant teaches or are some *believers* simply seeking a loophole in the Word of God to justify their own greed? We will soon find out. Let God be true, and all the rest—**liars**!

Destroyed Or Fulfilled?

> **(Matthew 5:17 NKJV)** ***Do not think*** that I came to *destroy* the Law or the Prophets. I did not come to destroy **but to fulfill**.

These are the words of our Lord Jesus Himself. He openly decreed that He did not come to destroy the Law or the prophets, but rather to *fulfill* the other side of the Law, namely grace and mercy. Many have said, "Jesus has done away with the Law, therefore we aren't under obligation to obey *any* part of it." It is sad to see such ignorance in the Church today. The "Law" that Jesus came to do away with was **the Law of Sin and Death**, which is that principle of Sin that *was* living in us **before** salvation (See chapter three: *Roman's Reconciliation Revelation*). It seems many have gotten their **Laws** confused. The Law of Sin and Death has been indeed destroyed, nonetheless, the Law of Moses is still *in many ways* in effect.

This does not mean we have to live by Jewish Law. Rather, certain parts of the Law of Moses have been rendered void by the Death, burial, **and** resurrection of Jesus; (such as: making sacrifices for cleansing, circumcision, and meats sacrificed to idols). These are all outlined in the New Covenant as no longer applicable. Yet nowhere is it written that tithing has been done away with. The only verse that I've read concerning tithing in a negative light came out of the mouth of Jesus Himself in the book of Matthew.

(Matthew 23:23 KJV) Woe unto you, scribes and Pharisees, hypocrites! for ye **pay** tithe of mint and anise and cummin, and have omitted the *weightier matters* **of the law**, judgment, mercy, and faith: these ought ye to have done, *and not to leave the other* **undone**.

Jesus spoke against the Scribe's and Pharisee's unbalanced lifestyle in regard to tithing. They were *excessively* concerned about tithing, but very unconcerned about other parts of the Law such as judgment, mercy and faith. After Jesus rebuked them, He also told them to practice judgment, mercy and faith, and also *to continue* to tithe. A man once told me that Jesus could not have spoken against tithing, *because* it was a requirement of the Law; and He hadn't gone to the cross to pay the price. I understand this man's reasoning, yet why did Jesus make statements against other items of the Law, such as hand washing or working on the Why didn't He speak against tithing if it isn't for us? Paul made a few negative statements regarding circumcision.

(1 Corinthians 7:18,19 NKJV) "Was anyone called while circumcised? Let him not become uncircumcised...Circumcision *is nothing* and uncircumcision *is nothing*, but **keeping the commandments of God is what matters**."

It appears both Paul and Jesus Himself had no qualms about speaking against areas of the Law that were overemphasized or void. Hence, this form of logic is void of strength to support itself. Furthermore, the commandments of God are given to us in the Bible **from** Genesis **through** Revelation. God's Word was given as our guidebook for *victorious living*, **not** a decree of bondage. However, when one is rebellious against God's Word, then it will become bondage in *their eyes*. Jesus gave **His** commandment to us concerning taxes and tithing in Luke chapter 20:

(Luke 20:22-25 NKJV) "...'Is it lawful for us to pay taxes to Caesar or not?' But He perceived their craftiness, and said to them, 'Why do you test me? Show me a denarius. Whose image and inscription does it have?' They answered and said, 'Caesar's.' And He said to them, 'Render therefore to Caesar the things that are Caesar's *and to God* the **things that are God's**.'"

The statement of Jesus in this passage of Scripture is very clear. He was addressing the subject of money. If I were a citizen of that day it would be easy for me to know what belonged to Caesar, as far as my taxes were concerned. Likewise, it would be also easy for a citizen of that day to know what belonged to God. Why is it so difficult for some in our world today to understand what is God's? The *only* financial statements I've read in God's Word are where He clearly says that the tithe, and in some cases the offering, are His. Not one writer of the New Covenant (including Jesus) made any statement against tithing to the New Covenant Church. Nowhere have I read **"Thou shalt not tithe,"** before **or** after the cross. The reason for this is because tithing still applies to us today. On the other hand, I have read statements in the Word of God which clearly show me that God's Word/will is forever unchangeable, such as:

(Hebrews 13:7,8 NKJV) *Remember* those who rule over you, who have spoken the word of God to you, whose faith follow, considering the outcome of *their* conduct. Jesus Christ is **the same** yesterday, today **and** forever.

This says loud and clear, that God's plans for man have not changed since the Garden of Eden, to include tithing. It's not legalistic to tithe *honorable* people do it out of love.

After Which Priesthood Is Jesus Ordained?

(Hebrews 7:1,2,6,8,9;17) "For this Melchizedek, king of Salem [and] priest of the Most High God, met Abraham as he returned from the slaughter of the kings and blessed him, And Abraham gave to him *a tenth portion of all* [the spoil]...But this person who *has not* their Levitical ancestry received tithes from Abraham [himself] and blessed him who possessed the promises [of God]. Furthermore, **here** [in the Levitical priesthood] tithes are received by men who are subject to death; while **there** [in the case of Melchizedek], they are received by one of whom it is testified that he lives [perpetually]. A person might even say that Levi [the father of the priestly tribe] himself, who received tithes (the tenth), paid tithes *through Abraham*...For it is witnessed of **Him, You** are a Priest **forever** *after the order* (with the rank) *of* ***Melchizedek***."

Melchizedek was a priest about 400 years prior to Levi's priesthood. Therefore, Melchizedek's priestly line *was the first priesthood* to be established by God. Also, Hebrews chapter seven verse eight says the Church was tithing during *its* writing, "**here** tithes are received by men." The book of Hebrews shows that the New Covenant Church was tithing in AD 65, the *approximate* time in which *Hebrews* was written.[1] In other words, the Church was tithing approximately 35 years after the ascension of Jesus Christ, proving that tithing was not merely some *discontinued* Jewish Law. If this were the case, the writer of Hebrews would have had no need to write concerning the principle of tithing. Tithing was taking place before the Law being written, and years after Jesus ascended.

Also, in Hebrews we read, "A person might even say that Levi himself, who received tithes, paid tithes *in* Abraham." This statement displays that in God's eyes Abraham gave tithes on behalf of the Levitical priesthood, prior to its existence. Thus, the requirement of tithing (*which became law*), was being met in Abraham. One could say the tithe began with Abraham in an "official" sense.

Finally, which priesthood did Jesus our Lord rise up from? It is documented in the Word of God that Jesus was of the tribe of Judah. However, the Jewish priesthood began with the tribe of Levi, *not* Judah. This is probably the *main* reason the religious leaders of Jesus' day did not attempt to receive Him. Thus, God ordained Jesus as a Priest after the order of Melchizedek, according to Hebrews chapter seven verse seventeen. Hence, the Body of Christ is **also** ordained as priests unto God, after the priestly line of Melchizedek.

The first **official** tithe was given to the first priestly line, which was the priesthood of Melchizedek. Furthermore, since Jesus and His Body are ordained into this same priestly line, and since Jesus is alive forevermore, His Priesthood **lives on today**, *which includes* the principles of tithes & offerings.

Why should the principles of tithes and offerings be included? Because they have their origin (root) under another priesthood, which was completely separate from that of the Levitical priesthood. God started these principles under His **first** priesthood then He carried them over into His second priesthood (Levi's). It was an **eternal** priesthood (verse 17).

WHEN THE HOLY SPIRIT REVEALS

Now that we have killed the sacred calf that opposes tithes and offerings, it is time to move on to another controversial topic.

Malachi Three: Whom Is It Written To?

(Malachi 3:1-3 NKJV) Behold, I send My messenger, And he will prepare the way before Me. And the Lord, whom you seek, Will *suddenly* come to His temple, Even the Messenger of the covenant, In whom you delight…But who can endure the day of His coming? And who can stand when He **appears**? For He is like a refiner's fire And like launderer's soap. He will sit as a refiner and a purifier of silver; He will *purify the sons of Levi*, And purge them as gold and silver. That they may offer to the Lord An offering in righteousness.

Many Christians believe Malachi chapter three is under the Old Covenant, and therefore no longer applies to the Church. However, upon closer examination of these verses of Scripture one can *see* otherwise. The first verse speaks of John the Baptist. Who prepared the way for Jesus to come? Then in part two of verse one we see the words, "And the Lord whom you seek, Will **suddenly** come *to His temple*." Point one is this: Jesus did not come to this earth as a baby in a *sudden* manner. On the other hand, His second coming will be a sudden coming. Likewise, Jesus in His earthly ministry rejected the temples of men, but in His second coming He will finally set up His earthly kingdom and temple. This will take place when we come back *with* Him for the 1,000 year reign.

This prophetic chapter *actually* prophesies about the modern-day Church, which is waiting for the soon coming King. Despite the ignorance of some believers, Malachi chapter three is in fact a prophetic look at the condition of the modern day Church. We have met *all of* the conditions this chapter clearly speaks about.

In verse three of chapter three, it states that Jesus is going to purify His priesthood, so we can offer Him an offering in righteousness. This is *exactly* where we are in God's last days time schedule. God is purifying His priesthood (the Church), so we can offer an offering in righteousness.

(Malachi 3:5,6 NKJV) "And I will come near you **for judgment**; I will be a swift witness Against sorcerers, Against adulterers, Against perjurers, Against those who exploit wage earner and widows and orphans, And *against those who turn away an* *alien*...'For I am the Lord, *I do not change*; Therefore you are not consumed....'"

Malachi writes in verse five that Jesus will come near for judgment. Judgment was not the mission of Jesus' first coming, peace from God toward man was; but in His second coming He will come for judgment. Malachi also says that He will move swiftly against those involved in sorcery (witchcraft and drugs), and that He will be against adulterers and liars. Hence, this Bible passage does not describe Jesus' first coming, but rather His **second coming**.

Furthermore, He also says that He will judge those who *exploit a wage earner*. Many Christians do this every Sunday. Perhaps you are asking, "How do *believers* do this every Sunday?" We do this **every time** we enter the doors of our local church, and fail to give of our tithes and offerings.

Most local pastors are not "hired," however; they do work for a living serving the people of God. Therefore, we exploit that man or woman of God every time we make a conscious decision to disobey the Word of God concerning tithes and offerings. God will judge all who fit into the classification of an exploiter of wage earners, unless they repent.

We also exploit widows, orphans, and aliens by our refusal to give of our tithes and offerings. We're guilty of this if we continually allow the offering plate to pass by without putting something in. Thus, the finances simply aren't available to *effectively* run the local church, much less take care of widows, orphans, and the homeless. I believe debt is the single biggest reason why we don't give. Jesus made a powerful statement in the book of Matthew chapter twenty-five referring to this.

> **(Matthew 25:45 NKJV)** "...Assuredly, I say to you, inasmuch as you did not do it to one of the least of these, **you did not do it to Me**."

Without repentance, *many* believers will be judged by God for their lack of obedience and compassion for those less fortunate than they! God's perfect will for the Church is that we are *blessed to be a blessing* to all nations of the earth.

> **(Malachi 3:7-9 NKJV)** "'Yet from the days of your fathers You have gone away from My ordinances And have not kept them. *Return to Me, and I will return to you*,' Says the Lord of hosts. But you said, 'In what way shall we *return?*' '*Will a man rob God?* **Yet you have robbed Me**!' But you say, 'In what way have we

robbed You?' **In tithes and offerings**. *You are cursed with a curse,* Even this whole nation."

Here, God is telling us we have been robbing Him since *the Church* began. This was written originally to the Israelites, however, this portion of Scripture is a prophetic look at the stewardship of the Church today. This applied to Israel; nevertheless, it applies to us today **even more.**

A survey was taken some time ago showing that approximately **18%** of the Church is faithful in tithing.² Can you believe that, *only* 18%? No wonder the lost have not yet been reached for Christ. Only 18% of heaven's windows are open over the end time Church. This means that **82%** of heaven's windows **are closed** over the Body of Christ. It is no wonder **the Anointing** isn't moving in many of our meetings. He cannot move in a temple that has closed its doors to widows, orphans, and the homeless. I believe that it's time that we repented; because the Anointing of Almighty God **will not** manifest Himself among an assembly of temple robbers!

God was specific when He told Malachi what we were doing wrong. He said, "You are robbing Me of tithes **and** offerings. You are cursed with a curse." The curse mentioned here *is not* the curse of the Law, but rather a curse that **we bring upon ourselves** by withholding our giving. God did not say, "You are cursed with **the** curse;" but rather with **a** curse. It is one that we have caused through disobedience.

Heaven's Windows: How Are They Opened?

(Malachi 3:10,12) "Bring all the tithe (**the whole tenth of your income**) into *the storehouse*, that there may be food in My house, and **prove Me** now by it, says the Lord of hosts, if I will not *open the windows of heaven* for you and pour you out a blessing...And I will rebuke the devourer [insects and plagues] for your sakes and *he* shall not destroy the fruits of your ground, neither shall your vine drop its fruit before the time in the field, says the Lord of hosts. And **all** nations shall call you *happy and blessed* for you shall be a land of delight, says the Lord of hosts."

God makes His requirements for financial prosperity and protection clearly known. He says if we will be faithful stewards of that which belongs to Him, then He will open heaven's windows over us and pour out such abundant blessings that we will end up having to give much away. God has placed within our hands our own financial destiny. He is telling us today in this *prophetic word* exactly what we need to do in order to prosper. If we are faithful with our tithes and offerings, **then** He will give us abundance. However, there's a *tragic* reason why *many* don't give— nor receive.

> **(Malachi 3:13,14)** Your words have been **strong** *and* **hard** against **Me**, says the Lord. Yet you say, What have we spoken against You? You have said, *It is useless to serve God*, and **what profit is it if we keep His ordinances** and walk gloomily *and* as if in mourning apparel before the Lord of host?

This is one of the main reasons many in the Body of Christ do not tithe or receive. They have said in their hearts, "It is worthless to serve God, since we *see* no immediate financial profit." Many Christians give up on tithes and offerings simply because they've given to God once or twice and have not experienced an ***immediate*** flood of blessing. They do not realize that the flood of blessing God is referring to only comes to those who have been faithful in their giving *as well as their daily confession*. There are no "get rich quick schemes" with heaven's economics. God's prosperity comes by faithful obedience to His Word, and keeping watch over our tongues. The latter is **considerably** more troubling than the former in most believers lives.

More On The Offering

The Word of God gives detailed instructions concerning how we should give offerings. God does not set a *specific amount*, but rather allows us to choose how much blessing we want *to receive back* from Him. The degree of prosperity in which we live, is **entirely** dependent upon *our faithfulness* in obeying God's instructions concerning abundance.

> **(2 Corinthians 9:6,7;10)** "[Remember] this: he who sows sparingly *and* grudgingly will also reap sparingly *and* grudgingly, and he who sows generously [***that blessing may come to someone***] will also reap generously *and* with blessing. *Let each one* [give] *as he has made up his mind and purposed in his heart*, not reluctantly or sorrowfully or under compulsion, for God loves (He takes pleasure in, prizes above other things, and is unwilling to abandon or to do without) a cheerful (joyous *"prompt to do it"*) giver [whose heart is in his giving…And [God] Who provides **seed for the sower** and bread for the eating will also provide and multiply your [resources for] sowing and increase the fruits of your righteousness [*which manifests itself in* active goodness, kindness, and charity]."

God makes Himself perfectly clear: "If you give little, you will receive little; if you give big, then you will receive big!" In verse seven of chapter nine God reveals to us, that we are the ones who choose how much we will give when it comes to our offerings. He has placed our financial destiny in our own hands. We choose how much God **will be able** to bless us in return, by the way in which we give our tithes and offerings. As a result, we **cannot** blame God if we are not experiencing abundant financial harvests. It's time to *grow up* and accept responsibility for our own spiritual and financial actions, instead of blaming God when everything doesn't go as planned. **That** is the same type of foolishness that the people in Malachi three (v: 13-14) exhibited against God.

A Closing Scripture

(Matthew 22:21 NKJV) Render therefore to Caesar the things which are Caesar's and unto God ***the things*** that are God's.

11

ESCHATOLOGY 101
(The Rapture—Tribulation & Second Coming)

In Expectation of His Return

(John 14:1-3 KJV) Let not your heart be troubled: ye believe in God, believe also in me. In my Father's house are many mansions: if it were not so, I would have told you. I go to prepare a place for you. And if I go and prepare a place for you, *I will come again, and receive you unto myself*, that where I am, there ye may be also.

Jesus Himself promised us (the church) that He would return for us after He had prepared a place for us in heaven. We have this expectation of His triumphant return (at any moment), as our *blessed hope*. No man knows that day or hour—nevertheless, the promise is sure!

(1 Thessalonians 4:13-18 KJV) But *I would not have you to be ignorant*, brethren, concerning them which are asleep [dead], that ye sorrow not, even as others which have no hope. For if we believe that Jesus died and rose again, even so them also which sleep [die] in Jesus will God bring with him. For this we say unto you by the word of the Lord, that we which *are alive and remain unto the coming of the Lord* [the rapture] shall not prevent them which are asleep. For the Lord himself shall descend from heaven with a shout, with the voice of the archangel, and with **the trump** *of God*: and the dead in Christ shall rise first: Then we which are alive and remain shall be **caught up together** with them in the clouds, to meet the Lord <u>in the air</u>: and so shall we ever be with the Lord. Wherefore **comfort one another with these words**.

Notice in this above passage of Scripture that Paul (and the Lord) does not want us to be *ignorant* (misinformed) about the Rapture of the Church and those who have died prior to its expected arrival. Jesus will descend toward earth with a shout and with **the trump** of God *still* blowing. We will then be **caught up into the air** to meet Him. Please note that this passage says we will meet the Lord **in the air**.

This means that He **will not** touch down on earth at the event called the Rapture or the catching away of the Church. Please not that the term Rapture is not found in the English Bible—it is a Latin term which means: *Catching away or caught away*. However, the word "Rapture" is encoded in the Hebrew language version of the Old Covenant—called *the Bible Code*. Finally, the passage of Scripture tells us to "comfort one another with these words."

It wouldn't be very comforting to us if this passage said, *"You will just have to wait to be with Me, until you have been tried and test in the Tribulation,"* now would it? No way! No one wants to go through the Tribulation of those days, because the Bible says that it will be like no other in history. So, since God is a Father—a God of love, I see no way that He would *will* His people to go through the most terrible time history.

Hope of His Return Helps To Purify Us!

(1 John 3:2,3 KJV) Beloved, now are we the sons of God, and it doth not yet appear what we shall be: but we know that, when he shall appear, we shall be like him; for we shall see him as he is. And every man *that hath this hope* in him **purifieth himself**, even as he is pure.

I have heard people say, *"the most effective thing God uses to purify the church is persecution, and tribulation."* This sort of logic is actually saying the same thing as, "God uses sickness, disease and poverty to teach us something. Both lines of logic are absolute nonsense. God uses His Word and His precious Holy Spirit to teach and purify our hearts of sinful thoughts and actions not the wrath of Satan or even God. The hope of His return motivates us to purify ourselves. It is true that there is a possible chance the church may experience persecution, imprisonment or even death for the Name of Jesus. However, IF any of this happens, it will take place before the actual Tribulation (the whole 7-year period), begins. Many believers have died for the faith, and that same possibility is available to us today. However, I totally believe that we will not be here on this earth during it.

Eschatology 101

An Unknown Hour?

(Luke 12:35-40 KJV) Let your loins be girded about, and your lights burning; And ye yourselves *like unto men that wait for their lord*, when he will return from the wedding; that when he cometh and knocketh, they may open unto him immediately. Blessed are those servants, whom the lord when he cometh **shall find watching**: verily I say unto you, that he shall gird himself, and make them to sit down to meat, and will come forth and serve them. **Be ye therefore ready** also: for the Son of man cometh at an hour *when ye think not*.

Jesus told His people (Himself) that it would be to our advantage if we remain like people who wait for their lord. He also said that those who He finds watching will be blessed (empowered to prosper). How will those who are watching be blessed? I believe they will be blessed by watching for Him and when He comes they will be prepared to receive Him at the Rapture, as well as they will most likely receive a special reward at the Judgment Seat of Christ. His return is imminent—meaning, *it is sure and it's coming closer and closer* daily. Those who teach Mid-Tribulation, Post-Tribulation and the Pre-Wrath Rapture; all mock or at least *attempt to nullify* the idea of the fast approaching return of Jesus. This is a debasement of the words of Jesus Himself in (Lk. 12:35-40). Jesus is coming Church—and we had better be watching. Jesus said that those who are watching for His return would be blessed—empowered to prosper.

The GREAT Tribulation Lasts 3 ½ Years

(Daniel 12:9-11 KJV) And he said, Go thy way, Daniel: for the words are closed up and sealed till the time of the end. Many shall be purified, and made white, and tried; but the wicked shall do wickedly: and none of the wicked shall understand; but the wise shall understand. And from the time that the daily sacrifice shall be taken away, *and the abomination that maketh desolate set up*, there shall be **a thousand two hundred and ninety days** (3 ½ years).

When Daniel speaks of the Abomination that makes desolate, he referring to the time when Antichrist walks into the temple of Jerusalem and proclaims himself to be "God." This marks *the half way point* of the Tribulation period, and the beginning of the second three and one half years. The Tribulation period will last a total of 7-years; however, it will *all* be a time of judgment and wrath from God. It will be a terrible time to live on this earth. Note: we are not appointed unto wrath, *however*, the Bible also says that IF we judge our selves—*then we will not be judged*. It is our calling to keep judging our lives in the light of God's Word.

The Mystery of The Ages Revealed

(1 Corinthians 15:49-55 KJV) And as we have borne the image of the earthy, we shall also bear the image of the heavenly. Now this I say, brethren, that flesh and blood cannot inherit the kingdom of God; neither doth corruption inherit incorruption. **Behold, I show you a mystery**; We shall not all sleep, but we shall all be changed, *In a moment, in the twinkling of an eye,* at *the last trump: for trumpet shall sound,* and the dead shall be raised incorruptible, and we shall be changed. For this corruptible must put on incorruption, and this mortal must put on immortality. So when this corruptible shall have put on incorruption, and this mortal shall have put on immortality, then shall be brought to pass the saying that is written, Death is swallowed up in victory. O death, where is thy sting? O grave, where is thy victory?

In order to examine *the whole picture* of the Rapture one must consider *five* important passages of Scripture: 1). Jn. 14:1-3. 2). 1 Cor. 15:49-55. 3). 1 Thess. 4:13-18. 4). 1 Thess. 5:1-5, 8-11. 5). 2 Thess. 2:1-9, 12,13. We will not address all of these passages of Scripture at this point in our study, but I do suggest that the reader review the above listed passages.

In (1 Cor. 15:49-55), Paul says that the teaching of the Rapture is a "mystery" to all those listening to Paul's letter to the Corinthians. He also says that we will be gone in the twinkling (blink) of ones eye. At that speed one would completely disappear in a split-second of time. [*We will deal more with the speed factor of the Rapture later*].

Notice further, that this will take place at the last trump blast (of God's trumpet). This is not referring to the trumpets that are addressed in the book of Revelation. Those trumpets are for the judgment and wrath of God. In Revelation there are several trumpet that are sounded, but here in 1 Corinthians 15:49-55; there is *only one* trumpet mentioned. These two events are not one in the same!

The Rapture isn't a time where the Church experiences God's judgments or wrath, rather a time of great expectation and reward. The Bible calls the Rapture, "The **blessed** hope." If it is a "Blessed hope" then there must be reason for the Body of Christ to have *hope*.

Eschatology 101

A Brief Chronology of Rapture Events

1. The Lord will descend from heaven to gather His Church. He will descend with a mighty trumpet shout. (1 Corinthians 15:51,52 / John. 14:1-3 / 1 Thessalonians 4:16).
2. The Lord will resurrect those who have died in Him (1 Corinthians 15:52 / 1 Thessalonians 4:14-16)
3. We which are alive and remain will be changed and caught up with them. (1 Corinthians 15:51-53)
4. This complete event will take place in the twinkling [blink] of an eye (1 Corinthians 15:52)
5. We shall *always* be with the Lord (1 Thessalonians 4:17)

There should be no doubt in ones mind as to what will take place during the catching away of the Body of Christ. This will be the most glorious event in the history of the Church—*Our home coming party!*

The Rapture v. The Glorious Appearance

The Rapture and the Glorious Appearance **are not** the same events. The Glorious Appearance is when Jesus (and all His saints) come back for the Battle of Armageddon and the 1,000 year reign. It is otherwise referred to as *the Second Coming*. In the Rapture we meet Jesus *in the air*. He never touches down on the earth. This is a vital point to remember. Furthermore, in the 2nd Coming, Jesus (along with the Church) touches down on the earth and after the Battle of Armageddon is finished; He and His Body will rule the earth for 1,000 years—seven day (millennium) rest.

In the Rapture Jesus is **only** seen by believers who are ready and waiting for His victorious return—unbelievers are not able to see the Rapture of the Church. Those who miss the Rapture are *only able to see what is left behind* by the believers who have departed i.e. their vacant clothes, cars and homes. In the Second Coming, Jesus is seen *by all*. Also, in the Second Coming, the Body of Christ *will be with Him* coming in the air back to the earth.

Moreover, the Rapture will take place in what the Bible calls "*a twinkling of an eye*," or in the blink of an eye; which is at and above the Speed of Light.

"Light travels at **186,272 miles per second**. Which equals 6 million million, or 5.88 trillion miles in one year. If you could travel at the speed of light, time would stop. This is called the 'time dialation' theory and is based on Einstein's Law of Relativity…If you were to speed up until you were traveling at 99.99 percent the Speed of Light and traveled into outer space for a total of sixty years, when you return you would find that FIVE MILLION years had passed while you were gone…if you could travel at 100 percent the Speed of Light, time would stop and the moment "now" would be forever."[1]

Kept *From* The Hour of Temptation

(Matthew 24:21,22 KJV) For then shall be *great tribulation*, such as was not since the beginning of the world to this time, no, nor ever shall be. And except those days should be shortened, there should no flesh be saved: but **for the elect's sake** those days shall be shortened.

The Tribulation period will be unlike **anything** that this earth has ever experienced in the past. It will be a time of God's judgment **and** wrath for unrepented sin. [See: the complete chapter of Matt. 24 & Lk. 21:7-35 for more details about the conditions of the Tribulation Period]. The Tribulation period will literally be "**hell on earth!!!**"

(Revelation 3:7-11 KJV) And to the angel of the church in Philadelphia write; These things saith he that is holy, he that is true, he that hath *the key of David*, he that *openeth, and* **no man** *shutteth*; and shutteth, and **no man** openeth; I know thy works: **behold, I have set before thee an open door**, and no man can shut it: for thou hast a little strength, and hast kept my word, and hast not denied my name. Behold, I will make them of the synagogue of Satan, which say they are Jews, and are not, but do lie; behold, I will make them to come and worship before thy feet, and to know that I have loved the Because thou hast kept the word of my patience, ***I also will keep thee from the hour of temptation***, which shall come upon all the world, to try **them that dwell upon the earth**. Behold, I come quickly: hold that fast which thou hast, that no man take thy crown.

Now let's examine (Rev. 3:7-11), for a moment and see what insight we can gain from this passage of Scripture. First of all, Jesus begins in this portion of the book of Revelation by telling us that *He* holds the Key of David (See also: Isa. 22:22). What does Jesus mean by His having **the Key of David?** Perhaps this verse of Scripture has brought to mind another verse with a reference to keys. Matthew 16:19 tells us, that we have been given "the keys of the kingdom" to bind and loose spiritual forces. Now the words "key or keys," symbolize authority (honor) given by God.

Therefore, at this point in Scripture, Jesus takes **full** authority (the key/keys) over the earth. Why does He need to take authority again? It's because of man's 6,000 year lease on the earth expires with the "6th" Church (Philadelphia)? Philadelphia (the sixth Church in Revelation 3), represents the end of man's authority over the earth, *which is in **our** generation*. Hence, Jesus is saying that He has been given the "Key of David," or the authority of God **as a King** to open and close anything He desires in Heaven, earth or hell—***sole*** authority. He delegated His Messianic authority (keys) after He rose (so we share it with Him). But, *here*, He is referring to Him having sole (*not* shared) authority on the earth.

Jesus continues by saying, "behold I have set before thee and open door." Here again He is informing us of His (sole) authority over planet earth, which He receives back, at the close of man's earth lease found in Rev. 3:7,8. Furthermore, Jesus says that because we have kept the word of His patience He will **keep** us ***from*** *the hour of temptation* that will come upon the whole world. What is meant by the word "keep?" According to concordance *keep* means:

"**5083**. ***tereo***, *tay-reh'-o*; from teros (a watch; perh. akin to G2334); to guard (**from loss or injury**, prop. **by keeping the eye upon**"[2]

Thus Jesus was saying that He promises to keep (guard us from loss or injury), all those who keep there eyes fixed on His coming—by living their lives in a proper manner. This in no way suggests that we will be kept "through" the Tribulation period but rather away ***from*** it completely. He said He would keep us from the day of temptation. *Therefore*, seeing that Jesus said the Tribulation period would come upon ALL those who DWELL (live) on the earth. I believe we can safely say that we *will not* be living on this earth at that time.

An Open Door In Heaven

(Revelations 4:1,2 KJV) After this I looked, and, **behold, a door was opened in heaven**: and the first voice which I heard was as it were of *a trumpet* talking with me; which said, ***Come up hither***, and I will show thee things which must be hereafter. And **immediately** I was *in the spirit*; and, behold, a throne was set in heaven, and one sat on the throne.

WHEN THE HOLY SPIRIT REVEALS

Now let's examine how **Revelation 3:7-11** flows right in to chapter four verses one and two. In chapter 3 verse 8, Jesus tells that He has set before us *an one door* that *no man* can shut; and then in chapter 4 verse 1, the manifestation of that open door is clearly shown. Jesus already told us that He has sole authority and power to open this door and then He proves this point by clearly showing the manifested "open door" in heaven. What do you think this open door in heaven represents? I believe that this is speaking of a ***literal door*** or entrance way in the Spirit realm for us in heaven, and there is only one way that we can get there. By Super-natural departure! Note that Jesus is the Door & the Way for us.

Next, John the apostle, hears a "trumpet talking" to him saying, "Come **UP** thither;" and **immediately** he is *in the Spirit* and is **translated** into heaven. We are already familiar with 1 Cor. 15:52:

> "In a moment, in the twinkling of an eye, at the *last trump*: for **the trumpet shall sound, and the dead shall be raised incorruptible, and we shall be changed...."

Most prophetic teachers recognize this passage of Scripture as one of the main portions of Scripture that describes the Rapture in extreme detail. Seeing that both passages refer to a trumpet blowing (calling) and then they are transported into heaven. I can confidently say that Revelation 4:1 is a composite picture of 1 Corinthians 15:52. Finally, as soon as John Heard the words "come up thither," he was immediately in the Spirit—which is reminiscent of the phrase "in the twinkling of an eye."

Remember what we said about the Speed of Light—that it travels in 186,272 miles per second. This speed has been recorded at approximate the blink of an eye, or what *the King James Version* calls, "the tinkling of an eye." Therefore, I believe one can boldly say that *immediately* in this verse of Scripture is approx. 186,272 miles per second, or as fast as the blink of an eye. Here again confirming that (Revelation 4:1,2) is referring to the same event of **1 Corinthians 15:52**. The similarities of these two verses are to perfect and too synchronized not to be the ***exact*** same event.

Delivered *From* The Wrath To Come

(1 Thessalonians. 1:10 KJV) And to wait for his Son from heaven, whom he raised from the dead, even Jesus, which delivered us from the wrath to come.

Eschatology 101

There is little argument about whether or not we are delivered from God's wrath as children of God. However, there seems to be great debate about our being delivered from the first three and one half years of the Tribulation. I would never attempt to say that we are exempt from tribulations, persecutions and even death for Jesus name.

However, I personally believe that the root of this debate is founded in *carnal thinking* formulated by people with a strange idea that man some how can be able to "pay" for our sins by suffering. This is the typical "earn your way to heaven" lie of Satan. Such fleshly ideas are in direct opposition to all that Jesus Christ came to this earth to do. His Substitute Sacrifice was **and still is** all that is needed to "pay" for man's Sin. We could suffer in hell **for eternity** and never pay in full the debt that we owe to our Lord and Savior.

Moreover, the Tribulation will be like NO other period in history. Therefore, I believe that this is a time reserved for the unbelieving world and not for the born-again child of God. Moreover, the whole Tribulation will be a time of judgments from God and then the second half (the GREAT Tribulation), a time of even greater wrath.

We already know that we are not appointed unto wrath, but have you ever realized that we are also not appointed unto judgment. The Bible says in 1 Corinthians 11:31, "…if we would judge ourselves, we should not be judged." The Judgments of God, **which begins in the first half of the Tribulation**, has not been scheduled for believers.

Besides, the Bible says in Revelation 3:10 that the Tribulation will affect **all** those who dwell on the earth. Thus, this implies that if we are living here on earth at that time there is a great possibility that we would experience the judgments/wrath of God. Hence, I believe there is no possible way that the Church of Jesus Christ will be here during any phase of the Tribulation period. He's promised to keep us **from** it—*not through it!*

Finally, the book of Revelation details three distinct judgments of God in the Tribulation period. In Revelation chapter 6-8, John tells us of *the 7 Seal Judgments*. Similarly, in Revelation chapters 8 & 9 we see *the 7-Trumpet Judgments* of God. Last, but not the least, in Revelation 15 & 16 we read about *the 7-Vial Judgments*. Thus as a result, I believe that this time period should be extremely clear in ones mind as to what judgments will be taking place and when these judgments will come. These judgments will begin shortly after chapter 4 which is believed to depict the Rapture of the Church. *Please spend some time and re-read these verses.*

WHEN THE HOLY SPIRIT REVEALS
The Coming of The Lord—Our Gathering Unto Him

(2 Thessalonians 2:1-12 KJV) Now we beseech you, brethren, *by the coming of our Lord Jesus Christ,* **and** *by our gathering together unto him,* That ye be not soon shaken in mind, or be troubled, neither by spirit, nor by word, nor by letter as from us, as that **the day of Christ** is at hand. Let no man deceive you by any means: for **that day** shall not come, *except there come a falling away* (apostasia—means a departure), *first,* **and** that *man of sin be revealed,* the son of perdition; Who opposeth and exalteth himself above all that is called God, or that is worshipped; so that he as God sitteth in the temple of God, showing himself that he is God. Remember ye not, that, when I was yet with you, I told you these things? And **now ye know what withholdeth** that he might be revealed in his time. For the mystery of iniquity doth already work: *only he who now letteth will let, until he be taken out of the way.* **AND THEN** shall that Wicked be revealed, whom the Lord shall consume with the spirit of his mouth, and shall destroy with the brightness of his coming: Even him, whose coming is after the working of Satan with all power and signs and lying wonders, And with all deceivableness of unrighteousness in them that perish; *because they received not the love of the truth,* that they might be saved. And for this cause God shall send them **strong delusion**, *that they should believe a lie*: That they all might be ***damned*** [the mark will damn] who believed not the truth, but had pleasure in unrighteousness.

Look at verse one of 2 Thessalonians 2 where it says, "the coming of the Lord AND our gathering unto Him. According to Hobart Grazer [*a professor of Greek at Valley Forge Christian College in Pennsylvania*], said this statement made by Paul is actually in reverse order chronologically. He said further that Paul is referring too two separate events—the Second Coming of Jesus & the Rapture of the Church. I personally witnessed Mr. Grazer teaching on this at a church in up state New York I attended sometime in 1981. He said that because of the Greek construction of this verse, noun **and** noun construction, Paul would have had to be speaking of two separate events. I personally believe the reason why Paul referred to the Second Coming before the Rapture is because the people involved in this situation were afraid the Tribulation was already beginning. The people of Thessalonica were frightened that the Rapture had already taken place. Therefore, Paul responded to that concern first but he continued by reminding them of the proper order of prophetic events.

Paul clarifies this by saying that *"the day of Christ"* (the Second Coming of Christ), can not come until the *apostasia* first takes place **and** then the man of Sin will be revealed and finally *the day of Christ* will take place. Unfortunately, there have been many Bible scholars, who have translated the word **apostasia** *merely* as "falling away," as if to say that millions of born-again believers will fall away from the faith before the Antichrist is revealed.

However, *apostasia* is also translated in a much more positive light.

"Let no man deceive you by any means for (that day shall not come), except there come a departing first…(Geneva Bible)."³

"Do not begin to allow anyone to lead you astray in any way, because that day shall not come except the aforementioned departure [of the Church to heaven] comes first (Kenneth S. Wuest—An Expanded Translation)."⁴

What Does *Apostasia* Also Mean?

"John Dawson, A.B., indicates that apostasia means *a departure from any place.* John Parkhurst in is Lexicon defined it as, '*Property, a departure. A divorce or dismission.*' Robert Scott (Oxford Press) defines apostasia as 'Departure; disappearance—second meaning.'"⁵

As one can see, *apostasia* does not necessarily refer to a "Great falling away" of millions of Christians, but rather to the "**Great Departure**" of the Church with Jesus to heaven. This is radically different from the traditional teaching. Finally, according to a foot note in *the Amplified Bible Expanded Edition* concerning the word **apostasia**, it says, "A possible rendering of the Greek apostasia is: 'departure [of the church].'"⁶

More On The Wrath To Come

(1 Thessalonians 1:10 KJV) And to wait for his Son from heaven, whom he raised from the dead, even Jesus, which delivered us **from** the wrath to come.

(1 Thessalonians 5:9 KJV) "For God hath **not appointed us to wrath**, but to obtain salvation by our Lord Jesus Christ…."

This wrath referred to in (1 Thess. 1:10) is intended for *unbelievers*; thus, there is absolutely **no reason** for a believer to remain on earth once

God's judgments and greater wrath have begun. God's wrath isn't stored up to be expended up on His Church, but upon the disobedient world.

When Does God's Wrath Begin?

(Revelation 6:1,2 KJV) "And I saw *when the Lamb opened one of the seals*, and I heard, as it were the noise of thunder, one of the four beasts saying, Come and see. And I saw, and behold a white horse: and he that sat on him had a bow; and a crown was given unto him: **and he went forth conquering, and to conquer.**

(Revelation 6:16,17 KJV) "And said to the mountains and rocks, Fall on us, and hide us from the face of him that sitteth on the throne, and from **the wrath of the Lamb**: For *the great day of his wrath* **is come**; and who shall be able to stand?"

According to these passages of Scripture, the wrath of the Lamb (God) will begin to be poured out at the *beginning* of the sixth chapter, and *officially declared* by the end of that same chapter. This is much sooner than believers who teach that we'll be Raptured in the middle of the Tribulation period usually acknowledge. Therefore, here is the grand picture which Jesus painted for us through the apostle John. The apostle John is "caught up" in to heaven in the beginning of chapter 4, (*a symbol of the Rapture of the Church*).

And then, by the beginning of chapter 6, *the wrath of the Lamb* has already begun to be poured out—which is officially identified as such by the end of the same chapter. Revelations chapters four and six, plainly explain that the wrath of the Lamb will begin very shortly after the Rapture, "Coming up thither" of the Church, seen in chapter four verse one and two. [Please compare the difference between (Rev. 3:6) and (Rev. 13:9), and ask yourself why God's address no longer includes the churches? *Note that* His address to the Churches stopped at chapter 3 verse 22].

The book of Revelation is also quite plain concerning how the Church is not found in its pages from chapter four verse three until chapter nineteen verse one. What could explain this space of silence concerning the Church? I believe, it's because we are no longer living on the earth, and the earth (and its people) are the focus of God and His wrath—in the Tribulation. Once we are out of this mess down there, God will begin to increase His focus upon the earth and all its wickedness by His judgments. Revelation is clear in telling us that the wrath of the Lamb begins in chapter 6:1.

Eschatology 101
The Tribulation Period

(Daniel 9:24-27 KJV) "Seventy weeks are determined upon thy people and upon thy holy city, to finish the transgression, and to make an end of sins, and to make reconciliation for iniquity, and to bring in everlasting righteousness, and to seal up the vision and prophecy, and to anoint the most Holy. Know therefore and understand, that from the going forth of the commandment to restore and to build Jerusalem unto the Messiah the Prince shall be seven weeks, and threescore and two weeks: the street shall be built again, and the wall, even in troublous times. And after threescore and two weeks *shall Messiah be* **cut off,** [separated] **but not for himself:** and the people of the prince that shall come shall destroy the city and the sanctuary; and the end thereof shall be with a flood, and unto the end of the war *desolations are determined.* **And he shall confirm the covenant with many** *for one* **week:** [a seven year treaty] and *in the midst of the* [in the middle of the seven year period—3 ½ yrs.] week he shall cause the sacrifice and **the oblation to cease**, and for the overspreading of abominations he shall make it desolate, even until the consummation, and that determined shall be poured upon the desolate".

The prophet Daniel predicted that the Tribulation period would be 1 week or **seven years** long—each day in this week represent one year. Daniel says also that in the middle of this 70th week (middle of the seven year Tribulation), that the Antichrist will break *the 7-Year Treaty of Peace* which he will sign with Israel. Once he does this, he will then make the Temple in Jerusalem desolate by proclaiming that he is "the messiah" (God); along with setting up once again a system of blood sacrifices. Notice that this takes place at the **mid-point** of the Tribulation period, and according to the book of Revelation this does not actually take place until chapter 13. The Antichrist (the man) rules the earth as a dictator for 3 ½ years. Also, at the mid-point of this period, Satan *himself* possesses this man called the Antichrist and he declares himself to be "God." Satan is pulling his strings during the whole Tribulation period, but he does not "incarnate" the man until the mid-point, which is when the GREAT Tribulation begins. Satan will *imitate* the incarnation of Jesus, by indwell the Antichrist. He has always merely copied that which God has created and ordained.

Who Are Those In White Robes?

(Revelation 7:13-14 KJV) And one of the elders answered, saying unto me, What are these which are arrayed *in white robes*?

and whence came they? And I said unto him, Sir, thou knowest. And he said to me, These are they which came **out of** *great tribulation*, and have washed their robes, and made them white in the blood of the Lamb.

As I read (Rev. 7:13,14) it reminded me very much of (Rev. 6:8-11). Therefore, I decided to research this out a bit further with *The Spirit-Filled Life Bible*,[7] and I discovered that it used a side-note on (**Rev.7:14**) which points one to (**Rev. 6:9**). Revelations 7:12-14 is the culmination of all believers who are to be "beheaded" for their testimony of Jesus during the tribulation and Great tribulation period. Furthermore, the multitude of saints referred to in (**Rev. 7:14**) came **out of** the Great tribulation. Thus, we will in no way be here to see this—except to watch it *from above*. Hence, those in white robes are the saints that are killed during the Tribulation.

Moreover, *the Kenneth Copeland Reference Edition Bible*[8] [Cambridge Bible], also uses a side note on (Rev. 7:14), which directs the reader to (Rev. 6:9—those **slain** for the Word of God).

(Revelation 6:8-11 KJV) And I looked, and behold a pale horse: and his name that sat on him was Death, and Hell followed with him. And power was given unto them **over the fourth part of the earth, to kill with sword,** and with hunger, and with death, and with the beasts of the earth. And when he had opened *the fifth seal*, I saw under the altar (v.9) **the souls of them that were slain for the word of God**, and for the testimony which they held: And they cried with a loud voice, saying, How long, O Lord, holy and true, dost thou not judge and avenge our blood on them that dwell on the earth? And **white robes** were given unto every one of them; and it was said unto them, that they should rest yet for a little season, *until their fellowservants also and their brethren, that* **should be killed** as they were, should be fulfilled.

As I said earlier, Revelation 7:14 is referring to the same people as Revelation 6:9, and the people that are discussed in (Rev. 6:9), are all those who were beheaded (killed) during the Tribulation. Therefore, these people could not possibly be the *Raptured* Church. Why? This is because the Raptured Church isn't killed before it enters heaven. **It will escape physical death all together**. This is why Paul says, "Grave where is thy victory—death where is thy sting." If those of us who are alive today are honored to live until the rapture (assuming that is takes place within the next 1-40 years), we will have had a privilege that even Jesus Christ Himself didn't experience. What is that privilege? We will have lived this life and never have had to die physically. **Remember**, the Raptured believers escape physical death! Jesus, on the other hand, experienced both Spiritual and physical in our place **through His death at Calvary and the 3 days & nights in the center of the earth or hell.** Wow! What an honor from God!

A Brief Look At Various Rapture Teachings

The Post-Tribulation view, the church will go through **all** of the Tribulation. They view the rapture and Glorious Appearance as one in the same event. This view teaches that Jesus will return, rapture the remaining church; and then will come back down with Him for the Battle of Armageddon. This position also believes that the church will remain here to "usher in the Kingdom." They hold the so-called "Kingdom Now" theological position.

The Mid-Tribulation view is much like the pre-Tribulation teaching except it teaches that the Rapture will take place in the middle of the Tribulation. It also teaches that the *two witnesses* in Revelation are literal people. This teaching attempts to emphasize that the wrath of Satan is released in the 1st half of the Tribulation and then God's wrath in the second half. It is almost identical to the Pre-Wrath teaching.

The Pre-Wrath view, according to this position the Church will be Rapture shortly before the wrath of God is poured out—believed to be approx. 5 ½ years into the Tribulation. It also denies the teaching of the imminent [fast approaching] return of Jesus for the Church.

The Pre-Tribulation view teaches of a seven-year Tribulation period called ***Jacobs*** (Israel's) Trouble. The Church will be raptured before the Tribulation, where we will be able to watch Tribulation events from a *safe* distance. [There is another branch of the Pre-Trib. view that teaches only those who are living *Super-Christian lives* will make it in the Rapture. **As if we can please God by our works**. Those who are not (*in their view*) will have to endure the Tribulation because of their failure to be ready].

The various Rapture positions opposed to the Pre-Tribulation Rapture teaching have always criticized the Pre-Tribulation teaching because *they say* it is only approx. 170 years old and started in the early 1800's. However, today there is documented proof that the Pre-Tribulation Rapture teaching is most likely *the oldest view* in existence. I do not believe that the age of a view point makes it true and reliable, however; this new evidence does help to bolster the Pre-Tribulation position in a new way because it proves that this teaching has been around for some time. It also shows that this view point was most likely the first position.

THE PRE-TRIBULATION RAPTURE *WAS* TAUGHT APPROXIMATELY 1,650 YRS. AGO

I have had the privilege of reading a book by Grant Jeffrey, who has been an Anointed teacher on the subject of prophecy for many years. He has discovered vital information that clearly proves that the Pre-Tribulation Rapture teaching *did not* originated in the early 1800's.

"In my ongoing research into recent archeological discoveries and into writings of early Church leaders I have made several exciting new discoveries that I want to share...While the ultimate resolution of this discussion [Pre-Trib. Teaching in early times], must be based on our interpretation of Scripture, it is important to answer the errors of our opponents who disparage "the blessed hope" of the Rapture with misinformation about the modern rediscovery of the truth about the pre-tribulation rapture...The only problem with their argument is that they are totally wrong, [by saying the Pre-Trib. Rapture view is 170 yrs. old]."[9]

Ephraem's Teaching—
On The Pre-Tribulation Rapture

"For all the saints and Elect of God are gathered, PRIOR TO the tribulation that is to come, and taken to the Lord lest they see the confusion that is to overwhelm the world because of our sins." (Original source*: On the Last Times, the Antichrist, and the End of the World*, by Ephraem the Syrian, **A.D. 373**)."[10]

That places Ephraem's writings at approximately 1,650 yrs. from today.

"The early Christian writer and poet, Ephraem the Syrian, (who lived from **A.D. 306-373**) was a major theologian of the early Byzantine Eastern Church...he also wrote a large number of commentaries that have never been translated into English. Ephraem's fascinating teaching on the Antichrist has never been published in English until now. This critically important prophecy manuscript from the fourth century of the Church reveals a literal method of interpretation and a teaching of the pre-millennial return of Christ."[11]

In other words, He returns in the Rapture for us **before** He returns in the Glorious Appearing or 2nd Coming. There has been confusion surrounding this area of Scripture for years and years, and Ephraem clearly addresses the issue.

> "...he [Ephraem] taught that the War of God and Magog would precede the tribulation period. I discovered another text by Ephraem, called *'The Book of the Cave of Treasure,'* that revealed he taught that Daniel's Seventieth Week will be fulfilled in the final seven years at the end of this age that will conclude with Christ's return (2nd Coming) at the Battle of Armageddon to establish His [earthly] Kingdom...key passages from Ephraem's important text, written about A.D. 373, [343 years after Jesus' ascension], were translated by Professor Cameron Rhoades, of Tyndale Theological Seminary, at my request...."[12]

The Second Coming—
With Ten Thousands of His Saints

(Jude 1:14-15 KJV) And Enoch also, the seventh from Adam, prophesied of these, saying, Behold, *the Lord cometh* **with ten thousands** [ten thousand(s) is plural] **of his saints**, To execute judgment upon all, and to convince all that are ungodly among them of all their ungodly deeds which they have ungodly committed, and of all their hard speeches which ungodly sinners have spoken against him.

Jesus is coming back to this earth to set up His earthly kingdom with more than ten thousand saints—it says ten thousand(s) of His saints. Meaning it is an innumerable number of saints.

This proves the Post-Tribulation view to be misguided. If the Church was here in the Tribulation, I dare say over 75% would be massacred before Jesus returned.

Pray Always That You May Be *Accounted* Worthy

(Luke 21:36 KJV) Watch ye therefore, and pray always, that ye may be accounted worthy to escape all these things that shall come to pass, and to stand before the Son of man.

In my opinion the translation of this verse is extremely poor, because it almost leaves one with the idea that we are to pray to be **made** worthy or something of that nature. Jesus has already *made us worthy* in God's sight. So all we need to do is live repented lives, and pray that we will be *accounted* worth to go in the Rapture. Remember that anything God does for or to us is not based on our worthiness. It is based solely upon His grace and it's **always** by faith. I'm *not* suggesting that we should live like *spiritual-pigs* just because God's gifts are by grace. Because, when we stand before the throne, those who tried to *play church*, will loose many great rewards.

The main point that I wish to make with (Luke 21:36), is that Jesus said that we will be able to escape all this (Matt. 24/Lk. 21:7-35), which will take place on this earth and stand before the Son of man. Luke clearly states that we are to pray to be found (not made) worthy to escape **all** those things. Therefore, no believer has to be left on this earth during this horrible of Tribulation. Why would God force the people He loves to go through *unspeakable* horrors?

Jesus—A Thief In The Night?

(1 Thessalonians 5:2-4 KJV) For yourselves know perfectly that *the day of the Lord [the Second Coming of Jesus]* so cometh as a thief in the night. For when they shall say, Peace and safety; then sudden destruction cometh upon them, as travail upon a woman with child; and **they** *shall not escape*. But ye, brethren, are **not** in darkness, that *that day* should overtake you as a thief.

Jesus' return, in the Rapture and the 2nd Coming, will be without warning *for all those who walk in darkness*. Only the born-again believers will see and be ready for the Rapture. One thing we must realize is this: just because we have prayed the Sinners Prayer down at the altar does not *necessarily* mean we are born-again. Mouthing words that we really do not mean doesn't get the job done in God's eyes. I can say this because God knows the heart of every human being, whether they are truly repentant—honest repentance is the key. The Word says, "Examine yourselves to see if you be in the faith." Our daily re-examination is the key to being *accounted worthy*! It's not about trying to be accepted by God or trying to earn His love, we could never do that. True repentance brings about a change in our lifestyle.

At this point in our study of Eschatology (prophetic end time events), I believe that we *need* to examine some of the problems that can arise when the Rapture teaching is misused or misunderstood.

Eschatology 101
Ignorant Misuse of the Rapture Teaching

To some the idea of believers misusing the Rapture teaching is almost inconceivable, one might even say impossible. On the contrary, I have personally witness **many** believers worldwide ignorantly misusing the teaching of the Pre-Tribulation Rapture. This is not to say that the other Rapture view-points have not also been misused, but God has lead me to focus specifically on the misuse of the Pre-Tribulation Rapture view-point. One might wonder, "How could some one misuse the teaching of the Rapture, and if so why would they even want to?" First of all, I want to inform you that this misuse has been done in ignorance—in other words, those that have done this are not aware of the misuse. Their motivation for doing this is subconscious, therefore, hidden to even them. It is unfortunate, but this same form of misuse takes place in the lives of many well-meaning believers, and has even infiltrated into our pulpits.

On that account, in what way have many born-again believers ignorantly misused the teaching of the Pre-Tribulation Rapture? Most of the believer's who misuse this teaching, are preaching and teaching the soon return of Jesus Christ with an improper motive. I have witnessed two specific misuses of this teaching since my relationship with Jesus Christ began. I remember when I first asked Jesus to come into my life at the age of eleven I experienced the first type of misuse that I would like to address. When I accepted Jesus I did so because I heard that if I did not except Him I would go to hell, and of course they also added that Jesus could come at anytime. These people made sure to inform me that Jesus could come again (at any time), and if I waited I would be left here to face the Antichrist without God. I listened to what they told me and gave my life (at least what I understood of it) to Jesus. My motivation for accepting Christ was improper. Why? It's because, I made this decision primarily because I didn't want to go to hell, or face the Antichrist without Jesus.

Many Christians do not understand that this is a form of misusing the Rapture teaching. Why is it a form of misuse? Because, when I (and those in my situation), except Jesus under these conditions, we are merely excepting Him as a "fire-escape," and not out of true heart felt repentance. *Fear* was my motivation instead of *faith*. Hence, most of us in these situations end up back sliding from Jesus, because our heart was not truly involved in the confessions that we made! However, I praise God for my parents who saw to it that I was discipled in the things of God, and I later understood exactly what I had committed my life to. Had I not been brought to church on a regular basis, I very possibly would not have continued in the life of faith—**Thank you very much Mom & Dad!**

All though this form of evangelism is not deceptive because the claims are Biblically true. On the other hand, this *is* improper because it is often used as *a scare tactic* to push (or manipulate) people into accepting Jesus Christ, and hence adding "new converts" to the church tally. Thus, numbers become the name of *our game* instead of reconciliation. As I said earlier, these improper motives are done without ones realization. One thinks he is doing a great work for Jesus, but in reality his motivation is twisted (wicked), therefore, it will not prosper.

The second reason that many believers improperly use the teaching of the Rapture is because they have allowed the cares (pressures) of life to cause them to loose the joy of their salvation. "How do Christians allow this to take place?"

For example, have you ever seen a believer who is worn out from the attacks of Satan which have come against them? In most of these cases they react in one of two ways. First, they become discouraged and angry at God, and they finally feel like *giving up* altogether. Next, if Satan can not get them to fall in line with that lie, he will attempt to convince them to *relax their stance* of spiritual warfare...and to look *forward* to the Rapture in an unbalanced manor. To these believers the Rapture becomes *their **only hope** of ever having a better life.*

I have even heard some of them say, "I think I'll just quite my job and wait for the Rapture." When a Christian who is *in this sort of mindset* begins to preach and constantly push the Rapture, they are doing so with ignorant, improper motives. It appears to be "spiritual," because it is a valid Bible doctrine. However, these people end up misusing this teaching as a way of feeding their (flesh) own discouragement and laziness. In reality, they are discouraged, depressed and unmotivated to continue living—possibly even suicidal!

Jesus *never* called us to give up living on this earth just because the Rapture is coming. Jesus said, "Blessed is the man whom his Lord finds **working** when He comes." I don't care who the believer is, if he gives up on his job, his vision from God...*purely because* Jesus is coming soon; then he is in reality **a defeated coward**. He has lost the joy of salvation! Now, don't misinterpret what I said. I *did not* say one *should not* quite his job to go into full-time ministry because the Lord has *specifically* told him to do so. I am solely addressing those who do such foolishness with the Rapture as their motive.

Eschatology 101
Why Hasn't It Happened Yet?

At this point you might be thinking, "Don't you believe that Jesus is coming, and that His return is coming ever closer?" Without a doubt—Yes! However, we must remember that *"No man knows the day or the hour."* Jesus is coming very soon—*this is true*—but the Bible **also** speaks of one specific thing that holds His return back.

> **(Acts 3:20,21)** "And that He may send [to you] the Christ (the Messiah), Who before was designated *and* appointed for you—even Jesus, Whom heaven **must** receive [**and retain**] *until the time for* **the complete restoration** *of all that God spoke* by the mouth of all His holy prophets for ages past [from the most ancient time in the memory of man].

The above passage of Scripture clearly shows that Jesus will be coming back, however, this will not take place *until* the Church has experienced an abundant time of Restoration. In *the King James Version* Bible restoration is called *restitution*, which according to the concordance means:

> "**Apokathistemi**, from G575 and G2525; **to reconstitute** (*in health, home* or *organization*):--**restore** (*again*)."[13]

God has given us a sure promise that before He sends Jesus in the event called the Rapture, He will restore **all** things that the devil has stolen. This is to include our health, finances, our home—be it the actual house, or those who live in it. A tremendous time of restoration will take place in the Body of Christ just moments before the Rapture. God is going to literally sweep many unsaved people during this time. The Holy Spirit has spoken to us very clearly about the timing of Jesus' return through the apostle Luke, therefore, we must realize the **He** wrote (Acts 3:20,21), and plan our lives in accordance with Him. God's Word says that we are to not only believe for the rapture, but also *for the fulfillment of our days*.

Saints of God, we shouldn't give up on whatever God has us doing. We must maximize our remaining time in prayer for the lost (our family members, friends; and the world). It is time for us to be motivated to win them with evangelistic campaigns that the Lord places within our spirits—rather than be slothful. However, we shouldn't attempt to win the world in our flesh (own strength). It's time to use the Anointing God has given us (as He leads) to reach as many for Jesus as possible before

He really returns, it will be too late to do so! Let's redeem the time for the days are evil.

Scriptures For Meditation

(Revelation 3:10 KJV) Because thou hast kept the word of my patience, *I also will keep thee* **from** *the hour of temptation*, which shall come upon all the world, to try them that dwell upon the earth.

(1 Corinthians 15:51-52 KJV) Behold, I show you a mystery; We shall not all sleep, but we shall all be changed, In a moment, in the twinkling of an eye, at *the last trump*: for the trumpet shall sound, and the dead shall be raised incorruptible, and we shall be changed.

(Matthew 25:13 KJV) "Watch therefore, for ye know neither the day nor the hour...."

(Acts 3:20,21) "And that He may send [to you] the Christ ...Whom heaven **must** receive [**and retain**] *until the time for* **the complete restoration** *of all*...."

SPIRITUAL DEATH AND THE CROSS

For some time, I have been hearing the various *heresy hunters* complaining about the Word of Faith's teaching concerning Spiritual Death. I was unable to get my hands on much information regarding this subject. So being the curious person that I am, I resolved to do some research on Spiritual Death for my own knowledge. This extensive, detailed chapter is the result of my research. I suggest that the reader set aside time to *thoroughly* research it for one's self and ask God for His Wisdom and revelation.

Thou Shalt *Surely* Die

Genesis 2:15-17: And the LORD God took the man, and put him into the garden of Eden to dress it and to keep it. And the LORD God commanded the man, saying, Of every tree of the garden thou mayest freely eat: But of the tree of the knowledge of good and evil, thou shalt not eat of it: **for in the day** *that thou eatest thereof* **thou shalt surely die**.

Does God ever waste words or make *idle* threats? Of course the answer is without a doubt, no! God told man that **in the day** that he ate of the tree he would die; however, Adam lived a total of 930 years. If God truly meant what He said, then why didn't Adam die on the day that he ate of the tree of knowledge? Did God make an *idle threat*, or did Adam actually *die* just as God warned him that he would? God's prophetic Word came to pass just as He said, and Adam **literally** died. However, the death that he experienced had little to do with the death of his physical body. At the *exact* moment of his disobedience, man partook of *Spiritual Death*. A death took place in man but it was in the realm of his spirit. Man had spiritually disconnected from God. He was, therefore, unable to receive revelation from God.

WHEN THE HOLY SPIRIT REVEALS
What Is Spiritual Death?

Romans 6:23: "For *the wages of sin* **is death**...."

The above verse explains Spiritual Death perfectly. The wages (price paid) for Sin is [Spiritual] Death. **Spiritual Death** is the wages, reward, or the result of a life of sinning, which is *ultimately* eternal separation from the Presence of the Living God. The very day that man ate of the fruit, he experienced spiritual separation from his Father.

Genesis 3:9, 10 (TAB): But the Lord God called to Adam and said to him, Where are you? He said, I heard the sound of You [walking] in the garden, and *I was afraid* because I was naked; and I hid myself.

Fear of God was the immediate result of Adam experiencing Spiritual Death. Those who are Spiritually Dead have a "built-in" *fear of God*. They do not have a respectful fear of God, but rather a frightful fear that He will punish them because their guilty (sinful) heart condemns them. Before sin entered the earth Adam & Eve had never experience fear.

Jesus Was Our *Substitute Sacrifice*

Matthew 27:46: And about the ninth hour Jesus cried with a loud voice, saying, Eli, Eli, lama sabachthani? that is to say, My God, my God, **why hast thou forsaken me**.

Why did Jesus cry out to God concerning His being forsaken? According to the concordance, *forsake* denotes: "to leave behind in some place, **to abandon**:--*forsake*, *leave*, reserve; to leave down, behind, by impl. To abandon, forsake; leave...."[1] Why would God the Father abandon, forsake or leave His *faithful* Son? We will answer this question gradually as we continue through this chapter. We have lot of background information to address in order for the biblical perspective to come into light. We need whole Bible context.

Psalms 22:1-11: *My God, my God, why hast thou forsaken me?* **why art thou so far from helping me, and from the words of my roaring?** *O my God, I cry in the daytime,* **but thou hearest not;** and in the night season, and am not silent. *But thou art holy*, O thou that inhabitest the praises of Israel. Our fathers trusted in thee: they trusted, and thou didst deliver them. They cried unto thee, and were delivered: they trusted in thee, and were not confounded. **But I am a worm**, *and no man; a reproach of men, and despised of the people*. All they that see me laugh me to scorn: they shoot out the lip, they shake the head, saying, He trusted on the LORD that he would deliver him: let him deliver him, seeing he delighted in him. *But thou art he that took me out of the womb: thou didst make me hope when I was upon my mother's breasts*. I was cast upon thee from the womb: thou art my God from my mother's belly. *Be not far from me;* **for trouble is near***; for there is* **none to help**.

According to *the Amplified Bible Expanded Edition*, Psalm 22 is called "The Psalm of the cross."[2] It is *theoretically possible* that Jesus quoted this very Psalm while He was nailed to the cross.[3] Also, this Psalm is prophetic of the many things that Jesus suffered (sacrificially) in our place, from before the cross to His resurrection.

Hank Hanegraaff has troubled the Word of Faith preachers, especially Kenneth Copeland, for saying that Jesus was a "worm." **However**, Jesus plainly stated this in Psalm 22:6. Nonetheless, again note that this Psalm is a prophetic picture of the many things that Jesus would have to suffer in our place. Thus, Jesus confessed, "I am a *worm* and no man...." The word *worm* denotes "a crimson color,"[4] or a blood red color. Seeing that Jesus shed His *precious* blood on our behalf, it is easy to understand why He said he was a "worm." And if Jesus said it was so, then it was so. It is impossible for God to ever lie.

What Trouble Is Near?

Psalm 22:11: Be not far from me; **for trouble is near***; there is none to help.*

Could there possibly be anything more troubling than the cross of Calvary? Was Jesus speaking of something far more shameful and terrible than even the cross? I believe that Jesus was referring to the three days and nights that He would spend *captive by man's Spiritual Death* in the belly of the earth.

K. R. "Dick" Iverson has also given us an insightful commentary on Psalm 22 in *The Spirit Filled Life Bible*:

"My God, My God: while on the cross, the tortured Jesus cried out those words (Matt. 27:46; Mk. 15:34). Hell is **total separation** from God as a **punishment** *for unrepented sin*, **a state of**

being forsaken. Jesus went through this hell experience *in our place* for our sins, so we will not have to."⁵

Iverson believes Psalm 22 as a proclamation of Jesus' experiencing *total separation* from His Father, **on the behalf** of His creation. He also notes that this separation did not only take place while He was on the cross, but rather *also* while He endured our punishment in hell itself. He paid the *complete* price, not just half of it!

Chastisement & *Substitute* Suffering

Isaiah 53:5-9: But he *was* wounded for our transgressions, *he was* bruised for our iniquities: **the chastisement** of our peace *was* upon him; and with his stripes we are healed. All we like sheep have gone astray; we have turned every one to his own way; and the LORD hath laid **on him** *the iniquity of us all*. He was *oppressed*, and he was *afflicted*, yet he opened not his mouth: he is brought as a lamb to the slaughter, and as a sheep before her shearers is dumb, so he openeth not his mouth. He was *taken from prison and from judgment*: and who shall declare his generation? for **he** *was cut off out of* **the land of the living**: *for the transgression of my people was he stricken*. And he made his grave with the wicked, and with the rich *in his death*; because he had done no violence, neither *was any* deceit in his mouth.

The time has come for us to examine Isaiah 53 in the light of what the Bible actually says *instead of* by the doctrines of our traditional Sunday school lessons. It's time for the Body of Christ to stop fooling around with the *Substitute Sacrifice* of Jesus Christ. He paid an **awesome** price to redeem us from Sin, and we need to acknowledge the price He paid. The later portion of Isaiah 53:5 tells us, *"the chastisement* of **our** peace was upon him...." The concordance defines *chastisement* as: "to chastise, lit. (*with blows*) or fig. (**with words**); hence to instruct: **bind**, chasten, **correct**, **punish**, reform, **reprove**...."⁶ Jesus, therefore, received *our* punishment, correction, and reprisal for Sin. Still, how does the Bible define the punishment for Sin?

Ezekiel 18:4b: "...the soul that sinneth, it shall **die**." [Also: Gen. 2:17]

Romans 6:23a: "For the wages of sin is **death**..."

The Bible does not teach that the *complete price* for Sin is physical death, although that's part of it, rather it teaches that Spiritual Death (*sepa-

ration from God's Presence) **is** the **ultimate** price that one will have to pay for rejecting the Substitute Sacrifice of Jesus. Furthermore, Ezekiel 18:4 (in my Bible) gives a cross-reference to Romans 6:23 tying them both directly together. Jesus Christ paid this *complete* price of Sin—spirit, soul, as well as body.

Jesus took our chastisement [punishment] upon Himself so that we could have peace with God. That kind of peace can only come through a renewed relationship with our God. He was punished with our separation (Spiritual Death) so that we would never have to be punished/separated from God for Sin. This is why Romans 8:35 can *legally* say: "Who shall *separate us* from the love of Christ…?"

Imprisonment—Judgment & *Substitute* Suffering

Isaiah 53:8—emphasis added: "He was taken *from prison and from judgment*: and **who** shall declare his generation? [**Why**?] for he was cut off **out of** the land *of the living*: for [*because of*] my people was he stricken."

Most traditionally-minded Christians would argue that this verse of Scripture is merely talking of Jesus' imprisonment prior to His crucifixion. I can understand why they would say this, and I believe that this sort of reasoning is partially true. However, in order to receive the *full* revelation of what this is saying, we must read the whole verse. Isaiah asks "Who shall declare his generation?"

The question we must now ask ourselves is: "Why did Isaiah ask who will declare his generation—(with the implied) *for Him*?" If we were to read the next sentence, then we'd find out the answer. He asked this question **because** Jesus was "cut off **out of** the land of the living." In other words, He was in the land of the Dead (departed spirits), otherwise known as Hades.

Furthermore, I believe that Jesus "began" to be *cut off out of* [from] the land of the living while He hung on that cross (spiritually speaking). He was made to be Sin **after** He had made Atonement for man's Sin.

Moreover, why was Jesus cut off out of the land of the living? The next sentence tells us, "for [or because of] my people was he stricken." Jesus was cut off out of the land of the living (Spiritual Death) because He became Sin, and our Sin **caused** Him to be separated from

His father (**after** *He made Atonement*). Believers understand that Sin **always** causes separation from God's Presence. *It's Spiritual Law!*

Seeing that Sin puts into motion *the Law of Spiritual Separation*, and God's Laws work the same way **no matter who** is affected by them, then why would our Sin affect Jesus any differently than it does us? Some would say, *"Jesus was God; therefore, Sin couldn't possibly affect Him like it does us."* **Correction**—Jesus was **fully** man *as well as* God, but He voluntarily *limited* Himself so that He could be a man. Jesus (the Man) had the same limitations that we had. The only advantage that He had over us was the fact that He had never sinned, but He took care of *our disadvantage* by paying the complete price for Sin.

As we have seen, Jesus was taken from prison and from judgment. But, what does the Bible mean by prison and judgment? The concordance defines prison and judgment as:

"[Prison] to inclose; by anal. to hold back; also to maintain, rule, *close up*, **detain**, *fast, keep (self close*, still), **prevail**, *refrain*, **reign**, **restrain**, *retain*, shut (up), slack, stay, stop, *withhold* (self)."[7]

"[Judgment] *a sentence or* **formal** *decree* (human or [partic.] **divine law**, individual or collect.), the act the place, the suit, *the crime*, **and the penalty**, to be judged."[8]

Jesus was imprisoned [in closed, detained, kept; restrained by the devil] in hell because of our Sin, the same as we would have been *had we gone* to hell for our Sin. Jesus received the divine sentence and penalty of Death (separation without God) in our place, because we could never possibly pay the *complete price* for our rebellion. Jesus paid our debt in His spirit, soul and His body.

Perhaps you're thinking "Fine, but show me some more Scripture to prove that Jesus was imprisoned for me!"

Acts 2:27, 31; 24 emphasis added: Because thou wilt not leave *my* [Jesus'] *soul in hell*, neither wilt thou suffer thine Holy One to see corruption. He [David] seeing this before *spake of the resurrection of Christ*, that *his soul was not left in hell*, neither his flesh did see corruption. Whom God hath *raised up*, having **loosed the pains of death**: because it *was not possible* that he should be holden of it.

David the Psalmist spoke prophetically of Jesus' resurrection, stating that God would not leave His soul in hell [Sheol or Hades].[9] We could get into a lengthy debate concerning the terminology used here to describe hell, but *perhaps* we can take this up at a later date. David *could not* have been referring to Abraham's bosom, **because** there was *no pain or punishment* where Abraham dwelt. **No**! Whether we want to face the truth or not, David *was* talking about **the pit** itself.

The Bible goes on to say that Jesus was loosed from the pains [*birth throws, sorrow, travail*] of Death.[10] It is impossible for me to have a baby, but from my own limited experience with birth, I can *see* that the throws of birth are not very pleasant. Why?

It's because they are extremely painful. Jesus (at His resurrection) was released from the spiritual birth throws that are beyond man's ability to communicate or understand. And He voluntarily did all of this for us! A majority of traditionally-minded believers would aggressively argue against this point; nevertheless, they have nothing scripturally to prove their disagreement to the contrary.

God Was Pleased—*Substitute* Suffering

Isaiah 53:10-12: Yet *it pleased the* LORD to bruise him; he hath put him to grief: when thou shalt **make his soul an offering for sin**, he shall **see his seed**, he shall *prolong his days*, and the pleasure of the LORD shall prosper in his hand. He shall *see of the* **travail of his soul***, and shall be satisfied*: by his knowledge *shall my righteous servant* **justify** *many*; for he shall **bear their iniquities**. Therefore will I divide him a portion with the great, and he shall divide the spoil with the strong; *because he hath* **poured out his soul unto death**: and he was *numbered* **with** *the transgressors*; and *he bare the sin of many*, and made intercession for the transgressors.

Was Jesus offered by God *only* in a physical sense? Isn't man a three part being—*spirit, soul & body* (1 Thess. 5:23)? Therefore, the real man *is not* what we see (the body), but the spirit which is merely housed by that body of flesh.

Thus, for Jesus to be *completely* offered by God, wouldn't He have had to be offered in spirit **and** soul *and* body? In order for Jesus to redeem the *complete* man from Sin's control, He would have had to been offered up completely—spirit, soul, as well as body. We must remember that Sin is not a physical aliment. Sin is an aliment of the spirit and soul. The Bible says that God made Jesus' *soul* an offering for Sin. Did God mean His soul (mind, will & emotions) *only*, or did this offering go even further? In the Old Testament *soul* is defined as:

"[*Nepes*] soul; self; person; heart…The inner person is *nepes*, while the outer person, or reputation, is *sem*…."[11]

Consequently, the Bible dictionary denotes *Nepes* as both soul **and** spirit. It's because the center (heart) of every human being is the spirit. And the Word of God many times refers to the inner person (man) as *the spirit of man*. In addition, the **only** "thing" that is capable of dividing (separating) the difference between soul and spirit is the Word of God because they are an **inseparable unit**. Only God and His Word can separate them.

The prophet Isaiah goes on to tell us that once God had made an offering of Jesus' soul (and spirit) God the Father saw the *travail* [labour, pain, sorrow, trouble][12] of His soul and then He was *satisfied* [to have enough, fill, be weary of].[13]

Moreover, the Scripture clearly teaches that God *made* Jesus to be Sin, that we might be *made* the Righteousness of God in Christ. He *took* our Sin, and we *received* His Righteousness: "For he hath **made** *him to be* **sin** *for us*, who knew no sin; that we might be *made the righteousness of God in him*" (2 Corinthians 5:21). The Bible dictionary defines *made* as "to become."[14] Thus, God caused Jesus to become Sin with our Sin so that we could become righteous with His Righteousness. You might be thinking, *"How could a sinless man become Sin?"* A sinless man could become Sin if he voluntarily accepted the Sin of the whole human race [*and its punishment*] upon Himself. In like manner, this was precisely what Jesus Christ agreed to do with the Father.

His Sorrow Was Unto *Death*

Matthew 26:38: Then saith he unto them, My soul is exceeding sorrowful, *even unto* **death**: tarry ye here, and watch with me.

Jesus, when He was in the Garden, said that He was under the pressure of such sorrow that it was about to kill Him. Jesus was experiencing extreme heaviness (oppression) or pressure by an attack of sorrow. Why was Jesus attacked with so much pressure from sorrow? It was because His heart was despising the very **thought** of being separated from His Father, especially for a group of people like us.

Hebrews 12:2: "…who for the joy that was set before him **endured** [*stayed under a curse*] the cross [*exposure to death*], **despising** [*to think against*] the shame…."

Matthew 26:39: And he went a little farther, and fell on his face, and prayed, saying, O my Father, *if it be possible*, let **this cup** *pass* from me: *nevertheless not as I will, but as thou wilt.*

Jesus put Himself under the cruse or allowed Himself to be exposed to Death—physical & Spiritual. He was resistant to the *thought* of going through this separation, yet He did it so that we could be joined once again to His Father. As a result, the pressure of that sorrow was **literally** about to kill Him because He was struggling with His own will. It's obvious that if there had been another way to accomplish the Father's plan, Jesus would have taken it. But once He surrendered His (human) will, He received a peace that empowered Him to go through with God's *master plan of the ages*. When He surrendered His will to the Father, the pressure of sorrow was broken and peace ruled.

Jesus desired that the **cup** might pass from Him. What did He mean by this "cup?" *Cup* [poterion] is defined by the concordance as "a drinking vessel, the contents thereof; fig. a lot or fate."[15] If God's will for Jesus was **only** that He go into the protected place in hell (Abraham's bosom), then why was Jesus abhorring thought of drinking it? Was He *afraid* of the cross? *No way!* Jesus detested drinking that cup because He knew exactly what it represented—Spiritual separation!

The very fact that Jesus would be nailed to a cross (tree) meant that He would be brought under a curse (the curse of the Law), because the people that He was to redeem were under the same curse. In order to redeem a cursed people He had to be cursed in our place.

Galatians 3:13-14: Christ hath redeemed **us** *from the curse of the law*, being **made a curse for us**: for it is written, *Cursed is* **every one** *that hangeth on a tree*: That the blessing of Abraham might come on the Gentiles through Jesus Christ; that we might receive the promise of the Spirit through faith.

I can hear someone, even now, saying *"How could Jesus Christ, God's only Son, ever be cursed by Him?"* First of all, the Word of God states that every one who is hung on a tree is cursed. I didn't write Galatians chapter three verse fourteen; however, the One Who holds Supreme Authority did! Hence, **if God said it then it is so!**

It is time for the Body of Christ to stop believing what *they think* happened and believe what God Himself *actually said* happened. Next, Jesus was brought under the dominion of a curse because God's creation was in bondage under a curse. He received our curse (*and its punishment*), so that we could be released from the curse of the Law, and be dominated by a New Law—*the Law of the Spirit of Life*. Moreover, in John. 19:30, *"received"* denotes the act of taking something,[16] and the sour wine (mixed with gall) represented **a curse**.

Was There *Virtue* In The Cross?

Many in the Body of Christ today speak of *the cross* of Christ as if *it* were almost some kind of "god." They sing songs about *it* nearly every Sunday. They speak concerning *it* as if *it* were **sacred**. However, is *the form* of death which our Lord experienced really worthy of all the religious hype that the crucifixion has received? They cling to the **"old rugged cross,"** more than they cling to *the Christ* of that cross. The cross represents a curse. We are to cling to Jesus!

Before you contemplate that I'm belittling what happened to Jesus at the cross of Calvary, please let me explain myself. Jesus paid an awesome price to reconcile us to God. *Nevertheless*, was there any virtue (purity, uprightness) in **the act of the crucifixion** *itself*? The best way that I know to answer this is by referring to a servant of God whom I love and respect deeply—Dr. Morris Cerullo:

> "There is no virtue in the cross. When Jesus Christ died on the cross, there was nothing virtuous *in that cross*. It was a piece of wood. The fact that he died on a cross was not virtuous; *there were thousands of people who died on crosses* in their day. Today, Jesus might have been hanged, put in a gas chamber, or electrocuted in the electric chair. Would we then **venerate** *the electric chair* by having it reproduced in gold charms to wear about our necks? The virtue was not in the cross, but **the virtue was in Jesus Christ** *Who died on the cross*. That was the thing *that was different* from the other deaths on crosses...the person!"[17]

This shocking thought was included in order to cause us to wake up and stop deifying the cross of Calvary. The *only* real significance that "the cross" (the *literal* form of dying) actually had is that God the Father prophetically spoke of it as being the way the Messiah would be Sacrificed. He could have said Jesus would be Sacrificed by having His throat slit so that He would shed His blood. Crucifixion merely happened to be the chief form of execution in Jesus' day. This is why God said He would be crucified.

Another thought simulating question. "Did Jesus *literally* offer the **physical** blood that He shed on Calvary **in heaven**?" When I ask this question, I mean, "Was the actual *physical* blood that poured out of His veins, and dried on His body as well as on the wood, offered in heaven?" Jesus **did** indeed offer His blood to the Father while on the cross.

However, His blood was also preserved and contained *in the realm of the Spirit*, so that He could offer it to His Father in heaven **after** He died, went into hell and was resurrected. In other words, this took place *after* He was released (resurrected) from Hell. Jesus did not ascend to the throne of God until **after** He'd been resurrected (released) from hell itself.

Jesus Paid The Price To Redeem— The *Complete* Man!

"Death is always, in Scripture, viewed as *the penal consequences of sin*—it was as *the Bearer of sin* that the Lord Jesus submitted thereto on the Cross. And while the physical death of the Lord Jesus was of the essence of His sacrifice, **it was not the whole**— He was left alone in the Universe, **He was forsaken....**"[18]

The price for Sin's penalty **must always** be paid—which is Death (physical & Spiritual). Jesus paid *our complete penalty*, which was Death—in body, in soul & in spirit. This is because, man is more than merely a physical body. He is a complete unit (*spirit, soul & body*).

Therefore, Jesus was ordained by God to redeem man *in his totality*, with His own (human) spirit, soul & body. Jesus received the penalty of *our* Sin (**Spiritual separation from God**), because He was the only Way to God. He was the **only** One qualified to pay the price (make compensation for), our complete penalty since He lived a **sinless life** here on earth, hereby, fulfilling the Law as a human being. He fulfilled the Law (as a man) *on our behalf*.

The *Precious* Blood Jesus

1 John 1:7: But if we walk in the light, as he is in the light, we have fellowship one with another, and *the blood of Jesus Christ* his Son *cleanseth us* from **all** sin.

Romans 3:25: "Whom God hath set forth to be a propitiation through faith *in his blood*, to declare *his* righteousness for the remission of sins that are past...."

Romans 5:9: Much more then, being now justified *by his blood*, we shall be saved from wrath through him.

Revelation 12:11: And they overcame him by **the blood of the Lamb, and** *by the word* of their testimony; and they loved not their lives unto the death.

Having read this chapter thus far, you may be wondering, *"Does he even believe in the saving power of the blood of Jesus?"* Absolutely, I would be a complete fool not to, especially when the Bible clearly states that our Redemption is through faith in the blood of Jesus. I personally "plead" the blood of Jesus over the life of my family and many others on a daily basis.

However, a part of what Jesus' blood has redeemed us from was the bondage and penalty of Sin (the curse of Sin). We were not *just* redeemed from a sinful lifestyle. We were redeemed from the bondage (control) and penalty of Adamic Sin *which was* eternal bondage, punishment and separation for Him in hell. That is what Sin's wages truly are! Jesus' shed blood made the way for Him to redeem us back to God by His (spirit, soul & body) sacrifice from bondage, punishment and separation. He did this by taking the curse, our curse, upon Himself. He submitted Himself to Death—*not just the death of His physical body*, otherwise He would never have died physically.

Why? Because the Scripture says that the soul *that sins* shall die. Jesus never sinned; thus, He *could not* have possibly died, *apart from* taking upon Himself the Adamic Sin and its penalty. His blood is the key factor in our Redemption, but without Him receiving *the wages* of our Sin, we could never be made the Righteousness of God. It is because our Righteousness is in and through His *Substitute Sacrifice*. If He did not receive our wages (separation), then the Father could in no way see us as righteous. The curse of Sin was much more than just our living a ungodly lifestyle—*we were* **Dead!**

What Happened At His Resurrection

Hebrews 1:1-9: God, who at sundry times and in divers manners spake in time past unto the fathers by the prophets, Hath in these last days spoken unto us by *his* Son, whom he hath appointed *heir of all things*, by whom also he made the worlds; Who being the brightness of *his* glory, and the express image of his person, and *upholding all things by the word of his power*, when he had **by himself** purged our sins, **sat down** on the right hand of the

Majesty on high; Being made so much better than the angels, as he hath by inheritance obtained a more excellent name than they. For unto which of the angels said he at any time, Thou art my Son, **this day** *have I begotten thee?* **And again**, *I will be to him a Father*, *and he shall be to me a Son?* **And again**, when he bringeth in **the first begotten** *into the world*, he saith, And let *all the angels of God worship him*. And of the angels he saith, Who maketh his angels spirits, and his ministers a flame of fire. But unto the Son *he saith*, Thy throne, O God, *is* for ever and ever: a sceptre of righteousness *is* the sceptre of thy kingdom. *Thou hast loved righteousness, and hated iniquity*; **therefore** God, *even* thy God, hath anointed thee with the oil of gladness *above thy fellows.*

Please note the latter part of verse three where we read, "...*when he had* **by himself** *purged our sins*...." Here the writer of the book of Hebrews is saying that once Jesus had purged us (or the temple) *by His Substitute Sacrifice*, He sat down at God's right hand. *The Amplified Bible* says it this way: "*When He had by offering Himself accomplished our cleansing of sins* **and** *riddance of guilt....*" Exactly how did our Lord Jesus purge us "by Himself," or by "offering Himself" for our cleansing and riddance of guilt? He did it—**spirit, soul and body.** Jesus **unreservedly** said:

John 10:15b, 18a Emphasis Added: "...I lay down my *life* [spirit] for the sheep...No man taketh *it* [My spirit] from me, but *I lay it* [My spirit] **down**...."

Moreover, the Word of God also states in the book of James that without the spirit, the body will cease to live.

James 2:26 Emphasis Added: "For as the body without the *spirit* [life] is dead, so faith without works [*corresponding action*] is dead also...."

Thus, as a result, there is *no doubt* that when Jesus said, "*I lay down My* **life** *for My sheep,*" He was referring to the surrendering of Himself (spirit, soul and body) for the Redemption of His sheep (the Church). Jesus did not just lay down His physical body—He laid down the life (spirit) of that physical body which was His human spirit. He gave Himself completely!

He's No Longer Called The *Only* Begotten

Hebrews 1:5, 6: "For unto which of the angels said he at any time, Thou art my son, **this day** *have I begotten thee?* **And again**, I will be to Him a Father, and he shall be to me a Son? **And again**, when he bringeth in **the first begotten** *into the world....*"

Romans 8:29: For whom he did foreknow, he also did predestinate to be conformed to the image of his Son, *that he might be the firstborn* **among** *many brethren.*

Colossians 1:15, 18: "Who is the image of the invisible God, *the firstborn of every creature...*And he is the **head** of the body, the church: *who is* **the beginning, the firstborn from** *the dead;* **that in all things** *he might have the preeminence.*"

Since the resurrection, Jesus Christ ceased to be referred to as the *only* begotten Son of God. T*he Amplified Bible* calls Him "the Firstbegotten or the Firstborn from [among] the dead." What does the Bible mean when it calls Him the Firstbegotten or Firstborn?

[Firstbegotten—Firstborn: a composite definition] "firstborn, first (of all) former...to produce seed, as a mother, a plant, **be born**, *bring forth*, **be delivered**, be in travail."[19]

Colossians chapter one verse eighteen states that Jesus is the firstborn **from** the dead, that *in all things* **he** might have preeminence. Again, *the Amplified Bible* says, "the Firstborn from **among** the dead." In what way is He the firstborn "from among" the dead? Jesus was the first man to ever be born permanently **out of** death physically, and *especially* Spiritually. He has preeminence in all things—does He not? Therefore, He received what we received, *except* He received it all **first**. *What does all this mean?* It means that Jesus Christ was the first **man** to ever receive Spiritual Reconciliation with God the Father. In other words, He was the first to be reborn Spiritually *from Death to Life*, or more commonly known as *the new birth*. Jesus had to be Spiritually reborn (**spiritually brought back into *fellowship* with God**) because He had voluntarily received the Sin of the human race—which separated Him.

When I say Jesus experienced *the new birth*, I mean He experienced a rebirth, a resurrection, or a **reconnection** with His Father <u>in a spiritual sense</u>. Jesus' human spirit experienced a rebirth from the bondage of our Sin to God's righteousness. His human spirit was **protected** by God from being *corrupted* (He never saw corruption) by the Sin of the human race while He was in hell. Our Sin was wrapped around Jesus like paper wraps a present. His human spirit was protected inside that sin wrapping by the Father, so Sin could not control His nature—Righteousness. But He <u>wasn't</u> protected from the penalty (punishment) of Sin. The spirit of man had to be recreated because *it was* corrupted by Sin, but Jesus' spirit was not recreated because it *was* protected.

The New Birth Is *Spiritual Law*

John 3:3-6: "…Verily, verily, I say unto thee, *Except* **a man** *be born again*, he cannot see the kingdom of God…Verily, verily, I say unto thee, *Except a man be born of water and of the Spirit*, he cannot enter into the kingdom of God. That which is born of the flesh is flesh; and *that which is born of the Spirit* **is spirit**."

Jesus told Nicodemus **every man** (indicating that this is Spiritual Law) must be born-again in order to see the Kingdom of God. Nicodemus could not comprehend this so he asked, "How can a man be born again when he is old…?" I believe that when Jesus replied with "Except a man be *born of water* and of the Spirit," He was actually saying that a man must be first born of water (his mother), and then he must be born also of the Spirit. Some believe "of water" is referring to baptism, but that could not possibly be the case. Why? It would mean that no one could go to heaven *unless* they were baptized in water, but the Bible in no way supports this unreasonable notion.

Jesus clearly informed Nicodemus that **ALL** men, (including Jesus, Himself) had to receive the new birth, *from Death to Life* [from Sin to Righteousness]. How can I be so sure that He was including Himself? First, He said *every* man had to be born-again to see God's Kingdom. Next, He was as much man *as He was* God. Therefore, Jesus (*the Man*) was included in this statement. Jesus submitted Himself to every ordinance [Natural & Spiritual Law] of God and man. Our Sin caused Him to Die Spiritually.

Reconciliation Meant—The Suffering *of Death*

Hebrews 2:9-17: But we see Jesus, who was *made a little lower* than the angels *for the suffering of death*, crowned with glory and honour; that he *by the grace of God should* **taste death** *for every man.* For it became him, for whom *are* all things, and by whom *are* all things, in bringing many sons unto glory, to *make the captain of their salvation perfect through sufferings.* For both **he that sanctifieth** *and they who are sanctified* **are all of one**: for which cause **he** is not ashamed to call them brethren, **Saying,** *I will declare* **thy** *name unto my brethren, in the midst of the church will I sing praise unto thee.* **And again**, *I will put my trust in him.* **And again,** *Behold I and the children which God hath given me.* Forasmuch then as the children are partakers of flesh and blood, *he also himself likewise took part of the same;* that **through death** he might *destroy him that had the power of death,* that is, **the devil**; *And deliver them* who through fear of death were all their lifetime subject to bondage. For verily he took not on *him the nature* of angels; but *he took on him the seed of Abraham.* Wherefore in all things it behoved him to be **made like unto his brethren**, that he might be a merciful and faithful high priest in things *pertaining* to God, *to make* **reconciliation** *for the sins of the people.*

Jesus was made lower than the angels, because *Adam* had bowed his knee to a fallen angle—therefore placing himself under (in submission to) that fallen angel. Jesus took on this same position of authority, in order to elevate man back to his *original* position of authority as God's under-lord of this planet. Jesus has caused us to sit in heavenly places (positions of authority), with Himself. Jesus has not only given us back our original dominion, but He has also given us the ability to walk, live and act in the same authority that **He** had over Satan. I'm *in no way*, saying that man is "an equal" with Jesus Christ in His *present day* position of authority.

However, man is now able to live and walk in the image of Jesus Christ *as He lived* here on this earth. We **are not** God! We will **never** become God or a god (Supreme Creator). We are the creation; *He is the Supreme Creator.* He simply lives in us and empowers us for victory by faith in the Name and by the blood of Jesus Christ! The Word of God continues by telling us that Jesus was made a little lower than the angels [that includes Lucifer—*he's an angel*], for the suffering of *death* (spiritual). Why? That He should **taste death** *for* **every** *man. If* the form of death that is addressed here was physical death, then why do people still die physically? The Scripture says that Jesus tasted of death for **every** man. Anyone over the age of *ten* knows that physical death is inevitable…apart from the rapture. If this passage was referring to physical death, no other human being would ever have to die physically. However, physical death **is not** the subject of this passage of Scripture.

Hence, verse nine *could not possibly* be addressing physical death. If that were the case, *then* the Word of God wouldn't be *the Truth*, because men still die physically. *On the other hand*, born-again believers die once *to Sin* and never have to taste of *Spiritual Death* again **forever**. Spiritual Death would be the only form of death that Jesus could taste for every man. The people who do not accept His *Substitute Sacrifice* will end up "paying" their share of the wages of Sin themselves but it will be for eternity.

Hebrews 2:11-13: "…for which cause **he** is not ashamed to call them [us] brethren, [He is] Saying, I will declare thy [God's] name unto my brethren, in the midst of the church will I sing praise unto thee. **And again**, I [Jesus] *will* **put my trust** *in him* [God]…."

Please understand that Jesus Himself was the One Who said, "**And again**, *I will put my trust in Him*." Why would Jesus need to put His trust in God the Father "again." if there was not a separation between them? *But* if He [Jesus the Man] had been **disconnected** from the life of God by our Sin, then He would need to be spiritually reconnected *born-again* [or put His faith/trust back in Him]. God the Father and Jesus make the following statement in Hebrews chapter 1:

Hebrews 1:5, 6: "For unto which of the angels said he at any time, Thou art my Son, **this day** have I begotten thee? **And again**, I will be to Him a Father, and he shall be to me a Son? **And again**, when he bringeth in **the first begotten** *into the world*…."

Consequently, the Father was saying that Jesus had ceased to be connected to Him as His Son for a period of time, because we were the cause of His disconnection. God would not have said, "And *again* I will be to Him a Father and he shall be to me a Son," **if** there had not been a period of Spiritual separation between them. According the concordance, the word *again* in this verse means "once more."[20] Moreover, the Bible dictionary defines *shall* as "are to, must." Thus, this would be better understood if it were read like this:

Hebrews 1:5b, 6a: *"And again* [once more], I will be to Him a Father and he shall [are to, must] be to me a Son? *And again* [once more], when he bringeth in **the first begotten** *into the world*…."

God the Father [*once again*] became a Father to Jesus and Jesus, because He had never sinned, had to [are to, must] become reconnected to Him as His Son and there was nothing all of hell could do to stop it. Jesus had fulfilled the Law of God, walking and living **as a man**. Therefore, hell could not possibly hold Him past the Father's prescribed three days and nights. God gave Jesus so that we would never be separated from Him again throughout all eternity. This can legally take place in our lives because Jesus Christ took our punishment (separation) for us.

John 3:16: For God so loved the world, that he gave [delivered up, offer][21] his only begotten Son, that whosoever believeth in him should not perish, but have everlasting [eternal, non-ending] life.

God gave [delivered up] His Son [spirit, soul, and body] for us, that we would never have to be spiritually separated from Him again. The Father loves us with **the exact same love** as He loves Jesus. God gave Jesus up to Spiritual Death so that we would never have to be separated from Him *again* for all eternity. That's the loving God we serve!

He Took Part of *The Same*

Hebrews 2:14b, 15: "*…he also himself likewise took part of the same*; that **through death** he might *destroy him that had the power of death*, that is, **the devil**; *And deliver them* who through fear of death were all their lifetime subject to bondage."

Jesus likewise took part of the same. What "same" did He take part of? He took part of everything that we human beings had. He took part of our humanity, part of our physical limitations, and also took part in our Sin. This began when He was on the cross, while He made Atonement for Sin, and ended when He was resurrected. Why did Jesus go through all this horrible torment? "…that **through death** he might *destroy him that had the power of death*, that is, **the devil**; *And deliver them*." Jesus' main objective from the Father was for Him to partake of all that we **had**, so that He could go into hell as our substitute. And while He was there, He was to completely destroy him who **had** been given the power of Death (Spiritual), who *was* the devil.

Moreover, He accomplished His mission with one hundred percent success. The church of Jesus Christ (the Firstborn), is completely free from **all** of Satan's control. The only problem now is that most of us can't seem to comprehend that we really are free from Sin and **all** its demands. Many Christians see themselves as just saved sinners—how sad! Especially when the Word of God says He made a great exchange with us.

Hebrews 2:17: Wherefore *in all things* it behoved him to be *made like unto his* brethren, that he might be a merciful and faithful high priest in things *pertaining* to God, to make **reconciliation** for the sins of the people.

Our Lord and Savior, Jesus Christ, made reconciliation [to exchange mutually, to take for oneself][22] for us. He took upon Himself our sin, made a mutual exchange. What was that exchange? He took our Sin from us and then He gave us His Righteousness. This idea is disputed by *The Vines Expository Dictionary*. It says that *propitiation* is actually a more proper term than "reconciliation."

> "[*Propitiation*]*...in Heb. 2:17 'to expiate, to make propitiation for'...'to make propitiation' is an important correction of the KJV, 'to make reconciliation.'...Never is God said to be reconciled, a fact itself indicative that the enmity exists on man's part alone, and that it is man who needs to reconciled to God, and not God to man. God is always the same and, since He is Himself immutable, His relative attitude does not change towards those who change...[Propitiation] 'an expiation, a means whereby sin is *covered and remitted*."23

I can agree with the use of the word *propitiation* in the sense that Jesus made Atonement, indemnity, or payment for our Sin. We were the ones who needed to be reconciled. On the other hand, *Vine's* says that the Sin of man was *covered and remitted*; this is only partly true. Our Sin was not merely covered and remitted [forgiven].24

The Old Covenant saints' sins were merely covered, but Jesus' Substitute Sacrifice **literally** removed the Sin nature from within us who believe—as far as the east is from the west. He took our Sin upon Himself and in exchange for our Sin, He gave us His Righteousness. We have been made the Righteousness of God in Christ Jesus. Reconciliation means "to change or exchange hence, of persons, 'to change from enmity to friendship, to reconcile," according to the Bible dictionary. In order to see this more clearly, let us examine how *reconcile* (in reference to Christ's sacrifice) is used in other portions of God's Word. And he is the head of the body, the church: who is the beginning, the firstborn from [among] the dead; that in all *things* he might have the preeminence.

Colossians 1:18-20: For it pleased *the Father* that in him should all fullness dwell; And, having made peace through the blood of his cross, by him to reconcile [to reconcile fully and *to change mutually*], all things unto himself; by him, *I say*, whether *they be* things in earth, or things in heaven.

Ephesians 2:16: And that he might reconcile [same as above], both unto God in one body by the cross, having slain the enmity thereby:

Both of the passages of Scripture above are referring to *the same event* that Hebrews chapter two verse seventeen refers to. Again, a mutual exchange took place. He took our Sin upon Himself and we received His Righteousness in exchange. Thus as a result, the word *reconciliation* is in reality a better rendering than *propitiation*. Jesus paid the **full** price for our reconciliation—*spirit, soul and body.*

Spiritual Justification—And Jesus

1 Timothy 3:16: And **without controversy** great is the mystery of godliness: God was *manifest in the flesh*, **justified in the Spirit**, seen of angels, preached unto the Gentiles, believed on in the world, received up into glory.

1 Peter 3:18 (NKJV): For Christ also *suffered* once for sins, the just for the unjust, that He might *bring us to God*, being put to death in the flesh but **made alive** *by the Spirit*.

Romans 1:3, 4 (NKJV): Concerning His Son Jesus Christ our Lord, who was born of the seed of David according to the flesh, *and* **declared** *to be* the Son of God with power according to the Spirit of holiness, **by *the resurrection*** *from the dead.*

In 1 Tim. 3:16 it tells us that Jesus Christ was *justified* in the Spirit. The word *justified* as defined by the concordance means "to *render* just or innocent, [to render] to be righteous."[25] In addition, the word *render* from the Bible dictionary is "to give up or back, furnish, provide and supply,"[26] whatever is needed. **Consequently**, it could be said the Jesus was *justified* with [rendered—given, furnished with, provided and supplied], Righteousness by the Holy Spirit. The word *Spirit* in this verse of Scripture denotes "a spirit, **Christ's spirit**, as well as the Holy Spirit."[27]

I believe this verse is speaking of a binary (twofold) combination. The Holy Spirit had to declare, and furnish Him with Righteousness because He was under the curse of our Sin. I am in no way saying that He was "unrighteous," as if He had sinned. I am saying that *our Sin* caused Him to be **a substitute** for the unrighteous human race, for a period of time, until God's time period was fulfilled by Him in hell.

Then hell, Satan, and all his demons could not hold Him, because He truly was righteous. Sin's complete bondage was destroyed by the Holy Spirit *after* God's set time period was fulfilled. Furthermore, in 1 Pet. 3:18 the Bible says that Jesus was made alive by the Spirit. In *the King James Version* Bible, the phrase *made alive* is rendered "quickened." *Quickened* denotes "made alive, *to revitalize*, make alive, **give life**,"[28] so says the concordance. Hence, Jesus was made alive by, revitalized by, or given **life** by the Holy Spirit.

If Jesus Christ never Died Spiritually, then why did He need to be **given life**? **Zoe** is the God-kind of life—perpetual, *never* beginning/ending life. Zoe is the *real* part of God that "makes" God—God (never beginning, never ending life). If Jesus was living here on this earth **as God**, then He would never have needed to have life *given back* to Him. But the Word states that the Holy Spirit made Him **alive** again. He had to because Jesus was **dead in our sin** and cursed.

Moreover, the Word of God says in Romans 1:3, 4, that Jesus was declared to be the Son of God, according to the Spirit of holiness, by His resurrection from the Dead (physical/Spiritual). The term *resurrection* in the concordance means "raised to life again, rising again." Again I ask—if Jesus was living on this earth "as God," then why would He need to be raised back to *life*? God's life is never beginning, never ending.

It's because the word *life* denotes both physical and Spiritual Life. Jesus laid aside a portion of Himself (godly attributes) so that He could be a man. Jesus did not walk on this earth with all power, all knowledge, and the ability to be present in all places at all times. He was just as much man as He was God, but <u>never</u> acted on His own accord.

No He came to this earth as a man Anointed by the Holy Spirit specifically to walk the line of the Mosaic Law and bring *it* to completion on our behalf. This is why He was able to take our curse upon Himself and become spiritually separated from the Father. You might ask *"How could God 'lay aside' a certain portion of Himself?"* I don't know, but I do know that's what He did according to the Word of God. After all, He is God, isn't He, and He is capable of doing millions of things that we can't even comprehend. That's a part of the sovereignty of God. I do not understand how God could pull off such a mighty work, but He did it!

Spiritual Justification—*By Identification*

Romans 3:24; 28: Being *justified freely* by his grace through the *redemption* that ***is in Christ Jesus***: Therefore we conclude that a man is justified by faith without the deeds of the law.

1 Corinthians 6:16, 17 (NKJV): Or do you not know that he who is *joined* to a harlot is one body *with her*? For "the two," He says, "shall become *one flesh*." But he who is **joined** *to the Lord is* **one spirit** *with Him.*

Romans 6:6 (NKJV): "...knowing this, that *our old man was crucified* with ***Him***, *that the body of sin might be done away with*, that we should no longer be slaves of sin."

2 Timothy 2:11 (NKJV): *This* is a faithful saying: For if we died *with Him*, We shall also *live* ***with Him***.

We obtained our justification by *the Spiritual Law of identification* with Christ Jesus. Jesus identified with our SIN and we identified with His Righteousness. *Identification* denotes "an act of identifying: a state of being identified..."²⁹ and *identify* means "to cause to be or become **identical**...to be or become *the same*."³⁰ We became united in the realm of the Spirit with Christ, or became one with Him [*identical*—identified], so that the body of Sin might be destroyed by Christ Jesus. We died with Christ as He died—spirit, soul, and body and, therefore, we've also been raised again to new life *much like* He was. The apostle Paul said in Galatians 2:20 "I've been crucified with Christ...."

This event could only take place by identification. Jesus established our identity in Him as righteous, our Sin established His identity with us *as* unrighteous. Again, Jesus was righteous—*He* never sinned one time, but our Sin that He took upon Himself caused Him to identify with our unrighteousness. He became one with us in our Spiritual Death, in that we might become one with His never ending [Zoe] life. This **is not** to say, *in any way*, that we are now "God," but simply that we are *one with Him*, in the sense of possessing the promises of the Father which include **never ending** life.

Why Did Jesus Submit To The Baptism of John?

One Tuesday afternoon in September 1997, I was driving home from work in my car listening to a preaching tape when the preacher mentioned that Jesus went into the wilderness after he received *the baptism of John*. Normally a statement like that would not have shaken me to my shoes, but this day it did!

After the preacher made that statement, the Lord asked me, "*Why did I submit to the baptism of John?*" I said, "I don't know!" He then said, "What was the baptism of John?" I said, "It was a baptism **unto repentance**—the *precursor* to receiving the New Birth."

Then He said, "*Why would I need to submit to a baptism that was unto repentance—Seeing that I never committed Sin?*" I said, "I *really* don't know that one!" He then reminded me of Philippians 2:6, 7 in *the Amplified Bible*:

which basically says that Jesus laid aside His glory [*Omnipresence, Omnipotence, Omniscience*] to become a human being. He said, "*I was submissive to the same Laws that you are. I wasn't submissive to the Law of Sin and Death until I was made to be Sin for you, but I was submissive to every other ordinance of man—the same way that you are.* **It was because, I was submissive to the New Birth as I was submissive to the baptism of John—I did all of these things for you!**"

Jesus had to submit to these ordinances of God because He lived on this earth *as a man* Anointed by the Holy Spirit, instead of as "Superman." He had to rely upon the Anointing in the same way as we also must. Jesus didn't *call the shots* while on earth, but He rather followed His Father's leading. This is why He never performed a miracle until *after* He had been baptized. Then the Holy Spirit descended upon Him! Jesus was our example to follow. He received everything that we have received…only He received it all first.

Committed—Finished & Fulfilled

Luke 23:46 (NKJV): And when Jesus had cried out with a loud voice, He said, "Father, into Your hands *I* **commit** [commend—KJV] *My spirit.*" Having said this, He breathed His last.

John 19:30 (NKJV): So when Jesus had received the sour wine, He said, "**It** *is finished!*" And bowing His head, He **gave up** *His spirit.*

Matthew 5:17 (NKJV): *Do not think* that I came to destroy the Law or the Prophets. *I did not come to destroy* **but to fulfill**.

The Bible states in Luke 23:46 that Jesus commended His (human) spirit to the Father. *Commend* is defined as "to deposit (as a trust or for **protection**),"[31] according to the concordance. Why would Jesus say to His Father, "I entrust my spirit to You for protection," if He was only going to the place called Paradise? *He would not have needed any protection there.* Abraham's bosom was already a protected place. Jesus entrusted His spirit to the Father so that it would be protected while He was wrapped by our Sin, and as He entered into the lower parts of the earth or the pit of hell itself (Ephesians 4:9). Jesus needed His Father's protection because He had to go into hell and face the punishment, plus separation caused by our Sin. Similarly, Jesus, while on the cross, said, "**It is finished.**" Most theologians would say, "*Now see there—that meant that the sacrifice was complete.*" According to the Strong's Concordance, *finished* means "complete, conclude, *discharge*, accomplish, *fill up*, expire."[32] However, Jesus made this statement in Matthew 5:17: "I did not come to destroy **but to fulfill**." What did Jesus come to fulfill? He came to fulfill the words of the prophets of old, and to fulfill the Law of God.

When Jesus said, "*It is finished*," He was proclaiming that **He had fulfilled the Law of God as a human being**, and He was also proclaiming that because of *that*, Satan's control over man was finished. He wasn't saying that His Substitute Sacrifice was finished. If this were the case, why did He commit His spirit to His Father for Him to protect it? Jesus knew where He had to go, and that's why He asked for protection—not **from** punishment but through the punishment. **His human spirit was protected from the *corruption* of our Sin.** He *did not* become some demonic creature. Sin's punishment (torment & separation) had to be paid (or inflicted) and Jesus was the only One qualified to receive it. He was the only One Who could experience the punishment of Sin *and still be able to rise* from the pit—**victorious**!

Moreover, in that same verse of Scripture, it says that Jesus "*gave up His Spirit*." The Spirit of God worded is, this way for a reason. G*ave* denotes "to surrender, intrust, cast, commit, deliver (up); put in prison, *bestow, grant*."[33] Jesus asked His Father for protection through the punishment of hell, then He gave up or delivered up His (human) spirit to be put in prison for man's Sin. He surrendered to ***Death***!

When Was Eternal Redemption *Officially* Finished?

As I have noted, when Jesus said, "It is finished," He wasn't referring to the completion of His work for our Redemption. This notion couldn't possibly be true because ever since the beginning of the Law, *Atonement* (plus Eternal Redemption) was to be obtained by *more* than the shedding of the blood of the Sin offering. Kenneth E. Hagin sheds notable light upon understanding the meaning of Jesus' statement: "It is finished."

> "Many have thought that when Jesus said on the Cross, 'It is finished.' He was talking about our salvation. No! No! No! Our salvation wasn't finished when Jesus died. **Salvation wasn't complete until He ascended into the heavenly Holy of Holies to obtain eternal redemption for us**. (See Hebrews chapter 9)S When Jesus said "It is finished' on the cross, He was talking about the Old Covenant being finished. And when He said those words, the curtain that sealed off the Holy of Holies in the Temple was rent in twain — or torn in half — from top to bottom (Mark 15:38)." [34]

Based on Hagin's quotation, I believe that it is important that we further examine the passages of Scripture that he referred us to, in order to see the whole picture of what Jesus did to obtain *Eternal Redemption* for us.

Hebrews 9:6-8 (NKJV): Now when these things had been thus prepared, the priests always went into the first part of the tabernacle, performing *the services*. But into the second part the high priest *went alone once a year, not without blood, which he offered* for himself and *for* the people's sins *committed* in ignorance; the Holy Spirit indicating **this**, that the way into the Holiest of All was not yet made manifest **while the first tabernacle was still standing**.

Old Covenant *Atonement* came *after* the blood was offered in the Holy of Holies—*not before*. Jesus wasn't able to offer His blood in the REAL Holy of Holies until **after** He had resurrected from death and ascended. Furthermore, the earthly Holy of Holies in Solomon's temple had to be first abolished—FINISHED, before Jesus was able to enter into heaven three days and nights later.

Hebrews 9:11, 12 (NKJV): But Christ came *as* High Priest of the good things to come, with the greater and more perfect tabernacle not made with hands, that is, not of this creation. Not with the blood of goats and calves, but with His own blood *He entered the Most Holy Place once for all,* **having obtained** *eternal redemption.*

Hebrews 9:12 (TAB): He went once for all into the [Holy of] Holies [of heaven], not by virtue of the blood of goats and calves [by which to make reconciliation between God and man], but His own blood, **having found *and* secured** *a complete redemption* (an everlasting release for us).

Jesus entered into the Holy of Holies having obtained **Eternal Redemption**—***not*** just an Atonement (*or covering*). At the cross, Jesus atoned (made a covering) for our Sin. However, Atonement was the *precursor* to **Eternal Redemption**, which was "officially" declared **after** Jesus presented Himself to the Father and had poured out His blood in heaven.

Eternal Redemption wasn't possible without the full penalty being paid. *Separation and punishment* were an important part of how Adam's Sin was **blotted out!**

Hebrews 9:13-23 (NKJV): For *if* the blood of bulls and goats and the ashes of a heifer, sprinkling the unclean, sanctifies for the purifying of the flesh, how much more shall the blood of Christ, *who through the eternal Spirit offered Himself without spot to God*, cleanse your conscience from dead works to serve the living God? And for this reason He is the *Mediator* of the new covenant, **by means of death** [separation], for the redemption of the transgressions under the first covenant, that those who are called may receive the promise of the eternal inheritance. For where there *is* a testament, there must also of necessity be the death of the testator. For a testament *is* in force after men are dead, since it has no power at all while the testator lives. Therefore not even the first *covenant* was dedicated without blood. For when Moses had spoken every precept to all the people according to the law, he took the blood of calves and goats, with water, scarlet wool, and hyssop, and sprinkled both the book itself and all the people, saying, *"This is the blood of the covenant* which *God has commanded you."* Then likewise he *sprinkled with blood both the tabernacle and all the vessels of the ministry*. And according to the law almost all things are purified with blood, and without shedding of blood there is no remission. Therefore, *it was* necessary that the copies of the things in the heavens should be purified with these, **but the heavenly things themselves with better sacrifices than these**.

This is what Jesus did! Jesus' blood has needed to cleanse the heavenly temple, *the same as the earthly temple was cleansed* before the "official" declaration of Eternal Redemption could be proclaimed and made available to us.

Note that the cleansing of the temple was an important part of Old Covenant Atonement, the same as it was in our receiving Eternal Redemption. It was not complete without it!

Hebrews 9:24-28 (NKJV): For Christ has not entered the holy places made with hands, *which are* copies of the true, *but into heaven itself*, now to appear in the presence of God for us; not that He should offer Himself often, as the high priest enters the Most Holy Place every year with blood of another; He then would have had to suffer often since the foundation of the world; but now, once at the end of the ages, He has appeared to put away sin by the sacrifice of Himself. And as it is *appointed for men to die once*, but **after this the judgment**, so Christ was offered once *to bear the sins of many*. To those who eagerly wait for Him He will appear a second time, apart from sin, for salvation.

Jesus experienced Death and judgment on the behalf of the human race. He became Sin and bore our sicknesses and diseases in our place. Sin was not *officially* (for eternity) put away **until after** Jesus presented Himself before the Father, and poured His blood in the Holy of Holies. *Jesus experienced judgment—Spiritual Separation for all men*!

> **John 19:30 (NKJV)**: So when Jesus had received the sour wine, He said, "***It is finished***!" And *bowing His head, He gave up His spirit.*

> **Mark 15:37, 38 (NKJV)**: And *Jesus cried out with a loud voice, and breathed His last.* **Then** the veil of the temple was torn in two from top to bottom.

No one would argue that the above portions of Scripture are referring to the same historical event—Jesus' last words in human flesh. Mark fifteen verse 37 tells us that He cried out with a loud voice. What do you think He cried out? **"IT IS FINISHED!"** Immediately after He cried out those words, what happened? The Bible says the veil separating the Holy of Holies was torn from top to bottom, *denoting the meaning of Jesus' last words*. The earthly man-made temple, God's dwelling place, **was finished**!

However, man did not become His temple until the day of Pentecost, after Jesus went to heaven. Moreover, in John 20:17, Jesus said to Mary Magdalene: "*Touch Me not; for I am not ascended to My Father....*" **Why was Mary not to touch Jesus?** Still, *after* Jesus had ascended to His Father and offered His blood in the Holy of Holies He returned to earth and told His disciples to touch [handle] Him (Luke 24:39): "*Behold my hands and my feet, that is I myself:* **handle me***, and see; for a spirit hath not flesh and bones as ye see me have.*"

So, why was Mary told not to touch Him, but His disciples were told to do so **after** He had presented Himself and His blood to the Father? The reason for this was because if she (an unsaved person) had touched Him, she would have made Him unclean by her sinfulness **before** He had ascended to His Father. This openly shows that Eternal Redemption was not fully completed until *after* He presented Himself and His blood to the Father in heaven. Any other notion is illogical and a stretch at best. Eternal Redemption was *officially* proclaimed **after** Jesus died, went to hell, resurrected from *among* the dead, and appeared in heaven! Jesus gave His life (*His spirit*) for the sheep. Jesus obtained our forgiveness He obtained our freedom from Sin's bondage, obtained Eternal Life and Righteousness for us, **but He also** obtained our freedom from punishment—He was our *Scape-goat* (our Substitute Sacrifice). The word Substitute means *our exchange*, alternate, in our place, and replacement for what we deserved.

The Day of Atonement: God's Established Pattern—Eternal Redemption

The Bible plainly declares that God is the same yesterday, today, and forever; His plans, purposes, and ways **never** change (Heb. 13:8). Hence, it should be easy to see how God's Old Covenant pattern of *Atonement* was the *exact* picture of New Covenant *Eternal Redemption*, which Jesus made for the world. In order for us to gain tremendous understanding of all that we have discussed thus far, I believe it is very important that we examine God's *established* pattern of Atonement from its original Old Covenant foundation.

As we embark upon this almost overwhelming task of studying the Old Covenant pattern of Atonement, I need to remind the reader that in Jesus' day the Laws of the Sacrifice were very much in force. Therefore, all sacrifices for Sin would be conducted according to the Old Covenant pattern written in the Law of Moses. New Covenant Eternal Redemption was **no** exception! It was accomplished according to God's pattern!

> **Leviticus 6:24-26; 28, 30**: And the LORD spake unto Moses, saying, Speak unto Aaron and to his sons, saying, This *is the law of the sin offering*: In the place where the burnt offering is killed shall the sin offering be killed before the LORD: **it *is* most holy**. The priest that offereth it for sin shall eat it: in the holy place shall it be eaten, in the court of the tabernacle of the congregation. But *the earthen vessel* wherein it is sodden *shall be broken*: and if it be sodden in a brasen pot, it shall be *both scoured*, and rinsed in water. And no sin offering, whereof *any* of the blood is brought into the tabernacle of the congregation **to reconcile** *withal* in *the holy place*, shall be eaten: it shall be **burnt in the fire**.

In this passage of Scripture, God is instructing Moses concerning the Law of the Sin offering. Please notice the various details and consider how they apply to the crucifixion of our Lord Jesus. God tells Moses that the Sin offering is *most holy*.

The precious blood of Jesus was a Most Holy Sacrifice, which covered our Sin **and** blotted it out for eternity. In verse 28 of this passage, it tells us that the "earthen vessel…shall be broken." Jesus, Himself, is quoted in 1 Corinthians chapter 11 verse 24 saying that His body was to be broken for us. Finally in verse 30 of Leviticus 6, we are told that the Sin offering was to be burned with fire. How does this apply to the sacrifice of Jesus, you might ask? To answer this, consider the following verses of Scripture.

Psalm 86:13: For great *is* thy mercy toward me: and thou hast delivered my soul *from the lowest hell* [the pit].

Matthew 12:39, 40: But he answered and said unto them, An evil and adulterous generation *seeketh after a sign*; and there shall no sign be given to it, *but the sign of the prophet Jonas*: For as Jonas was three days and three nights in the whale's belly; so shall the Son of man be *three days and three nights* **in the heart** of the earth.

John 12:24-26: Verily, verily, I say unto you, Except a corn of wheat fall into the ground **and die**, it abideth alone: but *if it die*, it bringeth forth much fruit. He that loveth his life shall lose it; and he that hateth his life in this world shall keep it unto life eternal. If any man serve me, *let him follow me*; and where I am, there shall also my servant be: if any man serve me, him will *my* Father honour.

All three of the previous passages of Scripture are referring to the three days and nights that Jesus spent in the center of the earth (hell itself). I dare say that no one would question my saying that hell is a place of fire, heat, and burning. And seeing that Jesus took upon Himself *our punishment* for Sin, (eternal punishment in hell fire) He had to have experienced it.

Therefore, I believe one could say that Jesus experienced these things and worse during His three-day stay in hell. The price that Jesus paid for our freedom is *far greater* than anything the human mind can conceive.

Two Goats—*One* Sacrifice!

Leviticus 16:5-11: And he shall take of the congregation of the children of Israel **two** *kids of the goats for a sin offering*, and *one ram for a burnt offering*. And Aaron shall offer his bullock of the sin offering, which is for himself, and make an atonement for himself, and for his house. And he shall *take the two goats*, and present them before the LORD *at* the door of the tabernacle of the congregation. And Aaron shall cast lots upon *the two goats*; one lot for the LORD, and the other lot for **the scapegoat**. And Aaron shall bring the goat upon which the LORD'S lot fell, and offer him *for* a sin offering. *But the goat, on which the lot fell to be the scapegoat, shall be presented alive before the* LORD**, to make an atonement with him**, *and to let him go for a scapegoat into the wilderness.* And Aaron shall bring the bullock of the sin offering, which *is* for himself, and shall make an atonement for himself, and for his house, and shall kill the bullock of the sin offering which *is* for himself:

Carefully notice that God said Aaron was to take **two** goats to make **one** complete sacrifice for the sins of the people. One of those goats was used in the actual Sin offering itself, and the other was used as a "scapegoat." Now we know where the term "scapegoat" (one taking the place of another) came from. Jesus Christ was not only our Sin Offering, but He was also our **Scapegoat** from Sin, hell and Eternal Punishment.

Notice further that the priest made Atonement for himself as well. Through the three fold Substitute Sacrifice of Jesus, He also made Atonement for Himself (because He was to become Sin for us), so that He wouldn't have to remain under the bondage of *our* Sin for eternity. Again, that is in no way to say that Jesus ever committed any Sin; however, He did take our Sin upon Himself. Through His sinless life, plus His precious blood, He also made the way for Himself to be released from the punishment for the Sin of the world. In verse 9 of Leviticus 16, we are told that the scapegoat was to be offered *with* the goat for the Sin offering to make Atonement. It took *two* goats to make **one** Sin offering, and Jesus Christ was *the embodiment* of those two Old Covenant symbols. Most know what the goat for the actual blood offering symbolizes, but what does the *scapegoat* represent? Verse 10 of this same chapter answers this question. The scapegoat was to be released into the wilderness, or the *inhabitable parts* of the earth.

The Bible declares that our Sin is separated from us, as far as the east is from the west. This is the purpose of the scapegoat. It was literally released into an uninhabitable part of the wilderness. However, in spiritual terms, this is a parallel of our being separated from our Sin as far as the east is from the west. Moreover, the terms "wilderness" and "inhabitable parts of the earth" are used metaphorically to describe the pit of hell—the place of ultimate uninhabitability. Hell is the place of confinement where Jesus was held for three days and nights on our behalf. Jesus was our Scapegoat! We escaped the torment of hell *because* He went into it for us. Had Jesus not gone to hell and received our punishment for our

Sin, *we would still have to experience it*. Now, let us continue in our study of the Old Covenant pattern of Atonement by examining Leviticus 16: 15-18:

> **Leviticus 16:15-18**: Then shall he kill the goat of the sin offering, that *is* for the people, and bring his blood within the veil, and do with that blood as he did with the blood of the bullock, and sprinkle it upon the mercy seat, and before the mercy seat: And he shall *make an atonement for the holy place*, **because of** *the uncleanness of the children of Israel*, and because of their transgressions in all their sins: and so shall he do for the tabernacle of the congregation, that remaineth among them in the midst of their uncleanness. And there shall be no man in the tabernacle of the congregation when he goeth in to make an atonement in the holy *place*, until he come out, and have made an atonement for himself, and for his household, and for all the congregation of Israel. And he shall go out unto the altar that *is* before the LORD, and make an atonement for it; and shall take of the blood of the bullock, and of the blood of the goat, and put *it* upon the horns of the altar round about.

Just as the blood of the Sin offering made Atonement (a covering) for the Sin of Israel, so Jesus' blood made a covering for Sin. However, His blood not only covered Adamic Sin, it also *completely removed* it—an **eternal** removal of Sin and its wages or punishment. The sacrifice for Sin found in the Old Covenant had to be repeated once a year. However, the *complete* Sacrifice that Jesus made purchased *Eternal Redemption* for all those who will believe upon Him and His precious, priceless blood.

As a child, I would cringe whenever I heard someone talk about "the blood of Jesus." Not because I was possessed or something like that, but rather because I did not understand the important significance of the blood of Jesus. It is because He shed His blood that we can be reunited to God the Father and spend eternity with Him! The blood of Jesus was the key to our Redemption, but there was more to the price of Eternal Redemption. *There was also an eternal sentence of Death* (separation from God) that went right along with the Offering for Sin. The price of Sin was *a multi-faceted tariff* that the human race could not possibly pay. This is why Jesus had to make **full** restitution for us. Wait, there's more!

> **Leviticus 16:20-22**: And when he hath made an end of *reconciling the holy place, and the tabernacle* of the congregation, and the altar, he shall bring the live goat [scapegoat]: And Aaron *shall lay both his*

hands upon **the head** *of the live goat, and* **confess over him all the iniquities** *of the children of Israel,* **and all their transgressions** *in all their sins, putting them upon the head of the goat, and shall send him away by the hand of a fit man into the wilderness:* **And the goat shall bear upon him all their iniquities unto a land not inhabited**: and he shall let go the goat in the wilderness.

In like manner, Jesus (our High Priest) made an end of reconciling the holy place and tabernacle, which is His Body, while upon the cross of Calvary. **After** this process was accomplished, the next phase of the multi-faceted tariff of Sin came into focus. God instructed Aaron (the priest) to lay his hands upon the scapegoat, *which was alive*, and confess all the iniquities and transgressions of the people over it. The scapegoat would *bear* the Sin into the inhabitable wilderness. The Bible states that our Lord Jesus bore (was covered with) the Sin of us all. Now, please consider **Isaiah 53: 5-9**:

But he *was* wounded for our transgressions, *he was* bruised for our iniquities: **the chastisement** of our peace *was* upon him; and with his stripes we are healed. All we like sheep have gone astray; we have turned every one to his own way; and the LORD hath laid **on him** *the iniquity of us all*. He was *oppressed*, and he was *afflicted*, yet he opened not his mouth: he is brought as a lamb to the slaughter, and as a sheep before her shearers is dumb, so he openeth not his mouth. He was *taken from prison and from judgment*: and who shall declare his generation? for **he was cut off out of the land of the living**: *for the transgression of my people was he stricken*. And he made his grave with the wicked, and with the rich *in his death*; because he had done no violence, neither *was any* deceit in his mouth.

Somewhere between life and death, **after** the Atonement (covering) for Sin had been accomplished, God the Father (the Chief High Priest) laid His hands upon the head of our "Head" and He confessed the Sin of the world over Jesus. Because of this *transference* of Sin, Jesus was killed spiritually, separated *temporarily* from His Father, to pay the full price of our Spiritual Death and all its punishment.

At this point, Jesus turned His human spirit over to Death (Spiritual separation), and He entered into the heart of the earth, where He was held captive *in our place* for three days and nights. Remember what the Word of God says, "We died with him (spiritually)," as well as resurrected. He went through all of this unspeakable horror in our place, on our behalf, because we could not have possibly been able to succeed in doing so on our own. He entered the wilderness of hell, the place where we deserved to dwell for eternity. He endured separation so that we would never have to experience it. Remember, He did all of this *in our place*...He never sinned! *That proves how much He really loves us.* We have already addressed the fact that Jesus *"burned in hell"* for you and I—what an extreme display of love. Hence, if Jesus went through all of this on our behalf, we are, therefore, extremely precious and highly prized by God! Contrary to what Hanegraaff and others like him think about this, what I am writing is *far from heretical*. It is the story of **the most-extreme** gift of love this world has ever known. If more people understood this story of Love, maybe they would treasure their salvation as the *most precious* prize known to men.

Leviticus 16:26-27; 30: And he that let go the goat for the scapegoat shall wash his clothes, and bathe his flesh in water, and afterward come *into the camp*. And the bullock *for* the sin offering, and the goat *for* the sin offering, whose blood was brought in to make atonement in the holy *place*, shall *one* carry forth without the camp; and **they shall burn in the fire** their skins, and their flesh, and their dung. For on that day shall *the priest* make an atonement for you, to cleanse you, *that* ye may be clean from all your sins before the LORD.

In the New Covenant, our Lord Jesus was crucified outside of the city, the same way that the Sin offering was made outside the camp (city). Notice again the fate of the Sin offering. The Bible says that it was to be *burned with fire*. Without a doubt, Jesus, *our Sin Offering*, also had to be burned with fire *in our place*. I realize that the very thought of such things makes one cringe in pain. One thinks, "How could a righteous Man be tortured and burned in hell?" Nonetheless, He was our **Scapegoat**!

Some *Prophetic* Words?

Job 29:12-18: Because I delivered the poor that cried, and the fatherless, and *him that had* none to help him. The blessing of him that was ready to perish came upon me: and I caused the widow's heart to sing for joy. I put on righteousness, and it clothed me: my judgment *was* as a robe and a diadem. I was eyes to the blind, and feet *was* I to the lame. I *was* a father to the poor: and the cause *which* I knew not I searched out. And *I brake the jaws of the wicked*, and plucked the spoil out of his teeth. Then I said, **I shall die in my nest**, and I shall **multiply *my* days as the sand**.

Job had to be prophesying about the torment that our Lord Jesus was to experience. Job *did not* brake the jaws of the wicked, however, Jesus came to destroy the works of the devil (1 John 3:8). Job *did not* multiply his days as the sand, but the Bible says of Jesus in Isaiah 53:10 that because of His Sacrifice, God prolonged His days forever! Job could not possibly have been literally referring to himself. Because he did not go through the sort of things that he was addressing. However, Jesus Christ did!

I would like to address one last long portion of prophetic Scripture from the book of Job:

Job 30:10, 15-30: They abhor me, they flee far from me, and *spare not to spit in my face*. Terrors are turned upon me: they pursue my soul as the wind: and my welfare passeth away as a cloud. And now *my soul is poured out upon me; the days of affliction have taken hold upon me*. **My bones are pierced in me** in the night season: and my sinews take no rest. *By the great force of* **my disease** *is* my garment changed: **it bindeth me** about as the collar of my coat. *He hath cast me into the mire, and I am become like dust and ashes*. I cry unto thee, and *thou dost not hear me*: I stand up, and thou regardest me *not*. *Thou art become cruel to me*: with thy strong hand thou opposest thyself against me. Thou liftest me up to the wind; thou causest me to ride *upon it*, and dissolvest my substance. *For I know that thou wilt bring me to death,* **and** *to the house appointed for all living*. Howbeit he will not stretch out *his* hand **to the grave**, though they cry in his destruction. Did not I weep for him that was in trouble? was *not* my soul grieved for the poor? When I looked for good, then evil came *unto me*: and when I waited for light, there came darkness. My bowels boiled, and rested not: *the of affliction prevented me*. I went mourning without the sun: I stood up, *and I cried in the congregation*. I am a brother to dragons, and a companion to owls. **My skin is black upon me, and my bones are burned with heat.**

No man living on earth past or present has ever experienced the torments that Job was speaking of, *including himself*. Job's trial period was rough, but it was nowhere near the description given in Job chapter 30. Again, the words of Job here were prophetic in nature, in the same way that King David wrote prophetically of Jesus so many times in the Book of Psalms. Job mentioned spitting. Jesus had a whole legion of soldiers who spit on and in His face shortly before He was crucified. The Bible also says in Isaiah that Jesus poured out His soul unto Death. While Jesus hung on the cross, His bones were all out of joint and piercing through

Him. Again, the book of Isaiah says that Jesus bore our sickness, disease, and carried our pains, and the weight (pressure) of all of this caused His visage (garment/body) to be horribly disfigured. Job says, "I cry unto thee, and thou doest not hear me."

Jesus is the only individual Who God was completely forsaken. God is aware of all our cries, but if they *are not* cries of faith, God simply *ignores them*, but not in the case of Jesus. God the Father **could not** look upon Him, because His human spirit was covered with the Sin of the world. Jesus is the only One, *this side of the grave*, Who has been truly forsaken by the Father. Job says, "Thou art become cruel to me...." Isaiah speaks clearly of this taking place to Jesus, saying, "Yet it pleased the Lord to bruise him; he hath put him to grief." He is truly the only One that God the Father has ever given Sin, sickness, disease, and pain. But He did so, with the purpose of Jesus defeating it for us.

Pay close attention to verse 23: "For I know *that* thou wilt bring me *to* death, and *to* the house appointed for all living." Jesus knew before He started His journey into the Reconciliation of man that He would be going into hell itself, but He also knew that He would be resurrected and once again enter the house appointed for all living (heaven). Job, on the other hand, probably had no idea of what he was actually referring to. Job continues by saying, "Howbeit he will not stretch out his hand to the grave...." Was he in the grave? Not at all! However, the Lord Jesus was in the grave three days and nights without relief. Job continues with another shocking statement that also appears to be prophetic of Jesus' Substitute Sacrifice.

Job 30:30 (TAB): My skin falls from me in blackened flakes, and my bones are burned with heat.

Some may say, "This doesn't say that Jesus burned in hell." "But, did Job's bones literally burn with heat?" Without a doubt no. However, Jesus our Lord was detained in the place of eternal flames and heat by the Sin of the world covering His spirit. Job could not have possibly experienced the torment that was illustrated here.

He Was God—But He Lived *As A Man*

Philippians 2:5-7 (NKJV): Let this mind be in you which was also in Christ Jesus, who, being in the form of God, **did not** *consider it robbery to be* **equal with God**, but made Himself of no reputation, taking the form of a bondservant, *and* coming in the likeness of men.

Many Christians read the above verse of Scripture and think "See, He lived here 'as' God. I never could live the same way He did." This verse reads that Jesus **did not** consider (think) it was robbery to be **equal** with God. That, basically, is saying that He had a *Super-natural advantage* over us. Therefore, we could not possibly live how He lived. However, does the above verse really interpret Jesus the way He really was, while here on the earth? I suggest that we look at another translation to make a comparison.

Philippians 2:6, 7 (TAB): Who, although *being essentially on with God and* in the form of God [possessing *the fullness of* **the attributes** which make God God], **did not think** this equality with God was a thing *to be eagerly grasped or retained*, But *stripped Himself* **[of all privileges and rightful dignity]**, so as *to assume* the guise of a servant (slave), in that *He* became like men *and was born a human being.*

The Amplified Bible translates Philippians 2:6, 7, in a tremendously freeing way. It tells the life of Jesus the way He told it. He said things such as, "It's not Me—It's My Father in Me, *He does the works*..." In this version, it says that Jesus did not think equality was something to be retained while He was in human form. Therefore, **He** stripped Himself of all those privileges that most traditionalists attempt to ascribe to Him, during His earthly ministry. Notice that Jesus was the One Who did the "stripping" of Himself of all the advantages He had *before* He came to earth.

Most traditional religious people probably hate *the Amplified Bible* just for these two verses alone, because it blows their theological and philosophical doctrines apart. Jesus is and was God, but He walked this earth with the same limitations as other men only He never sinned one time. However, He stripped Himself **of all privileges and rightful dignity** for the purpose of becoming a human being. Had He not done this, He would have defeated Satan as God **and not as a human being** (the Last Adam). Hank Hanegraaff has claimed that Jesus did not give up or give away His attributes and privileges, but that He simply covered them (or veiled them).[35]

On the contrary, *The Amplified Bible* **totally** contradicts such thinking. The Bible does not teach that Jesus *hid* His glory while on earth; it says He **stripped Himself,** in order that He could come to earth as a man. Remember what God said to Moses, "You can not see my face and live." So, how could the people of Jesus' day see "the face of God" and not die, if He did not temporarily strip off His glory (attributes & privileges) while here on earth? How did He do it? ***I have no idea***, but He was and is God, so I *know* that He was more than capable of handling the situation without a problem. Hanegraaff attributes so much of his theological perspective to the sovereignty of God, and this is one of the theological areas where one definitely needs to think of it in terms of God's sovereignty.

Finally, there is a lost and dying world who needs to know that God loves them every bit as much as He loves Jesus. If this were not true, then He would not have given Jesus up to Spiritual Death and torment, so that we would never have to experience it.

This is the message that will bring the lost people in by the millions. God loves them <u>*in their sins*</u>, just as much as He loves us <u>in His Righteousness</u>. Consider this before you go out "witnessing" the next time to your unbelieving family and friends! Salvation is a tremendously precious and high priced gift from God!

When The Holy Spirit Reveals

End Notes

END NOTES

Chapter 1: What's In A Word?
1. *The Spirit-Filled Life Bible, New King James Version*, (Copyright © 1992 by Thomas Nelson Publishers Inc., Nashville, TN), 711. Used by permission. All rights reserved.
2. *The New Strong's Exhaustive Concordance of the Bible*, (Copyright © 1990 by Thomas Nelson Publishers Inc., Nashville, TN; word # 2009).
3. Ibid., word # 2005.
4. Ibid., word # 7200.

Chapter 2: Visualization: Is It Scriptural?
1. By permission. From The Webster's Dictionary, Copyright © 1994 Merriam-Webster, Inc.
2. *The New Strong's Exhaustive Concordance of the Bible*, (Copyright © 1990 by Thomas Nelson Publishers Inc., Nashville, TN; word # 1254).
3. Ibid., word # 6754.
4. By permission. From The Webster's Dictionary, Copyright © 1994 Merriam-Webster, Inc.
5. *The New Strong's Exhaustive Concordance of the Bible*, (Copyright © 1990 by Thomas Nelson Publishers Inc., Nashville, TN; word # 7200).
6. Ibid., word # 4487.
7. Ibid., word # 3049.
8. Ibid., word # 3850.
9. Ibid., word # 8176
10. Ibid., word # 5341.
11. Ibid., word # 3820.
12. Ibid., word # 8444.
13. Ibid., word # 3049.
14. Ibid., word # 4295.

Chapter 3: Romans: Reconciliation Revelation
1. *The Compact Bible Dictionary*, (Zondervan Publishing

House, Grand Rapids, MI, 1967), 491.
2. *The Vine's Expository Dictionary of Old & New Testament Words*, (Fleming H. Revell, Grand Rapids, MI, 1981), 33.
3. *The New Strong's Exhaustive Concordance of the Bible*, (Copyright © 1990 by Thomas Nelson Publishers Inc., Nashville, TN; word # 2673).
4. Ibid., word # 3049
5. *The Vine's Expository Dictionary of Old & New Testament Words*, (Fleming H. Revell, Grand Rapids, MI, 1981), 229,230.
6. Ibid., 54.

Chapter 4: Temptation: What's Its Purpose?
1. *The New Strong's Exhaustive Concordance of the Bible*, (Copyright © 1990 by Thomas Nelson Publishers Inc., Nashville, TN; word # 974).
2. Ibid., word # 7287.
3. *Holman's Bible Dictionary* software for Windows on CD-ROM (by Parsons Technology, Inc. 1994). Used by permission.
4. By permission. From The Webster's Dictionary, Copyright © 1994 Merriam-Webster, Inc.
5. *The New Strong's Exhaustive Concordance of the Bible*, (Copyright © 1990 by Thomas Nelson Publishers Inc., Nashville, TN; word # 5281).

Chapter 5: Waiting In His Presence
1. By permission. From The Webster's Dictionary, Copyright © 1994 Merriam-Webster, Inc.
2. *The New Strong's Exhaustive Concordance of the Bible*, (Copyright © 1990 by Thomas Nelson Publishers Inc., Nashville, TN; word # 3427).

Chapter 6: What About Paul's Thorn?
1. *The New Strong's Exhaustive Concordance of the Bible*, (Copyright © 1990 by Thomas Nelson Publishers Inc., Nashville, TN; word # 1325).
2. Ibid., word # 32.
3. Ibid., word # 2852.
4. Ibid., word # 5485.
5. Ibid., word # 714.
6. Ibid., word # 1411.
7. *The Vine's Expository Dictionary of Old & New Testament Words*, (Fleming H. Revell, Grand Rapids, MI, 1981), 175.
8. *The New Strong's Exhaustive Concordance of the Bible*, (Copyright © 1990 by Thomas Nelson Publishers Inc.,

Nashville, TN; word # 769).
9. *The Vine's Expository Dictionary of Old & New Testament Words*, (Fleming H. Revell, Grand Rapids, MI, 1981), 204,205.
10. Ibid., 257.
11. *The New Strong's Exhaustive Concordance of the Bible*, (Copyright © 1990 by Thomas Nelson Publishers Inc., Nashville, TN; word # 3986).
12. *The Vine's Expository Dictionary of Old & New Testament Words*, (Fleming H. Revell, Grand Rapids, MI, 1981), 190.
13. *The New Strong's Exhaustive Concordance of the Bible*, (Copyright © 1990 by Thomas Nelson Publishers Inc., Nashville, TN; word # 3444).
14. Ibid., word # 3468.
15. Ibid., word # 4991.
16. Ibid., word # 5375.
17. Ibid., word # 2483.
18. Ibid., word # 4341.
19. Ibid., word # 7495.
20. Ibid., word # 4148.
21. Ibid., word # 7965.

Chapter 7: Whoever Said, "Women Can't Preach?"
1. *The New Strong's Exhaustive Concordance of the Bible*, (Copyright © 1990 by Thomas Nelson Publishers Inc., Nashville, TN; word # 1135).
2. Ibid., word # 435.
3. Ibid., word # 5383.
4. Ibid., word # 2980.
5. Ibid., word # 149.
6. Ibid., word # 1249.
7. Ibid., word # 444.
8. Ibid., word # 4398.
9. Ibid., word # 4396.
10. Ibid., word # 444.
11. Ibid., word # 3588.
12. *The Vine's Expository Dictionary of Old & New Testament Words*, (Fleming H. Revell, Grand Rapids, MI, 1981), 221.
13. *The New Strong's Exhaustive Concordance of the Bible*, (Copyright © 1990 by Thomas Nelson Publishers Inc., Nashville, TN; word # 1248).
14. Ibid., word # 4368.
15. By permission. From The Webster's Dictionary, Copyright © 1994 Merriam-Webster, Inc.
16. *The New Strong's Exhaustive Concordance of the Bible*,

(Copyright © 1990 by Thomas Nelson Publishers Inc., Nashville, TN; word # 5293).

Chapter 9: Is Bible School "Required" For The Great Commission?
1. *The Amplified Bible Expanded Edition,* (Zondervan Publishing Inc. & the Lockman Foundation, Grand Rapids, MI, 1987), 734 Used by permission.

Chapter 10: To Tithe *Or* Not To Tithe?
1. *The Amplified Bible Expanded Edition,* (Zondervan Publishing Inc. & the Lockman Foundation, Grand Rapids, MI, 1987) 1424 Used by permission.
2. "Prosperity: Why God Wants To Prosper Us!," *The Believer's Voice of Victory* , (Fort Worth, TX: Kenneth Copeland Ministries © 1995) [February 9, 1995] quotation: Jerry Savelle. Used by permission.

Chapter 11: Escotology 101
1. *Another Look At The Rapture,* Copy right © 1982 by: Dr. Roy H. Hicks, D.D Published by Harrison House Inc. P.O. Box 35035 Tulsa, Oklahoma 74135.
2. *The New Strong's Exhaustive Concordance of the Bible,* Copyright © 1990 by Thomas Nelson Publishers, Inc., Nashville, Tennessee.
3. *Another Look At The Rapture,* Copy right © 1982 by: Dr. Roy H. Hicks, D.D Published by Harrison House Inc. P.O. Box 35035 Tulsa, Oklahoma 74135.
4. Ibid.
5. Ibid.
6. *The Amplified Bible, Expanded Edition,* Copyright © 1987 by Zondervan Corporation and the Lockman Foundation, Grand Rapids, Michigan, p.1403.
7. *The Spirit-Filled Life Bible, New King James Version,* Copyright © 1992 by Thomas Nelson Inc. Nashville, Tennessee.
8. *The Kenneth Copeland Reference Edition Bible, King James Version* Copyright © 1991 by Kenneth Copeland Ministries, Inc., Ft. Worth, Texas.
9. *FINAL WARNING - Economic Collapse and the Coming World Government* Copyright © 1995 by: Grant R. Jeffrey; Published by: Frontier Research Publications, Inc. Box 129 Station "U", Toronto, Ontario M8Z 5M4, p. 304,305.
10. Ibid., p. 306
11. Ibid., p. 306

12. Ibid., p. 307
13. *The New Strong's Exhaustive Concordance of the Bible,* Copyright ©1990 by Thomas Nelson Publishers, Inc., Nashville, Tennessee.

Chapter 12: Spiritual Death & The Cross
1. *The New Strong's Exhaustive Concordance,* (Nashville, TN: Thomas Nelson Publishing, Inc., 1990; word # 1459/2641), 375.
2. *The Amplified Bible Expanded Edition,* (The Zondervan Corporation and The Lockman Foundation,1987; See: footnote), 800.
3. Ibid., 800.
4. *The New Strong's Exhaustive Concordance,* (Nashville, TN: Thomas Nelson Publishing, Inc., 1990; word # 8438), 1237.
5. *The Spirit-Filled Life Bible,* K. R. "Dick" Iverson, (Nashville, TN: Thomas Nelson, Inc., 1992), 770. Used by permission. All rights reserved.
6. *The New Strong's Exhaustive Concordance,* (Nashville, TN: Thomas Nelson Publishing, Inc., 1990; word # 4148/3256), 186.
7. Ibid., (word #'s 6115 & 6113), 844.
8. Ibid., (word # 4941), 576.
9. *The Vine's Expository Dictionary of Old Testament & New Testament Words,* (Nashville, TN: Thomas Nelson Inc., 1984, 1996), (NT) 300.
10. Ibid., (NT), 455.
11. Ibid., (OT), 237.
12. *The New Strong's Exhaustive Concordance of the Bible,* (Nashville, TN: Thomas Nelson Publishing, Inc., 1990; word # 5999), 1115.
13. Ibid., (word # 7646), 912.
14. *The Vine's Expository Dictionary of Old & New Testament Words,* (Nashville, TN: Thomas Nelson Inc., 1984, 1996), (NT) 385.
15. *The New Strong's Exhaustive Concordance of the Bible,* (Nashville, TN: Thomas Nelson Publishing, Inc., 1990; word # 4221), 235.
16. Ibid., (word # 2983), 862.
17. Morris Cerullo, *Proof Producers,* (San Diego, CA: World Evangelism, Inc., 1984), 127,128.
18. *The Vine's Expository Dictionary of Old & New Testament Words,,* (Nashville, TN: Thomas Nelson Inc., 1984, 1996), (NT) 149.
19. *The New Strong's Exhaustive Concordance of the Bible,* (Nashville, TN: Thomas Nelson Publishing, Inc., 1990; word #'s 4416, 4413; 5088), 364.

20. Ibid., (word # 3825), 23.
21. Ibid., (word # 1325), 383.
22. *The Vine's Expository Dictionary of Old & New Testament Words*, (Nashville, TN: Thomas Nelson Inc., 1984, 1996), (NT) 513,514.
23. Ibid., (NT), 493.
24. *The New Strong's Exhaustive Concordance of the Bible*, (Nashville, TN: Thomas Nelson Publishing, Inc., 1990; word # 859), 869.
25. Ibid., (word # 1344), 578.
26. Ibid., (word # 591), 870.
27. *The Vine's Expository Dictionary of Old & New Testament Words*, (Nashville, TN: Thomas Nelson Inc., 1984, 1996), 523,524 (NT).
28. *The New Strong's Exhaustive Concordance of the Bible*, (Nashville, TN: Thomas Nelson Publishing, Inc., 1990; word # 2227), 856.
29. By permission. From Merriam-Webster's Collegiate® Dictionary, Tenth Edition ©1997 by Merriam-Webster, Incorporated. [Identification].
30. Ibid., [Identify].
31. *The New Strong's Exhaustive Concordance of the Bible*, (Nashville, TN: Thomas Nelson Publishing, Inc., 1990; word # 3908), 215.
32. Ibid., (word # 5055), 361.
33. Ibid., (word # 3860), 393.
34. Kenneth Hagin, *Zoe: The God-Kind of Life*, (Tulsa, OK: Kenneth Hagin Ministries, 1981, 1995, Sixth Printing), 44.
35. Hank Hanegraaff, *Christianity in Crisis*, (Eugene, OR: Harvest House, 1993), 140.

An Important Message

Dear Reader,

We believe it was no accident that you have come across this book. We want you to know that the Lord Jesus loves you and wants to bless your life <u>in every area possible</u>. He wants to give you **peace** and **joy** like you have never experienced before. If you desire to accept His free gift, we invite you to pray the following prayer:

"Dear Heavenly Father, I come to you in the Name of Jesus, and I ask you to forgive me of all of my sins. You said in Romans 10:9&10, that if I confess with my mouth the Lord Jesus and believe in my heart that You raised Jesus from the dead, that I would be saved (born a new).

I believe in my heart that Jesus is the Son of God. I believe He died on the cross for my freedom from sin and evil. I believe that You raised Him from the dead so that I would have a right relationship with You. I accept Jesus as my personal Lord and Savior. Jesus come into my heart and change me into the person You want me to be. I give you my life today.

Father, I thank You for accepting me as a member of Your family. Thank You for giving me Your peace and joy. I thank You for blessing every area of my life. Help me to live for You. I ask all these things in Jesus Name. Amen!"

If you have just prayed this prayer, accepting Jesus as your Lord and Savior, please email us at: **info@b2bablessing.org**. We would love to hear from you and help you grow in your new faith in Christ.

—Gregg & Emily Huestis

www.ingramcontent.com/pod-product-compliance
Lightning Source LLC
Chambersburg PA
CBHW060520100426
42743CB00009B/1391